SIMULATION TECHNIQUES
FOR DISCRETE EVENT SYSTEMS

Also in this series

1 An Introduction to Logical Design of Digital Circuits
  C. M. Reeves 1972

2 Information Representation and Manipulation in a Computer
  E. S. Page and L. B. Wilson, Second Edition 1978

3 Computer Simulation of Continuous Systems
  R. J. Ord-Smith and J. Stephenson 1975

4 Macro Processors
  A. J. Cole, Second Edition 1981

5 An Introduction to the Uses of Computers
  Murray Laver 1976

6 Computing Systems Hardware
  M. Wells 1976

7 An Introduction to the Study of Programming Languages
  D. W. Barron 1977

8 ALGOL 68 – A first and second course
  A. D. McGettrick 1978

9 An Introduction to Computational Combinatorics
  E. S. Page and L. B. Wilson 1979

10 Computers and Social Change
  Murray Laver 1980

11 The Definition of Programming Languages
  A. D. McGettrick 1980

12 Programming via Pascal
  J. S. Rohl and H. J. Barrett 1980

13 Program Verification Using Ada
  A. D. McGettrick 1981

Cambridge Computer Science Texts · 14

Simulation techniques for discrete event systems

I. MITRANI

Computing Laboratory, University of Newcastle upon Tyne

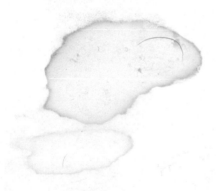

CAMBRIDGE UNIVERSITY PRESS

Cambridge

London   New York   New Rochelle

Melbourne   Sydney

Published by the Press Syndicate of the University of Cambridge
The Pitt Building, Trumpington Street, Cambridge CB2 1RP
32 East 57th Street, New York, NY 10022, USA
296 Beaconsfield Parade, Middle Park, Melbourne 3206, Australia

First published 1982

Printed in Great Britain at the University Press, Cambridge

Library of Congress catalogue card number: 82-4549

British Library Cataloguing in Publication Data
Mitrani, I.
Simulation techniques for discrete event systems
– (Cambridge computer science texts; 14)
1. Digital computer simulation
I. Title
001.42′4   QA76.9.C65
ISBN 0 521 23885 4 hard covers
ISBN 0 521 28282 9 paperback

CONTENTS

	Preface	vii
1	**Introduction to the simulation method**	1
	1.1 General background. Modelling	1
	1.2 Principal characteristics of Monte Carlo methods	3
	1.3 Simulation models. Classification	8
	1.4 A model of market fluctuations	10
	1.5 A model of a car washing station	12
	Exercises	15
2	**Construction of simulation programs**	16
	2.1 Basic approaches	16
	2.2 Data structures	23
	2.3 The implementation of event lists	31
	2.4 Simulation languages. SIMSCRIPT, GPSS and SIMULA	34
	2.5 Debugging of a simulation program	40
	Exercises	41
3	**Simulation examples**	42
	3.1 A versatile warehouse model	42
	3.2 The machine interference model	46
	3.3 A system with priorities	50
	3.4 A queueing network model	57
	Exercises	63
4	**Pseudo-random number sequences**	65
	4.1 Uniform variables	65
	4.2 Random sampling from different populations	69
	4.3 Statistical tests	76
	4.4 When to use what distribution	82
	Exercises	85
5	**Collection and analysis of simulation data**	86
	5.1 Estimation of parameters	86
	5.2 Confidence intervals	92
	5.3 Short-run and long-run performance	95
	5.4 The regenerative method	99
	5.5 Estimating distributions	103
	Exercises	105

6	**Variance reduction methods**	106
	6.1 Common random number streams	106
	6.2 Replacing random variables by their expectations	108
	6.3 Antithetic variates	111
	6.4 Control variables	113
	Exercises	115
7	**Design and analysis of simulation experiments**	116
	7.1 Analysis of variance	116
	7.2 Linear regression	121
	Exercises	126

Appendix 1	**A SIMULA primer**	128
	1. General features. Input/output	128
	2. The class concept	133
	3. Prefixing. Hierarchical structures	136
	4. Class *SIMSET*	139
	5. Class *SIMULATION*	143
	6. System-defined procedures	147

Appendix 2	**A probability theory primer**	150
	1. Sample points, events and probabilities	150
	2. Random variables	152
	3. Mean, Variance and Covariance. Inequalities	155
	4. Bernoulli trials. The geometric and binomial distributions	158
	5. The exponential distribution and the Poisson process	160
	6. The normal distribution and related topics	163
	7. Simple queueing systems	165
	Tables	169
	References	181
	Index	183

PREFACE

Computer simulation is partly art, partly science. The art is that of programming: a simulation program should do what its author intended, and should do it efficiently. However, it is not enough to write a correct and efficient program; one should also know how to use it to answer questions about the system being simulated. This is where the science comes in. A simulation study is essentially a statistical experiment, requiring statistical tools for the collection and analysis of data. Failure to use those tools properly can be just as disastrous to an investigation as an unnoticed error in the program logic.

This book is devoted in roughly equal proportions to the two aspects of the subject. The main treatment of general programming techniques relevant to simulation is to be found in chapter 2, while the special (but important) topics of random number generation are discussed in chapter 4. The process-oriented approach to simulation is illustrated by working out a number of examples (chapter 3). With the exception of chapter 3 and section 2.4, the presentation is not tied down to any particular programming language. Algorithms are given in an informal, ALGOL-like form of English, which should be self-explanatory. The wisdom of choosing SIMULA for the example programs may be disputed; one cannot please everybody. Personal preferences apart, I believe that a good case for SIMULA can be made on its merits (section 2.4).

The use of simulations to study system performance is examined in some detail in chapters 5, 6 and 7. The topics dealt with include different methods for the estimation of performance measures (chapter 5), methods for improving the efficiency of simulations (chapter 6) and methods for testing hypotheses and for performance prediction (chapter 7).

The book is intended as a student text (at either undergraduate or post-graduate level), but may also be used by practitioners in the field. The reader is expected to have some programming experience in a language of the ALGOL family, e.g. ALGOL 60, ALGOL 68, ALGOLW, PASCAL. That should enable him or her to master the SIMULA primer in appendix 1 easily. In addition, some background in probability is required for the understanding of the theoretical chapters. This need not be very solid, nor very recent; the relevant results are given in a concise form in appendix 2.

I. Mitrani
Newcastle, December 1981

ACKNOWLEDGEMENTS

The author wishes to thank all those who have helped him during the writing and production of this book. Special thanks are due to Professor C. M. Reeves and Dr E. S. Page: the first provided much of the initial impetus and both read the completed manuscript and made many valuable comments. A few errors in the example programs in chapter 3 were exposed and eliminated with the help of Dr P. J. B. King and a number of students. To Coreen Stenhouse goes the credit for the very efficient typing of the manuscript. Through the efforts of the Cambridge University Press staff, the production phase passed smoothly and painlessly.

Last, but not least, the Computing Laboratory of the University of Newcastle should be acknowledged for its support and stimulating work environment.

1. INTRODUCTION TO THE SIMULATION METHOD

1.1   General background. Modelling

To model a system is to replace it by something which is (*a*) simpler
and/or easier to study, and (*b*) equivalent to the original in all important respects.
If the real system interacts with the outside world in some way, that interaction
must be reflected in the model. The (simplified) logical equivalent is subjected
to the same, or similar, external stimuli as the original. It then produces outputs
which may be interpreted as the system's reaction to the stimuli (see figure 1.1).
Thus, by varying the model inputs and examining the corresponding outputs,
one attempts to study the behaviour of the real system.

That, in a nutshell, is a summary of the very large subject of modelling, with
applications in almost every branch of science and technology. Computer
simulation is a comparatively recent addition to the family of modelling method-
ologies. However, it is perhaps the most widely used (and, unfortunately,
misused) method today.

Before we go on to discuss simulation with respect to other modelling
methods, a few words concerning the terminology are in order. Several concepts
have already been introduced without having been formally defined, taking the
obviousness of their meaning for granted. For example, the notion of a 'system'
is fundamental to everything that follows, yet what is a system? The following
entry (from the *Pocket Oxford Dictionary*) probably gives as good an idea as
any: 'complex whole, set of connected things or parts, organised body of

Figure 1.1

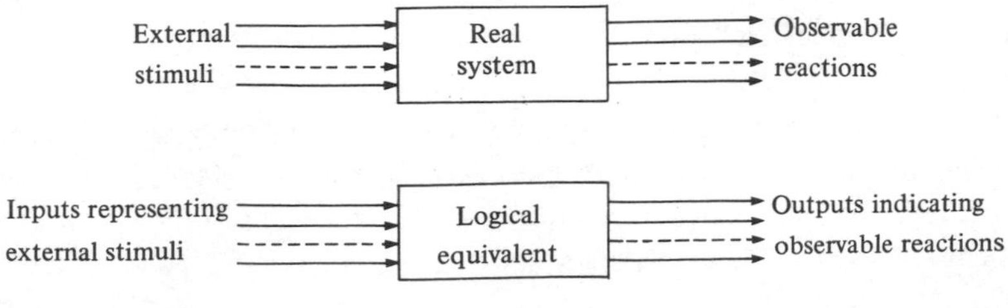

1

material or immaterial things'. Clearly, this is not a definition that would satisfy a mathematician; nor is it possible to give one that would. We shall continue, therefore, to leave concepts of a general nature to be defined by the context in which they are encountered.

A rough categorisation of the various approaches to modelling will help to put simulation in perspective (for a more detailed treatment, see Gordon [20]). The first and most basic distinguishing feature of a model is the nature of the logical equivalent used. That may be a physical system, in which case we talk of physical modelling, or it may be a set of abstract variables whose behaviour is controlled by a number of assumptions and equations; then the model is said to be mathematical. Physical modelling belongs primarily, although not exclusively, to the engineering domain: applications range from car and ship design, through aircraft testing in wind tunnels, to the training of astronauts in centrifuges.

The mathematical modelling methods can be divided into 'analytical' and 'numerical', depending on the approach to the solution. An analytical solution provides a closed-form expression for the desired system characteristics in terms of the defining parameters. Such solutions, while clearly advantageous, are usually unobtainable for any but the simplest models. On the other hand, a numerical solution can be applied to a model of arbitrary complexity, at least in principle. Moreover, as the processing power of digital computers increases, so does the area of feasibility of numerical solutions. These do, however, have the disadvantage of providing results only for isolated points in the parameter space.

The numerical modelling methods are divided further into 'deterministic' and 'stochastic'; the latter are also called 'Monte Carlo methods'. The terms 'deterministic' and 'stochastic' refer, respectively, to the absence or presence of random variables in the model. These may, or may not, reflect the absence or presence of random phenomena in the system being modelled. For instance, we shall describe in the next section a model of the number π involving random distances and angles. A numerical evaluation of π using that model will be classed as a Monte Carlo method, despite the fact that 'the system' π is deterministic.

For our purposes, simulation will be regarded as a type of Monte Carlo method. More precisely, it is a stochastic numerical modelling method applied to the study of systems which are (a) themselves stochastic and (b) dynamic. That is, the behaviour of the simulated system is influenced by random events occurring at different moments in time. The simulation is carried out by generating these events in a digital computer model, observing the resulting behaviour of the system and obtaining estimates for the required measures of performance. In the course of a simulation study, one has to exercise considerable skill in two main directions: first, the model must be a sufficiently close approximation to the target system; second, performance estimates must be obtained with a sufficient confidence in their accuracy and with a minimum of effort. There is also a

2

third objective, perhaps of lesser theoretical but great practical importance: the programming tools used should be such as to make the writing and verification of the computer programs reasonably painless. This book will be devoted largely to the various means available for achieving these three objectives.

The term 'simulation' is sometimes also applied to the numerical solution, by either analog or digital methods, of certain differential equations describing system behaviour. Such models are essentially deterministic in nature and (in the case of digital computers), classical numerical methods are used for their solution. The 'simulation' consists of constructing one or more functions that satisfy the differential equations for given initial conditions. That type of continuous modelling is outside our concern.

Why does one attempt to study a system through simulation? Or, for that matter, through any other kind of modelling? One, or both, of the following arguments may supply the motivation:

(i) It is too difficult, too hazardous, or too expensive, to observe the real system in operation. For example, one may wish to estimate the performance of a system which is not yet built (in the design of large computers, airport terminals, telephone exchanges, etc.). Alternatively, the object may be to assess the effect of a proposed major change in an existing system (new scheduling strategies, maintenance policies, addition of equipment, etc.).

(ii) There are questions that cannot be answered by observing the real system in operation; hypotheses about its internal structure may be checked by simulation. Models of some physiological, physical and genetic systems are of this type. Simulations are also used to examine the accuracy of analytical solutions obtained under simplifying assumptions.

Whatever the reasons, the decision to go ahead with a large-scale simulation should not be taken too lightly. Considerable expense, in terms of both human and computing resources, may be incurred and the pay-off may be minimal. An acquaintance with simulation techniques – the cost of applying them and the benefits to be derived from them – is essential.

1.2 Principal characteristics of Monte Carlo methods

At this stage, it will be instructive to illustrate the use of random numbers in modelling and, at the same time, to outline the main features of the stochastic approach. Two well-known examples will be described. Both concern deterministic static systems and therefore, according to the classification in the previous section, they are not simulations. However, they are simple, do not require system background, and yet display some important characteristics common to all Monte Carlo methods, including simulation.

The first example is a model of the number π, introduced by C. de Buffon in 1777 and known as Buffon's needle (e.g. see Shreider [38]). Imagine an infinite plane covered with a grid of parallel lines at a distance $2a$ from each other.

A line segment (a needle) of length $2b$ ($b \leqslant a$) is dropped at random on the plane. What is the probability p that the segment will cross one of the lines? The position of the segment on the plane is determined by the distance, Y, between its centre and the nearest line, and the angle, Φ, between the segment and that line; see figure 1.2. For reasons of symmetry, Y and Φ may be taken to vary in the intervals $0 \leqslant Y \leqslant a$ and $0 \leqslant \Phi \leqslant \pi/2$ respectively. Moreover, 'dropped at random' should be interpreted to mean that the random variables Y and Φ are independent and uniformly distributed on those intervals:

$$P(y \leqslant Y \leqslant y + dy, \quad \phi \leqslant \Phi \leqslant \phi + d\phi) = \frac{dy}{a} \frac{d\phi}{\pi/2}.$$

The segment crosses a line if $Y \leqslant b \sin \Phi$; the probability of that event is

$$p = \frac{2}{a\pi} \int_0^{\pi/2} \int_0^{b \sin \phi} dy \, d\phi = \frac{2b}{a\pi}.$$

Suppose now that the segment is dropped N times, and that on n of those occasions it crosses a line. According to the strong law of large numbers (see appendix 2),

$$\lim_{N \to \infty} (n/N) = p \tag{1.1}$$

with probability one. Therefore, an arbitrarily close approximation to π can be evaluated numerically by the following procedure:

1. Select values for a and b.
2. Generate N independent pairs of random numbers (y_i, ϕ_i), $i = 1, 2, \ldots,$ N, where y_i is uniformly distributed on $(0, a)$ and ϕ_i is uniformly distributed on $(0, \pi/2)$. Count the number n of those pairs which satisfy $y_i \leqslant b \sin \phi_i$.
3. Take the ratio $2bN/an$ as an estimate of π.
4. Assess the accuracy of the obtained estimate. If necessary, increase N and repeat from step 2.

This procedure is typical of Monte Carlo methods. A computer simulation study would normally go through phases that follow closely the pattern of steps

Figure 1.2. Buffon's Needle.

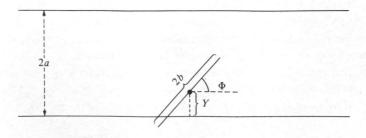

1–4 above:

1. Select parameter values.
2. Run the simulation program and collect statistics about the quantities of interest.
3. Use the collected data to obtain estimates of those quantities.
4. Assess the accuracy of the estimates. If necessary, make additional runs, repeating steps 2, 3 and 4.

Clearly, step 4 is of extreme importance. Suppose that the (unknown) value of the quantity of interest is μ, and that steps 1, 2 and 3 yield an estimate X for it. Since the procedure involves the use of random numbers, X itself is a random variable. There is not much point in obtaining a particular value for X (perhaps after a great deal of effort), if one has no idea how close that value is to μ. A probabilistic measure of the distance between X and μ should be derived, of the following type:

$$P(|\mu - X| < \delta) \geqslant \alpha, \quad 0 \leqslant \alpha \leqslant 1. \tag{1.2}$$

The interval $(X - \delta, X + \delta)$ is called a 'confidence interval' for μ; the probability α is the 'level of confidence'. In the Buffon's needle example, a confidence interval for the quantity $1/\pi$ can be obtained by applying Chebichev's inequality (appendix 2). This provides a bound for the probability that a random variable X deviates from its mean by more than a given amount, in terms of the variance of X:

$$P(|E[X] - X| > \beta) \leqslant \mathrm{Var}\,[X]/\beta^2.$$

By setting $\alpha = 1 - \mathrm{Var}\,[X]/\beta^2$, the above inequality can be rewritten in a form similar to (1.2):

$$P(|E[X] - X| \leqslant [\mathrm{Var}\,[X]/(1 - \alpha)]^{1/2}) > \alpha.$$

Consider now the random variable $X = (an)/(2bN)$; its mean and variance are given by

$$E[X] = 1/\pi, \quad \mathrm{Var}\,[X] = (a/2b)^2\, \sigma^2/N,$$

where $\sigma^2 = p(1-p) = (2b/a\pi)[1 - (2b/a\pi)]$ is the variance of the contribution to n of each toss of the needle (these expressions follow from the fact that we are dealing with a sequence of Bernoulli trials; see appendix 2). Applying Chebichev's inequality to this random variable yields a confidence interval for $1/\pi$:

$$P(|(1/\pi) - (an/2bN)| \leqslant (a/2b)\, \sigma/[N(1 - \alpha)]^{1/2}) \geqslant \alpha. \tag{1.3}$$

Unfortunately, the interval is given in terms of σ, which in turn depends on π, the quantity we are trying to estimate. In practice one would use an approximate confidence interval where σ is also estimated from the experimental data (e.g. $\sigma^2 \sim [n/(N-1)]\,(1-n/N)$).

It is obviously desirable that an estimate should be close to its target with a high probability. Therefore, having fixed the level of confidence, α (e.g. $\alpha = 0.95$

or $\alpha = 0.99$), the aim should be to reduce the width of the confidence interval as much as possible. Let us see how this can be achieved for the interval given by (1.3).

One possibility is to choose the parameters so as to minimise the quantity $(a/2b)\sigma = [(a/2b\pi) - (1/\pi^2)]^{1/2}$. Bearing in mind that the inequality $b \leqslant a$ must be satisfied, we see that the best choice is $b = a$. In other words, the best needle to toss is the longest permissible one. Another way of narrowing the confidence interval is to increase N, which means expending more effort in obtaining the estimate. From (1.3) it follows that, in order to halve the width of the confidence interval (i.e. double the accuracy of the estimate), the effort has to be increased four times.

This is a general phenomenon. When discussing the analysis of simulation results (chapter 5) we shall see that the width of a confidence interval is always proportional to the standard deviation of an individual member of the sample of observations, and it is inversely proportional to the square root of the sample size. That is why simulations tend to be expensive. That is also why several techniques have been devised for improving simulation efficiency by reducing the variance of estimates (see chapter 6).

The second example concerns the application of Monte Carlo methods to numerical integration. Suppose that we wish to evaluate the definite integral

$$I = \int_a^b f(x)\, dx, \tag{1.4}$$

assuming that the function $f(x)$ is non-negative and bounded: $0 \leqslant f(x) \leqslant c$ for $a \leqslant x \leqslant b$. Let R be the rectangle with base (a, b) and height c, and let S be the portion of R which is under the curve $f(x)$; the area of S is equal to I. If a point Q is dropped at random on R (i.e. its x and y coordinates are independent and distributed uniformly on (a, b) and $(0, c)$ respectively), then the probability p that Q falls in S is equal to the fraction of the area covered by S (figure 1.3):

$$p = I/(b - a)c.$$

If N points are dropped in this fashion, and n of them fall in S, then the fraction n/N will converge to p as N increases, with probability one. Therefore, I can be estimated by generating N independent pairs of random numbers (x_i, y_i), $i = 1$, $2, \ldots, N$, where x_i is uniform on (a, b) and y_i is uniform on $(0, c)$; counting the number of pairs, n, such that $y_i \leqslant f(x_i)$; taking $(b - a)cn/N$ as the estimate of I. Just as in (1.3), a confidence interval for I is given by

$$P(|I - [(b - a)cn/N]| < \sigma/[N(1 - \alpha)]^{1/2}) \geqslant \alpha, \tag{1.5}$$

where $\sigma = (b - a)c[p(1 - p)]^{1/2}$. Of course, in practice σ is unknown and has to be estimated from the sample.

Let us now demonstrate how a different approach to the problem can produce an estimate with a lower variance (and hence higher accuracy for the same amount of effort). Rewrite (1.4) in the form

$$I = \int_a^b \frac{f(x)}{g(x)} g(x) \, \mathrm{d}x, \qquad (1.6)$$

where $g(x)$ is an arbitrary probability density function on (a, b):

$$\int_a^b g(x) \, \mathrm{d}x = 1.$$

It follows from (1.6) that if X is a random variable with probability density function $g(x)$ and Y is the random variable defined by $Y = f(X)/g(X)$, then $I = E[Y]$. Therefore, an unbiased estimate of I can be obtained by generating N independent random numbers $x_1, x_2, \ldots, x_N$ from the density $g(x)$ and taking the mean:

$$\tilde{I} = \frac{1}{N} \sum_{i=1}^{N} [f(x_i)/g(x_i)].$$

The expression for the confidence interval would be as (1.5), with the estimate replaced by $\tilde{I}$ and σ replaced by the standard deviation of Y.

In particular, if the uniform density $1/(b - a)$ is chosen for $g(x)$, the estimate becomes

$$\tilde{I} = \frac{(b - a)}{N} \sum_{i=1}^{N} f(x_i),$$

where the random numbers x_i are independent and uniformly distributed on (a, b). Without going into details (see Hammersley & Handscomb [21]), it is

Figure 1.3. Monte Carlo integration.

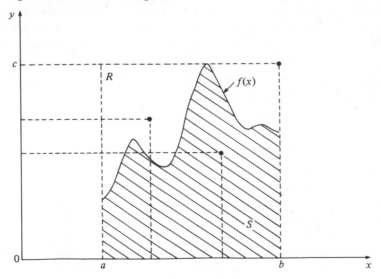

intuitively clear that this last estimate is more efficient (in the sense of having a lower variance) than the one in (1.5), since it involves one random number, x_i, per observation instead of a pair (x_i, y_i). Moreover, the variance can be reduced even further by an appropriate choice of $g(x)$: the idea is to generate the x_i values in such a way that the 'more important' values of Y are sampled more often. This particular variance reduction technique, called 'importance sampling', has only a limited application in simulation and we shall not return to it; the interested reader is directed to Kleijnen [29].

1.3   Simulation models. Classification

The time has come now to introduce some terminology particular to the subject of simulation. This will allow us to discuss system and model structures from the model builder's point of view. It will also help to sort the large family of simulation models into reasonably well-defined categories.

As a preliminary to the construction of a simulation, it is necessary to abstract from the real system all those components (and their interactions) that are considered important enough for inclusion in the model. The components thus selected are referred to as 'entities'. For instance, in a simulation of a railway station, the entities might be tracks, sidings, signals, platforms, passenger trains, goods trains, storage depots, fuel tanks, etc. Associated with each entity are zero or more 'attributes' – quantities that describe the state of the entity and whose value may or may not vary with time. In the example above, an attribute of a track might be the number of trains currently on it; trains may have as attributes length (or number of cars), departure and destination points, current delay time, etc.

The collection of all attributes (i.e. of all entity descriptors) at time t defines the 'system state', $\mathbf{S}(t)$. In general, $\mathbf{S}(t)$ is a vector of random variables. A particular realisation of that vector as a function of time over some region $\mathcal{T}$, $\{\mathbf{S}(t), t \in \mathcal{T}\}$, is an 'operation path' (sometimes also called a 'sample path') for the system over the 'observation period' $\mathcal{T}$. After a simulation model has been constructed, each run of the program corresponds to an operation path for the target system over some observation period.

In general, the system state changes in the course of an operation path; these changes of state are called 'events'. The instants of time at which events occur are referred to as 'event times'.

A 'continuous' system is one whose state varies continuously with time; i.e. both the effects of the events and the intervals between event times are infinitesimal. Such systems are usually described by sets of differential equations. Their operation paths (functions that satisfy the equations) are usually determined uniquely by the initial and boundary conditions. Problems in mechanics, electrical engineering and economics often give rise to continuous models. However, as mentioned already, these models are outside our field of interest.

Discrete stochastic models come in a variety of shapes and sizes, but may be divided into two broad categories according to their time and event parameters:

(a) Discrete time. The system is considered only at selected moments in time, $\mathcal{T} = \{t_1, t_2, \ldots\}$. Typically, these observation points are evenly spaced ($t_{i+1} - t_i = \text{const}, i = 1, 2, \ldots$); an appropriate choice of time unit makes them integer. Some economics models are of this type (we shall examine one in the next section), due to the fact that economics data usually become available at fixed intervals. The operation paths of discrete time models are sequences of system states, $\{S(t_1), S(t_2), \ldots\}$. Any changes of state are noticed only at observation points. It is as if events in the real system are allowed to occur only at the moments $t_1, t_2, \ldots$. It is obvious that a continuous system can be approximated by a discrete time model to any degree of accuracy by choosing a sufficiently small fixed time increment (this is exactly the way most continuous modelling packages work).

(b) Continuous time–discrete events. The time parameter is continuous, at least conceptually. The observation period is a real interval, usually taken to start at zero for convenience; $\mathcal{T} = \{t \in (0, T)\}$. An operation path is a (vector valued) function $\{S(t), t \in \mathcal{T}\}$ in which there are jumps of finite magnitude at event times $t_1 < t_2 < \ldots$. For example, suppose that a counter at a bank is being simulated, and that the system state is defined by a single attribute – the number of customers in the queue. The operation paths for this system are step functions. They jump up by one at the moments when customers join the queue and down by one at the moments when customers leave it (a similar system will be considered in section 1.5).

The characteristic feature of continuous time–discrete event systems is that an operation path is completely determined by the sequence of event times $t_1, t_2, \ldots$ and by the discrete changes in the system state which take place at those moments. In between two consecutive event times, (t_i, t_{i+1}), the system state may well vary continuously. Consider, for instance, a coal bunker of capacity C, serving a furnace which burns coal at a rate r. From time to time, loads of coal of different sizes are delivered and dumped into the bunker. If a complete load would cause an overflow, only the maximum possible amount is put in and the rest is taken away. When the bunker empties, the furnace is stopped, to be re-lighted again as soon as the next load is delivered. A typical operation path for this system (defining the system state as the amount of coal in the bunker) is illustrated in figure 1.4.

In this example, the discrete events that take place are coal deliveries: at time t_i an amount a_i is brought in ($i = 1, 2, \ldots$). There are also continuous events representing the burning of coal. However, the operation path is completely determined by the sequence of pairs $(t_1, a_1), (t_2, a_2), \ldots$.

Thus, although it is always possible to imitate the passage of real time by making small, fixed increments in the model's time variable and changing the system as required at each increment, this is not necessary for a discrete event system. The simulation model can advance its internal time directly from one discrete event moment to the next, taking on each occasion the appropriate actions dictated by the event and, if needed, projecting the system state to the next moment.

Techniques for constructing models will be discussed in greater detail in chapter 2. However, before considering the general problems, we shall attempt to give a flavour of what is involved in writing simulations by working out two examples, one with discrete time and one with continuous time–discrete events.

1.4   A model of market fluctuations

Consider the behaviour of the market in a certain commodity. It is generally assumed that, in the absence of political and strategic influences, that behaviour is controlled by the laws of supply and demand. These state, roughly, that

(i)   The demand for the commodity is low when its price is high and vice versa (demand law).

(ii) If a high price was obtained for the commodity over a period of time, the supply during the next such period will be high and vice versa (supply law).

Let us now attempt to construct a model of the market based upon a formalisation of laws (i) and (ii). There is a single entity – the commodity which is produced and sold. That entity has two attributes – the quantity Q placed on the market and the price P at which it is sold. The pair (Q, P) defines the system state. Market performance figures are published at fixed intervals (say once a month), so the system state is considered only at those selected points. Thus an operation path for the market is a sequence of states (Q_1, P_1), (Q_2, P_2), ..., (Q_i, P_i), ...

Figure 1.4. A coal bunker.

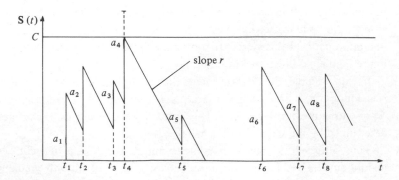

As a first approximation, the laws of demand and supply can be represented by linear relationships (Samuelson [37], Gordon [20]):

$$Q_i = -aP_i + b; \quad a, b \geqslant 0, \tag{1.7}$$

$$Q_i = cP_{i-1} + d; \quad c, d \geqslant 0. \tag{1.8}$$

In writing (1.7) and (1.8) the assumption has been made that the quantity put on the market in the ith observation interval is completely sold during that interval (demand = supply). The two lines $y = -ax + b$ and $y = cx + d$ are referred to as the 'demand line' and the 'supply line' respectively.

We shall introduce perturbation terms into (1.7) and (1.8) in order to account for random phenomena affecting the market. For example, the demand might be influenced by changing tastes, fashions, the appearance of competing products, etc., whereas the supply could depend also on the weather, industrial relations, breakdowns of equipment, etc. The laws of demand and supply then become

$$Q_i = -aP_i + b + \alpha_i; \quad a, b \geqslant 0 \tag{1.9}$$

$$Q_i = cP_{i-1} + d + \beta_i; \quad c, d \geqslant 0, \tag{1.10}$$

where α_i and β_i are random variables. The values of a, b, c and d, and the distributions of α_i and β_i (the latter are likely to be assumed independent of i) would have to be determined empirically.

The model is now specified. A simulation of the system can be carried out by a program implementing the following procedure:

1. Set $i = 0$. Fix a starting price P_0.
2. Increment i by one. Generate random β_i from the appropriate distribution. Using P_{i-1}, β_i and the supply law (1.10), calculate Q_i.
3. Generate random α_i from the appropriate distribution. Using Q_i, α_i and the demand law (1.9), calculate P_i. This determines the state (Q_i, P_i).
4. Repeat steps 2 and 3 for the required number of points in the operation path.

A possible history of this procedure is illustrated in figure 1.5. The consecutive system states are shown as points on the (P, Q) plane, with P plotted on the vertical axis according to established tradition. The effect of procedure steps 2 and 3, for the given demand and supply lines and the sequence of α_i, β_i values, is indicated by dotted lines. For reasons that are clear from the appearance of the diagram, these models are called 'cobweb models'.

The particular operation sequence in figure 1.5 represents what is called a 'stable market'. The fluctuations from one state to the next become smaller with time and the market eventually settles into an equilibrium regime where variations are caused only by the random phenomena. That equilibrium is independent of the initial conditions (i.e. the starting price P_0). Different model parameters may well result in an unstable market, with fluctuations increasing with time. Also, if the demand and supply laws are represented by curves instead of straight lines, the long-term behaviour of the market may depend on the initial conditions (see exercise 2).

Clearly, the model can be generalised to include several commodities whose quantity and price attributes are related. The demand and supply laws would become functions of several variables (plus random perturbations). The objective of a simulation would be to investigate the stability of the market and, perhaps, the rate of convergence to an equilibrium. The limiting values of the attributes could be estimated and confidence intervals obtained for them.

1.5   A model of a car washing station

Mr Benz, who owns a small garage, is toying with the idea of purchasing an adjacent piece of land and installing a car washing machine on it. He has a choice of two models: one rather slow and reasonably cheap, and the other much faster and much more expensive. In order to decide whether to go ahead with the deal, and if so which machine to choose, he needs an estimate of the average profit per unit time, P, associated with each alternative. On the basis that profit equals revenue minus cost, the following expression for P is arrived at:

$$P = aU - b; \quad a, b \geqslant 0, \tag{1.11}$$

where U is the fraction of time that the machine is busy washing cars; a and b are known constants reflecting the revenue per unit of busy time and the cost per unit time (running cost + depreciation), respectively.

Now the problem is to estimate the value of U. From his long experience at the garage, Mr Benz has a pretty good idea of the likely pattern of demands for washing. He can therefore make a reasonable assumption concerning the distribution of times between arrivals of customers (and if he cannot do it by himself, his brother-in-law, a specialist in operations research, is ready to help him). Also known, from the machine specifications, is the distribution of the

Figure 1.5. Market fluctuations.

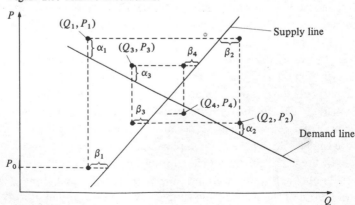

12

time it takes to wash a car. The area of the available land places an effective limit on the number of cars that can wait for washing at any one time; any car that finds that limit reached would go away immediately.

These parameters and assumptions are sufficient for the construction of a simulation model which can be used to obtain an estimate for U. Entities to be included in the model are cars, car washing machine and car park. As the problem is stated, the only attribute of interest is $N(t)$, the total number of cars in the station (waiting and being washed) at time t. If the limit on the number of waiting cars is M, then $0 \leqslant N(t) \leqslant M + 1$ for all t. A typical operation path over an observation period $0 \leqslant t \leqslant T$ is illustrated in figure 1.6.

There are two types of events: arrival events, at times $a_1, a_2, \ldots$, when $N(t)$ jumps up by one; departure events, at times $d_1, d_2, \ldots$, when $N(t)$ jumps down by one. If T_0 is the total time, during the interval $(0, T)$, that the operation path spends at level $N(t) = 0$, then T_0/T is an estimate for the fraction of time that the machine is idle; $\tilde{U} = 1 - (T_0/T)$ is an estimate of U.

The simulation program will maintain a 'current time' variable, t, and a 'current state' variable, N. The current time will be incremented from event to event and appropriate action will be taken at each increment. Since there are two event types, two additional variables, AT and DT, are required, to keep track of the times of next arrival and next departure, respectively. When the current time is at a departure instant, and there are customers still in the system, the next departure instant can be set by adding the service time of the next customer. If the queue is empty after a departure, then the proper setting of next departure instant will be postponed until the next arrival event. In the meantime, however, DT must be set to something; in order to make sure that the next event to occur is an arrival, it is set to infinity (in practice, the largest number available on the computer). If the current time is at an arrival event, the next arrival instant can be set by adding the next interarrival time. Also, if this arrival found the system empty, the proper value of the next departure instant is

Figure 1.6

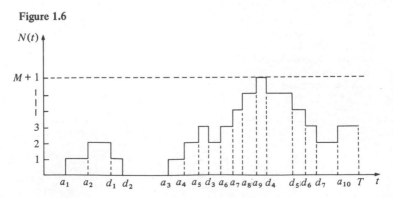

set and a variable *TO*, which is to contain the total idle time, is updated. The total simulation time is held in a variable *T* and the limit on waiting cars in a variable *M*. The variable *E* records the time when the system last emptied.

All actions of the program are displayed in the flow-chart in figure 1.7.

As shown, the simulation is started with an empty system. It would be just as easy to initialise *N* to a positive integer; perhaps on certain days cars queue up for washing before the opening hour. In that case, the initial value of *DT* would be finite.

A reference in the flow-chart to 'interarrival time', or 'service time', implies that a random number from the appropriate distribution is generated at that point. The operation path, and hence the estimate $\tilde{U}$ corresponding to a particular run of the simulation is determined by that sequence of random numbers. If Mr Benz desires a confidence interval for *U* as well as a point estimate (he

Figure 1.7

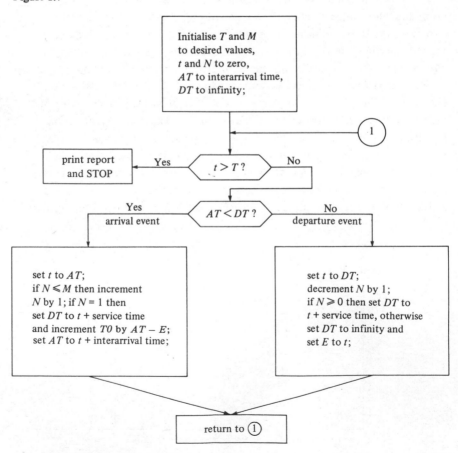

should insist on it, before making a decision), the program must be run several times with the same parameter values but different random number sequences, yielding a sample of estimates $\tilde{U}_1, \tilde{U}_2, \ldots, \tilde{U}_n$. The sample mean

$$U = \frac{1}{n} \sum_{i=1}^{n} \tilde{U}_i$$

will then be taken as the estimate of U; the width of the confidence interval will be proportional to the standard deviation of $\tilde{U}_i$ and inversely proportional to $n^{1/2}$ (see chapter 5).

The simulation structure described here is representative of the so called 'event-oriented' simulators. An alternative approach would be to program separately the actions of the 'processes', or 'activities', that cause events to occur and let these run in parallel. In this example, there would be a 'customer creation' process causing arrivals of cars, a 'service' process taking the waiting cars one after another and servicing them and a 'customer' process associated with each car, including the actions of joining the queue, waiting for servicing and departing. Both the event-oriented and the process-oriented approaches will be discussed in chapter 2.

Exercises
1. Devise and implement a Monte Carlo procedure for calculating the area of the ellipse $(x/a)^2 + (y/b)^2 = 1$; $\quad a, b > 0$. Apply the variance reduction technique of section 1.2 and observe its effect on the accuracy of the estimate.

2. Draw a cobweb model diagram corresponding to an unstable market. Give also an example (using non-linear demand and supply curves) of a market which may be either stable or unstable, depending on the starting price.

3. What modification would have to be made in the simulation program for the car washing station (section 1.5) if one wished to estimate the expected number of cars in the system? The expected number of cars turned away because the car park was full?

2. CONSTRUCTION OF SIMULATION PROGRAMS

2.1   Basic approaches

A simulation program has three main purposes. These are (*a*) to generate operation paths for the system being studied, (*b*) to collect statistics about various quantities of interest and (*c*) to obtain good estimates of the desired performance measures. The final aim is, of course, (*c*); in order to achieve that aim one needs (*b*), which in turn requires (*a*). When there is no danger of ambiguity, the part of the program that is devoted to the generation of operation paths will be referred to as 'the simulator'. Our concern now is with the programming techniques appropriate to the writing of simulators.

An operation path was defined as an instance of a behaviour pattern: the system state (which is a collection of attributes) as a function of time. Since the definition of the system state depends, in general, on the statistics that are to be collected, so does the structure of the simulator. In all cases, however, one has to keep track of the passage of time, generate the events that change the system state and implement the resulting changes. Thus every simulator should maintain an internal 'clock'; the passage of time is represented by incrementing the value of that clock.

The behaviour of a simulator clock may be very similar to that of a real one: at every 'tick', the value of the clock is incremented by a given (constant) amount. Such simulators are called 'fixed time increment', or 'synchronous'. Alternatively, since the operation path is determined by what happens at every event, the clock may be incremented directly from one event time to the next event time, no matter what interval separates them. Simulators of the second type are called 'variable time increment', or 'asynchronous'.

We thus have two possible simulation structures, outlined in figure 2.1. It is assumed that the current value of the clock is kept in a variable called *TIME*. In the case of synchronous simulators, the magnitude of each increment is ΔT.

Note that, among the actions implied by 'change the system state', is the setting of future event times, whenever possible. For instance, if the event that has just occurred was the arrival of an entity, then knowing the characteristics of the interarrival intervals, one can set the time of the next arrival.

16

Clearly, the choice of simulator structure is influenced by the nature of the system being simulated. Fixed time increments are appropriate to systems with discrete time, and also to those with continuous time–continuous events (in the latter case it is impossible to advance from event to event). One can use fixed time increment simulators for systems with continuous time–discrete events; however, they are then less efficient, in general, than the ones with variable time increments. To see why this is so, consider the effect of the size of time increment, ΔT. If ΔT is of the same order of magnitude as the intervals between events, or larger, then a fixed time increment simulator is probably too inaccurate: the inability to tell exactly at what point between two increments an event occurred becomes a significant drawback. If, on the other hand, ΔT is very small in relation to the intervals between events, then there are many clock increments in between event times. At each of those increments the possible event notices are examined, only to reveal that nothing has happened; that is unproductive effort as far as the simulation is concerned.

All currently available computer languages for the simulation of discrete event systems use variable time increments. They differ in their philosophy and in the logic of the control program; there are different ways of manipulating events and of updating the system state. In all cases, however, the actions that drive the simulation are performed at event times.

Scheduling of events

We shall begin by introducing the 'event-oriented' approach (which is used, for instance, in the language SIMSCRIPT; see section 2.4). In an event-oriented simulator there is a procedure associated with each type of event in the system: it performs the actions required to handle that type of event and it is invoked every time an event of that type occurs. Suppose that there are M event types, $1, 2, \ldots, M$, and let the corresponding procedures be $P_1, P_2, \ldots, P_M$. The simulator maintains what is called an 'event list'. Conceptually, this is an M-tuple

Figure 2.1

1. Initialise;	1. Initialise;
2. Increment *TIME* by ΔT;	2. Increment *TIME* to the time of the next event;
3. If any events have occurred, change the system state appropriately;	3. Change the system state appropriately;
4. Collect statistics;	4. Collect statistics;
5. If the simulation period has not expired, return to step 2;	5. If the simulation period has not expired, return to step 2;
6. Analyse collected statistics and produce report.	6. Analyse collected statistics and produce report.
Fixed time increments	Variable time increments

17

of event times, $(T_1, T_2, \ldots, T_M)$, where T_i is the instant when the next event of type i is going to occur. The incrementing of the clock is performed by finding the smallest T_i and taking it as the current clock value; the corresponding procedure P_i is then invoked.

The structure of an event-oriented simulation is summarised in figure 2.2 (again the value of the clock is held in variable *TIME*; the variable *PERIOD* contains the length of the simulation period).

A few words about the implementation of the event list are in order at this point (we shall return to the subject at greater detail later). The word 'list' implies a linear data structure and, indeed, most implementations use one. We shall see, however, that there are other possibilities worth exploring. Nor is it necessary to have an entry in the list for each event type at all times; given a suitable data structure, one can place events on the list and remove them from it. We are going to assume such an implementation in the example that follows.

Consider a system where a single machine services, in order of arrival, a stream of statistically identical jobs. From time to time the machine breaks down and suspends operation until it is repaired. When that happens, the job (if any) in service is returned to the head of the queue, to be restarted from the beginning when the machine becomes operative again. The distributions of inter-arrival intervals, service times, operative periods and repair times are given. The only performance measure of interest is the average response time – the time between the arrival of a job and the completion of its service.

We shall give a broad outline of an event-oriented simulation for this system. There are four event types: job arrival, service completion, machine breakdown and repair completion. The procedures associated with those event types will be called *ARRIVAL, SERVICE, BREAK* and *REPAIR* respectively. There will be

Figure 2.2. Event-oriented simulation.

Procedure *CLOCK*:	Procedure P_1:	.... Procedure P_M:
While *TIME* < *PERIOD*, repeat the following: find i such that T_i = min $(T_1, T_2, \ldots, T_M)$; set *TIME* = T_i, invoke procedure P_i;	Update system state; collect statistics; update event list; return to *CLOCK*;	Update system state; collect statistics; update event list; return to *CLOCK*;

Actions of main program:
1. Initialise event list and other variables; 2. Invoke procedure *CLOCK*; 3. Analyse collected statistics and produce report.

an entity *JOB* with a single attribute, *ARRTIME*, recording the time when the job arrived in the system; that attribute will be used to determine the response time for the job. Let us assume that the event list and the job queue are implemented as linked lists of records (see section 2.2) and that these are arranged in order of event times (for the event list) and in order of arrival (for the job queue).

The actions of the clock and event procedures are as follows:

Procedure CLOCK: while *TIME* < *PERIOD* do {set *TIME* to the time of the first event on the event list; remove that event from the list; invoke the corresponding event procedure};

Procedure ARRIVAL: create new *JOB* with *ARRTIME* set to *TIME* and enter it at the tail of the job queue; generate an interarrival interval from the appropriate distribution and insert next arrival event in correct position on the event list; if the queue was found empty and the server is not broken, generate a service time from the appropriate distribution and insert service completion event in correct position on the event list;

Procedure SERVICE: determine response time of the first *JOB* in the queue (by subtracting its *ARRTIME* from *TIME*) and accumulate it; increment number of completed jobs by one; remove first *JOB* from the queue; if the queue is not empty, generate a service time from the appropriate distribution and insert service completion event in correct position on the event list;

Procedure BREAK: if a service completion event is scheduled, remove it from the event list; generate a repair interval from the appropriate distribution and insert a repair completion event in correct position on the event list; set a flag to indicate a broken server;

Procedure REPAIR: generate an operative period from the appropriate distribution and insert a breakdown event in correct position on the event list; if the queue is not empty, generate a service time from the appropriate distribution and insert a service completion event in correct position on the event list; reset flag to indicate an operative server;

Note that the event list always contains an arrival event and either a breakdown or a repair completion event. A service completion event may not be present, either because the last departure left an empty queue or because the machine broke down during a service. If the system was such that an interrupted service was allowed to resume from the point of interruption, or restart without resampling from the distribution, then there would have to be a mechanism for remembering the remaining service time of a job; that could be included as another attribute of entity *JOB*.

Assuming that the system is started with the machine operative and an' empty queue, the actions of the main program are:

{Initialise job queue to empty; initialise event list to empty; generate an interarrival interval and place first arrival event on event list; generate an operative period and insert first breakdown event in correct position on the event list; initialise response time accumulator to zero, number of completed jobs to zero and *PERIOD* to the desired simulation period;

$$CL\dot{O}CK;$$

obtain average response time as the ratio of accumulated response time and number of jobs completed; produce report}.

In the event-oriented approach one takes a global view of everything that happens in the system; the manipulation of events is explicit. Alternatively, one could regard an operation path of a system as resulting from the interaction of a number of processes running in parallel. The management of events then becomes implicit in the management of processes. This viewpoint leads to the 'process-oriented' approach to simulation. Two widely used languages based on that approach are GPSS (section 2.4) and SIMULA (section 2.4 and appendix 1).

Scheduling of processes

A process is defined as a sequence of events, together with a set of actions accompanying each event. Thus the (potentially infinite) sequence of arrival events, together with the associated creation of new jobs, can be considered as a process. A particular event may be a member of more than one process sequence, but any given action belongs to at most one process. Moreover, if the control program itself is regarded as a process, then 'at most one' should be replaced by 'one and only one'.

The behaviour of a system can be represented by a set of processes whose event sequences, when merged, contain all events that occur in the system. Somewhere behind the scenes there is still a clock which is advanced from event to event, and the equivalent of an event list showing what is scheduled to happen when. However, the entries on that list are now processes, ordered according to the time of the next events in their respective sequences. After each advance of of the clock, the actions of the process at the head of the event list are executed. When there is more than one process scheduled for the same time instant (i.e. an event is a member of more than one process sequence), the actions of all those processes are executed, in the order in which they appear in the list.

The simulation support system (or the language) should provide primitives for placing processes at particular points on the event list, removing them from the list and re-scheduling them from one point on the list to another. A simulator is then written only in terms of process definitions describing the actions of the processes and employing the scheduling primitives (figure 2.3).

To illustrate these ideas, let us take the same example that we used before – the system with a machine subject to breakdowns – and apply to it the process-oriented approach. Four process definitions suggest themselves: a process to generate the arriving jobs, a process to perform the serving of jobs by the machine, a process associated with the machine breakdowns and a process for each job that comes into the system. Call these processes *ARRIVALS*, *MACHINE*, *BREAKS* and *JOB*, respectively. Suppose that the scheduling primitives available are (here we follow in the steps of SIMULA; for more details see section 2.4 and appendix 1):

ACTIVATE P [DELAY T]: schedule process P at $TIME + T$; if there is no *DELAY*, or if $T = 0$, then place P at the head of the event list (its actions will be executed immediately). This instruction is normally issued from another process. P is presumably not on the event list then. *TIME* is again the current clock value.

CANCEL P: remove process P from the event list. One process may cancel another scheduled process, or it may cancel itself.

HOLD(T): re-schedule the process which issues the instruction (that is the process at the head of the event list) to $TIME + T$.

The actions of our four processes can now be described as follows:

Process ARRIVALS:
{generate an interarrival interval, I, from the appropriate distribution;
HOLD(I);
create a new *JOB* process, J;
ACTIVATE J}; repeat;

Process MACHINE:
{while the job queue is not empty, do
       {let J be the first *JOB* in the job queue;
        generate a service time, S, from the appropriate distribution;
        HOLD(S);
        ACTIVATE J};
CANCEL this *MACHINE* (job queue is now empty)}; repeat;

Figure 2.3. Process-oriented simulation.

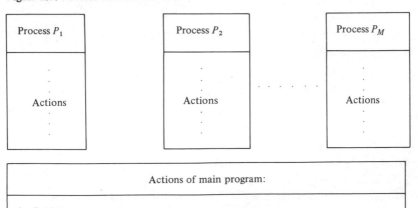

Process P_1		Process P_2		Process P_M
Actions		Actions	· · · · · · ·	Actions

Actions of main program:
1. Initialise;
2. Start one or more processes (i.e., schedule them);
3. Wait for the simulation period;
4. Produce report.

Process BREAKS:

{generate an operative period, *OP*, from the appropriate distribution; *HOLD(OP)*;
CANCEL the *MACHINE* process;
indicate, by setting a flag, that the machine is broken; if the job queue is not
empty, indicate by setting a flag, that there is an interrupted service;
generate a repair period, *R*, from the appropriate distribution; *HOLD(R)*;
reset flags; if there was an interrupted service then

> {generate a service time, *S*, from the appropriate distribution;
> *ACTIVATE* the *MACHINE* process *DELAY S*};

otherwise *ACTIVATE* the *MACHINE* process}; repeat;

Process JOB:

set *ARRTIME* to *TIME*; join at the end of the job queue; if the job queue was
empty before, and if the machine is not broken, then
ACTIVATE the *MACHINE* process;
CANCEL this *JOB* process (i.e. leave the event list until the job's service is
completed);
accumulate the response time of this *JOB* (it is equal to *TIME* − *ARRTIME*);
increment the number of completed jobs by one; leave the job queue; terminate
this *JOB*.

Main program:

initialise job queue to empty; initialise response time accumulator to zero,
number of completed jobs to zero and *PERIOD* to the desired simulation period;
create a new *ARRIVALS* process, *A*; create a new unbroken *MACHINE* process,
M; create a new *BREAKS* process, *B*;

> *ACTIVATE A*;
> *ACTIVATE B*;
> *HOLD(PERIOD)*;

obtain average response time as the ratio of accumulated response time and
number of jobs completed; produce report.

Note that there is no need for the main program to issue an *ACTIVATE M*;
that is done either by the first *JOB* process (if it finds the machine operative) or
by the *BREAKS* process (after a repair). Also, there is no need to build termination clauses into the *ARRIVAL*, *MACHINE*, and *BREAKS* processes; that is
done by the main program.

Clearly, in any given system, there may be several ways of apportioning events
and actions among processes. For instance, in the above simulator it was left to
the *BREAKS* process to restart a service that was interrupted by a breakdown.
Those actions could just as easily have been included in the *MACHINE* process.
Similarly, the jobs could have been defined as passive entities, rather than
processes; the actions of placing them in the queue and removing them from it

22

could have been part of the *ARRIVAL* and *MACHINE* processes respectively. Different decisions of this nature would result in different simulator structures. The net effect should always be the same, i.e. the same operation paths should be generated. What may be affected are the readability, ease of debugging, ease of modification and, perhaps, the efficiency of the program.

Scheduling of activities

There is a third approach to simulator construction which deserves a mention, although we shall not dwell on it. That is the 'activity-oriented' approach. The idea behind it is that the actions of the simulator are partitioned into segments called 'activities'. An activity does not span more than one event. With every activity is associated a condition which, at any moment of time is either satisfied or not, depending on the global system state and the value of an internal activity clock. As with the other variable time increment methods, the simulation progresses from event to event. At each event time, all activities are scanned and those amongst them whose conditions are satisfied, are executed. There is no event list.

The simulation languages CSL (Buxton [4]) and SIMON (Hills [23]) are based on the activity-oriented approach.

2.2 Data structures

We have seen that the work of a simulator is almost entirely devoted to manipulating various collections of data items, such as entity attributes, event lists, queues, etc. It is important, therefore, to examine at greater detail some of the more frequently encountered data structures. Their implementation will depend, of course, on the programming language used. We shall try to keep the discussion as general as possible, but will assume a language that provides a facility for creating composite data objects and for referring to them (e.g. ALGOL W, ALGOL 68, PASCAL, SIMULA). The examples will be in SIMULA.

Perhaps the simplest non-trivial data structure is the array. This is a named collection of items of identical type, arranged in a regular pattern. Individual elements of an array can be accessed directly by indexing: thus $A(I)$ is the Ith element of the linear array A and $B(I, J)$ is the element at the intersection of the Ith row and Jth column of the two-dimensional array B. The storage occupied by an array – determined by the type and number of elements – remains unchanged throughout the array's existence. In a given environment (or level of nesting, or scope), one name can be associated with at most one array.

Relaxing some of the restrictions governing arrays, one arrives at the notion of a 'record'. This is also a named collection of items but the latter are not ordered in any way and may be of different types. Individual items (or 'attributes', as we shall call them) within a record have names too, and can be accessed directly. There may be many instances of a record, all associated with the same name and having the same attributes, but with different values for those attributes. To get at the attributes of a particular instance, one needs a 'reference', a pointer to the piece of storage where that instance of the record is kept.

Suppose, for example, that we wish to define a record called *JOB*, with two attributes, *ARRTIME* (arrival time) and *REMTIME* (remaining execution time). An instance of *JOB* is to be created and its attributes are to be assigned the values of the variables *TIME* and *EXEC* respectively. Another instance of *JOB* is also to be created. In SIMULA, this could be done as follows:

```
class JOB;
begin real ARRTIME,REMTIME end;
ref(JOB)J1,J2;
J1:—new JOB;
J1.ARRTIME:=TIME;
J1.REMTIME:=EXEC;
J2:—new JOB;
```

Lines 1, 2 and 3 contain declarations: line 1 associates the name *JOB* with the record that is being defined (the 'class' concept is not, of course, limited to records); line 2 describes the 'body' of the record, specifying the names and types of its attributes; line 3 declares two variables, *J1* and *J2*, that can be used to refer to instances of *JOB*. In line 4, a new instance of *JOB* is created and a pointer to it is assigned to *J1*; since SIMULA initialises all variables, the *ARRTIME* and *REMTIME* attributes of that new instance are set to zero. Lines 5 and 6 modify those attributes;. access to the internal variables *ARRTIME* and *REMTIME* is via the pointer *J1*. In line 7, another instance of *JOB* is created (with attributes initialised to zero) and a pointer to it is assigned to *J2*. If we wished to access the attributes of this second instance of *JOB*, we would use *J2. ARRTIME* and *J2. REMTIME. SIMULA* also allows attributes to be passed as parameters to classes; that mechanism is sometimes more convenient than declaring them in the body.

It should be obvious from the above that records are well suited to representing single entities, event notices, etc: simple objects with a fixed number of different attributes. In addition, there is a need for structures representing ordered or unordered sets of entities (such as queues). Moreover, the membership of those sets should be allowed to change dynamically, with new elements being inserted and old ones removed from time to time.

Linked lists

A straightforward way of grouping elements together is to place them in a 'chain', with every element except the last having a unique successor and every element except the first having a unique predecessor. A 'linked list' is thus obtained – a structure that imposes a strict linear ordering among its elements. If those elements are records, the linked list can be implemented by including as an attribute of each record a pointer (a reference) to one (or both) of its immediate neighbours. One possibility is to have each record refer to its successor only; the result is a 'singly linked list', illustrated in figure 2.4.

Take, for example, the record *JOB*, defined earlier. That definition can be easily extended by including an attribute, say *NEXT*, which will be a reference to *JOB*:

> **class** *JOB*;
> **begin real** *ARRTIME,REMTIME*; **ref**(*JOB*)*NEXT* **end**;

Now if we are given the references to two instances of *JOB*, say *J1* and *J2*, and wish to link them so that *J2* is the successor of *J1*, the following assignment statement can be used:

> *J1.NEXT:–J2*;

JOB records can thus be placed into a singly linked list. Then, given a reference to the first record, say *HEAD*, all other records can be accessed by stepping along the pointers:

> *J:–HEAD*;
> **while not** *J.NEXT==***none do** *J:–J.NEXT*;

(a reference variable that does not point to anything has the value **none**; this is used to detect the end of the list).

Singly linked lists are often used to implement stacks and queues. The stack is a linear data structure where new elements are added at one end and the most recent ones are removed from the same end (Last-In-First-Out). These operations are easily performed with a singly linked list, given a reference to the first element; call it *TOP* (stacks are traditionally thought of as 'standing up'). In our example with the *JOB* records, to place a *JOB* (say *J*) on to the stack one writes

> *J.NEXT:–TOP*;
> *TOP:–J*;

Similarly, removing a *JOB* from the top of the stack and assigning it to *J* is accomplished by

> *J:–TOP*;
> *TOP:–TOP.NEXT*;

Figure 2.4. Singly linked list.

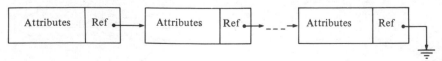

25

Note that if the above statements are executed when the stack is empty, the value of *TOP* will be **none** and *TOP.NEXT* will result in a failure.

The queue is a linear data structure with two distinguished ends: new elements are added at one end and old ones are removed from the other end (First-In-First-Out). Again, given a singly linked list and pointers to the first and last elements – call them *HEAD* and *TAIL* respectively – these operations are quite straightforward. In our example, to add a *JOB* (say *J*) to the tail of the queue we write

> *TAIL.NEXT:—J*;
> *TAIL:—J*;

and to remove a *JOB* from the head of the queue,

> *J:—HEAD*;
> *HEAD:—HEAD.NEXT*;

One can also insert new elements into, and remove old elements from, an arbitrary position of a singly linked list. The appropriate manipulation of pointers is shown in figure 2.5, (*a*) and (*b*) (for a more detailed presentation, see, for example, Page & Wilson [36]). The new pointers are indicated by dotted lines. It is important to realise, however, that while it is easy to insert a new element after a given element in the list, it is not so easy to do that before a given element. This is because each element points to its successor, but not to its predecessor. A similar remark applies to deletions: to remove an element from the list one needs a reference to its predecessor.

These difficulties can be avoided by including another reference in each element, pointing to the element preceding it (if any). The result is a 'doubly linked list', illustrated in figure 2.6. Now, given references to the two ends, the list can be traversed in both directions; insertions can be made either before or after any given element in the list; any element can be removed from the list without having to know its successor or predecessor.

Figure 2.5

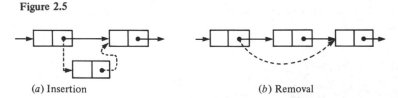

(*a*) Insertion   (*b*) Removal

Figure 2.6. Doubly linked list.

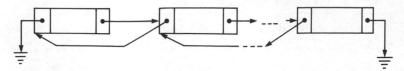

26

Directed graphs, trees and heaps

A finite set of elements, or 'nodes', together with a set of pointers, or 'arcs', from some of those nodes to others, is called a 'directed graph' (figure 2.7). Clearly, the singly and doubly linked lists are special cases of directed graphs. Other applications include representations of job shops, large computer systems, railway networks, production and supply networks, etc. (much of the terminology associated with directed graphs has network connotations).

If a directed graph is known to remain unchanged, then each node can be represented by a record containing the appropriate pointers to other nodes. Such a representation may be inadequate if the topology of the graph is liable to change: then one may wish to add new pointers to a node record, and that may be difficult once the record has been created. The alternative is to associate a linked list with each node and include in it an entry for every arc coming out of that node. Another linked list would contain pointers to the heads (and, perhaps, tails) of those linked lists. Nodes and arcs can then be added to, or removed from the graph.

Certain special types of directed graphs deserve particular attention. Before they are introduced, however, some more definitions are necessary. Let i and j be two nodes in a directed graph. If there is an arc from i to j then j is said to be 'immediately reachable' from i. Next, the concept 'reachable' can be defined recursively as follows: j is reachable from i if either j is immediately reachable from i, or there exists a node k such that j is immediately reachable from k and k is reachable from i. If no node in the graph is reachable from itself then the graph is said to be 'acyclic'.

In a directed acyclic graph, the nodes that can be reached from a given node are sometimes called its 'descendants'; those that are immediately reachable from it are its 'sons'. Similarly, the nodes from which the given node can be reached are called its 'ancestors'; those from which it can be immediately reached are its 'parents'.

A 'tree' is a directed acyclic graph which has the following properties: there is one, and only one node, called the 'root', which has no parents (all other

Figure 2.7. A directed graph.

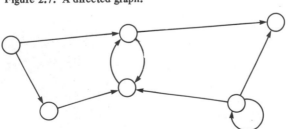

nodes are descendants of the root); every node except the root has exactly one parent.

A 'binary tree' is a tree in which every node has at most two sons; they are often distinguished by being referred to as the 'left son' and the 'right son'. A node without any sons is called a 'leaf'. These concepts are illustrated in figure 2.8 (according to established tradition, the root is placed at the top).

The implementation of a binary tree by means of records and references presents no problems. A declaration of the following type can be used:

    class *NODE*;
    begin ref(*NODE*)*LEFTSON,RIGHTSON*; 'other attributes' **end**;

There would be a pointer to the root of the tree, e.g.

    ref(*NODE*)*ROOT*;

The tree can then be built up (or down, depending on the point of view), starting at the root:

    ROOT:—**new** *NODE*;
    ROOT.LEFTSON:—**new** *NODE*; . . . .

Binary trees have the appealing property that isolating a node, together with all its descendants, produces another binary tree with a root at that node. This allows many operations on such trees to be performed recursively. For example, a binary tree can be traversed (i.e. all its nodes can be visited) by the following procedure which takes a pointer to the root as a parameter:

    procedure *TRAVERSE*(*R*); **ref**(*NODE*)*R*;
    begin if not *R.LEFTSON*==**none then**
        TRAVERSE(*R.LEFTSON*);

Figure 2.8. A binary tree.

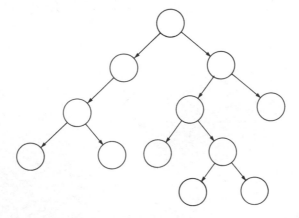

'visit R';
if not $R.RIGHTSON$==**none then**
$TRAVERSE(R.RIGHTSON)$;
end;

Just as in the case of linked lists, the manipulation of binary trees is facilitated by including in the node record a backward pointer to the (unique) parent node.

Apart from the fact that they arise quite naturally in many applications, binary trees are important because they lead to very efficient algorithms. Tasks such as searching among a set of n items, whose average execution time is O(n) (i.e. roughly proportional to n when n is large) when the items form a linear list, take on the average O(log n) time if a binary tree is used instead. In a 'complete' binary tree with n nodes, i.e. one with a maximum number of nodes at each level, the distance from the root to any leaf is approximately log n (base 2). Hence, any algorithm operating on that tree in a way that involves following a path from the root and stopping when a leaf is reached, will have a time complexity of O(log n).

A tree structure of special relevance to simulation (we shall refer to it when discussing event list implementations) is the 'heap'. This is a complete binary tree where each node has associated with it a real number. Moreover, the number of a son is always greater than or equal to that of his parent. Thus the smallest number in a heap is at the root and the largest one is at one of the leaves. Elsewhere in the literature (e.g. Knuth [31], Aho, Hopcroft & Ullman [1]) the inequalities are reversed and the largest number is at the root. We choose the present definition because of the event list application; there the numbers will be event times and the root will contain the earliest event. An example of a heap is shown in figure 2.9. Note that the leaves in the last, partially filled, level are 'packed to the left'. We shall assume that this is always the case.

Figure 2.9. A heap.

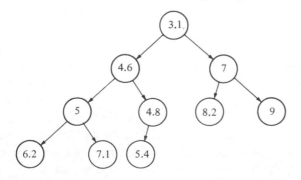

The operations of removing a node from a heap and inserting a node into a heap can be performed in O(log n) time, where n is the number of nodes. Consider first the removal of the root. Let L be the last leaf in the heap, i.e. the rightmost leaf on the level furthest from the root (in figure 2.9, L is the node marked 5.4). Having taken the root out, L is put in its place and the resulting binary tree is reorganised so that it becomes a heap again. The latter can be done by the following somewhat loosely described recursive procedure which takes a pointer to the root as a parameter:

> **procedure** *REMAKE(R)*; **ref**(*NODE*)*R*;
> **begin if** '*R* is not a leaf and the smaller of its sons, say *S*, is smaller than *R*' **then**
>> **begin** 'swap the contents of *R* and *S*';
>> *REMAKE(S)*;
>> **end**;
> **end**;

If a node other than the root (or L) is removed, the simplest way to proceed is to replace it by its parent, the latter by *its* parent, etc., until the root replaces one of its sons. The leaf L is then put in the place of the root and procedure *REMAKE* is invoked (one can improve on this slightly).

To insert a new node into the heap, we start by placing it in the first vacant position, i.e. the leftmost vacant position on the level furthest from the root (in figure 2.9 that is the brother of the node marked 5.4), or if that level is full the leftmost position of the next level. The resulting binary tree is then remade into a heap by a procedure similar to *REMAKE*, except that the new data now travels up the tree instead of down, stopping either when it finds a parent smaller than itself or when it reaches the root.

There remains the problem of how to find the last leaf or the first vacant position. One solution is to implement the heap as an array, A, of pointers: $A(1)$ refers to the root and if $A(i)$ refers to a node, then $A(2i)$ and $A(2i + 1)$ refer to the left and right sons of that node respectively. When there are n nodes in the heap, $A(n)$ refers to the last leaf and $A(n + 1)$ is the first vacant position. Such an implementation is very efficient with respect to time, but not necessarily with respect to space. In order to ensure that the array does not overflow, the most conservative estimates have to be made when declaring the bounds, which may cause large portions of the array to remain unused most of the time. If, on the other hand, the heap is implemented by pointers from parents to sons then the storage management is flexible but there is no direct reference to the last leaf. However, one can gain access to it easily enough, using the binary representation of n: the first bit corresponds to visiting the first level of the heap, the root; moving from the $(i-1)$th to the ith level, go left if the ith bit of n is zero, right otherwise. For example, the heap in figure 2.9 has 10 nodes; the binary representation of 10 is 1010. The path leading to the last leaf is: visit the root, go left, go right, go left. Similarly, to get at the first vacant position, one uses the binary representation of $n + 1$.

The important point about all these operations with heaps is that they involve no more than following a path from root to leaf and/or from leaf to root. Since the heap is a complete binary tree, the time complexity is in all cases $O(\log n)$.

2.3   The implementation of event lists

An 'event notice' is a data item associated with an event that has been scheduled. That item specifies the type of the event and the time at which it is to occur. In section 2.1 we saw that both event-oriented and process-oriented simulators use event notices – the first in order to decide which procedure to call next and the second in order to decide which process to activate next. The way in which the collection of event notices, i.e. the event list, is organised and manipulated may affect significantly the efficiency of a simulator.

The following simulator actions involve the event list:

(a)   Find the event notice corresponding to the most imminent event (this is done prior to every advance of the simulation clock; the event thus found becomes the current event);

(b)   Remove the current event notice from the list;

(c)   Insert a new event notice into the list;

(d)   Remove the notice associated with a given event type from the list (there can be at most one event of a given type scheduled at any one time).

Note that the rescheduling of the current or another event has not been mentioned explicitly. That is because such a rescheduling is conceptually equivalent to executing (b), or (d), followed immediately by (c).

All existing and proposed implementations of the event list have been designed so that (a) can be executed as quickly as possible, regardless of the number of notices present. A simple structure which suits that purpose very well is a linked list where the notices are placed in increasing order of event times. The following declaration could be used, for instance, to construct a doubly linked list of event notices:

> **class** *EVENTNOTICE*;
> **begin integer** *TYPE*; **real** *EVENTTIME*;
>   **ref**(*EVENTNOTICE*)*PREVIOUS,NEXT*;
> **end**;

Given such a linked list, actions (a) and (b) become very straightforward; they amount to accessing and removing the head of the list. To carry out (c), however, one has to scan the event list, starting either at the head or the tail, until the correct position for inserting the new event notice is found. With N notices in the list, the worst case time complexity of that operation will be $O(N)$. Similarly,

31

to carry out (d), the list has to be scanned until the appropriate event notice is found; again the worst case time complexity is $O(N)$.

It is much more difficult to determine how long operation (c) takes on the average. That depends, among other things, on the rate at which events are scheduled, the distribution of event times and the direction of scan. Consider, for example, the effect of the 'event offset time', i.e. the difference between the event time and the value of the clock at the moment when the event was scheduled. In the extreme case when all offset times are equal, the order of event notices in the event list is exactly the order in which they arrived for scheduling. Each new event notice must be placed at the end of the event list; there is no point in scanning the list from the beginning. Intuitively, if the variation of offset times is small, then it is better to scan the event list backwards, starting at the tail, whereas if that variation is large, it is better to scan forwards, starting at the head. Indeed, Engelbrecht-Wiggans & Maxwell [10] have shown that for Erlang distribution of offset times (coefficient of variation <1, see appendix 2) forward scan is better, for hyperexponential distribution (coefficient of variation >1) backward scan is better and for exponential distribution (coefficient of variation $= 1$) the two are equivalent.

In a large-scale simulation with many event types, scanning the event list at every scheduling instant may occupy a significant proportion of the total simulation time. That is why several event list structures have been proposed, whose aim is to improve the efficiency of executing (c) (one need not worry too much about speeding up (d); that is usually a much less frequent operation). Here we shall examine briefly some of these proposals.

Indexed list (Vaucher & Duval [40], Wyman [43], Engelbrecht-Wiggans & Maxwell [10]). The event notices are still placed in a linear list in increasing order of event times. In addition, another list of 'keys' is maintained; each key has a time attribute and points to a portion of the event list where the event times are larger than the value of that attribute (figure 2.10).

The procedure for inserting a new event notice into the list involves, first, finding the last key whose time precedes the event time of the new notice, and then scanning through the corresponding portion of the event list. If the number

Figure 2.10. An indexed list.

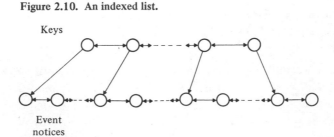

Keys

Event
notices

of keys is K and the maximum number of event notices between consecutive key pointers is M, then the worst case time complexity of an insertion is $C = O(K + M)$.

It is possible, of course, to keep the key pointers in an array, instead of a linked list. Then, provided that the index of each array element determines uniquely the range of event times in the corresponding portion of the event list, the appropriate key can be found directly, without a search. Given a sufficiently large array, the average time for an insertion will be a small constant, independent of N (for an analysis of this case, see Wyman [43]). It should be pointed out, however, that time is bought at the expense of space; the price paid may be too high, especially since much of the reserved space may remain unused for much of the time. Placing the keys in a linked list buys flexibility in space allocation, at the expense of the time spent searching that list.

One strategy for maintaining an indexed list is to keep K constant, with a fixed interval between consecutive key times. Then all event notices in the list may happen to fall in the first of those intervals. We have $C = O(N)$, the same worst case complexity as for the simple linked list. Alternatively, one could allow K to vary and ensure that M does not exceed a certain value. When a new event notice is to be inserted into a sublist which already contains M notices, either the existing key pointers are adjusted or, if that is impossible, a new key is added. With N event notices in the list, N/M keys would be used and the expression for C would be $C = O(M + N/M)$. That expression is minimised by choosing $M = N^{1/2}$, in which case $C = O(N^{1/2})$. To this one should add, however, the overhead of adjusting the key pointers and creating new keys.

Two-level indexed lists (Franta & Maly [14]). The two strategies described above can be combined by introducing 'primary' and 'secondary' keys. There is a constant number of primary keys with evenly spaced time attributes. These point into a variable list of secondary keys which, in turn, point into the list of event notices (figure 2.11).

Figure 2.11. A two-level indexed list.

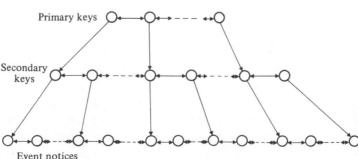

33

Inserting a new event notice into the list involves finding the appropriate primary key, then searching through the corresponding sublist of secondary keys for the appropriate secondary key, and then searching through the corresponding sublist of event notices for the appropriate insertion point. The list of secondary keys may have to be reorganised so that the number of event notices between two consecutive secondary key pointers does not exceed M.

Again, choosing $M = N^{1/2}$, the worst case time complexity of an insertion becomes $O(N^{1/2})$. The average complexity is unknown but there is no obvious reason why it should not also be $O(N^{1/2})$, although with a smaller coefficient of proportionality.

At this point it is natural to suggest that the number of primary keys be allowed to vary so that there are no more than M secondary keys between two consecutive primary key pointers. Then, choosing $M = N^{1/3}$, the worst case time complexity of an insertion can be reduced to $O(N^{1/3})$. With L levels of keys, one should in theory be able to achieve a worst case time complexity of $O(N^{1/(L+1)})$. In practice, however, a point of diminishing returns will be reached very quickly, as the overheads of reorganising all those pointers will begin to outweigh the advantages gained.

Heaps (Gonnet [18]). Significant improvement in efficiency can also be achieved by abandoning the linear ordering of event notices altogether and using a binary tree instead. The heap structure described in the last section is particularly suitable for the implementation of event lists. The current event notice is always at the root of the heap. We saw that removal of the root and insertion of a new node can be done in $O(\log N)$ time. This compares favourably with the $O(N^{1/2})$ worst case complexity of an insertion into an indexed list. Moreover, the problem of maintaining a balanced structure does not arise: the heap always remains a heap, i.e. a complete binary tree.

A disadvantage of the heap structure is that the natural 'successor' relationship among event notices is lost. To find the notice of the event immediately following an arbitrary event, one may have to traverse the whole heap. Also, the constant of proportionality implicit in that $O(\log N)$ bound may be quite large. Thus, although for very large values of N the heap is more efficient (as far as the worst case complexity of an insertion is concerned) than the indexed lists, the latter may well be better for moderate values of N.

2.4   Simulation languages. SIMSCRIPT, GPSS and SIMULA

One does not really need a simulation language in order to simulate. Any general purpose programming language can be used, with a greater or lesser degree of effort. What the simulation languages aim to do is to make life easier for the programmer by including some of the standard simulator components as language primitives. The facilities that a good simulation language should provide fall into five broad categories:

A. Entity manipulation. Creating new entities, destroying old ones, placing entities into, and removing them from, ordered and unordered sets (stacks, queues, etc.).

B. Time and event manipulation. Maintaining a clock and an event list, and executing the scheduling operations (a)-(d) described in section 2.3 (in the case of activity-oriented languages, these facilities are slightly different).

C. Random numbers. Sequences of numbers that appear to behave like independent and identically distributed random variables. Various discrete and continuous distributions should be provided, as well as the ability to both reproduce and change the sequences between different runs of the same program.

D. Collection of statistics. Data that can be used to obtain means, variances, frequency histograms and other quantities of interest. The collection may extend over entire simulation runs, or it may be restricted to separate portions of them.

E. Numerical computation. The ability to implement various numerical algorithms is required, e.g., in the statistical analysis of simulation output and in the construction of special random number generators.

In addition, a good simulation language should possess all those qualities that are desirable in any programming language, such as power, flexibility, simplicity, ease of use, readability, modularity, efficiency of compilation, run-time efficiency, good diagnostics, etc.

We shall examine now very briefly three popular simulation languages and comment on the way each of them meets the requirements outlined above.

SIMSCRIPT

The language that we shall refer to as SIMSCRIPT is in fact SIMSCRIPT II.5, the latest in a family of languages whose development began almost 20 years ago at the RAND Corporation (Karr, Kleine & Markowitz [26], Kiviat, Villanueva & Markowitz [27], [28]). SIMSCRIPT is organised as a five-level hierarchy: the first three levels provide a general purpose programming language having approximately the power of ALGOL; the fourth level contains entity manipulation features such as those outlined in category A above; the fifth level provides simulation facilities of categories B, C and D.

SIMSCRIPT is an event-oriented language. The general format of a simulation program in SIMSCRIPT is as follows:

PREAMBLE

'define variables, event notices, temporary and permanent entities together with their attributes, sets and the manner of their ordering, data to be collected'

35

END
MAIN

'initialise variables and sets, schedule the event notices
necessary to start the simulation'
START SIMULATION
'produce report'

END
EVENT name

'actions to be executed when an event of this type occurs'
RETURN

END

.
.
.

EVENT name

'actions to be executed when an event of this type occurs'
RETURN

END

To declare the types of events that occur in the system, a statement listing
the names (and possibly the attributes) of event notices is included in the
preamble. Thus, for the system described in section 2.1, one could write

EVENT NOTICES INCLUDE ARRIVAL, DEPARTURE,
BREAKDOWN, REPAIR AND ENDSIMULATION

For each event notice listed in the declaration there should be an event routine
of the same name. The event routine is invoked whenever an event of that
type occurs, i.e. whenever an event notice of that name comes to the head of the
event list.

An entity declaration specifies its name and its attributes. In our example, to
define an entity *JOB* with an attribute *ARRTIME* (a real variable) and with the
ability to join the queue, the following statements can be used:

TEMPORARY ENTITIES
EVERY JOB HAS AN ARRTIME AND MAY BELONG TO THE
QUEUE
DEFINE ARRTIME AS A REAL VARIABLE

For reasons of space allocation, SIMSCRIPT distinguishes between temporary
and permanent entities.

Global variables and sets are declared as belonging to the system, thus

THE SYSTEM OWNS A QUEUE
DEFINE QUEUE AS A FIFO SET

The entities in a set may be ordered according to the time of arrival (*FIFO*, First-
In-First-Out, or *LIFO*, Last-In-First-Out), or according to the value of a particular
attribute.

36

Having completed the declarations, one is ready to initialise the system and to start simulating. This is done in the main program. The statement *'START SIMULATION'* passes control to the SIMSCRIPT clock routine, which finds the next event, advances the clock, invokes the appropriate event routine, etc. When the clock routine finds an empty event list, control is returned to the main program (to the statement following *'START SIMULATION'*), at which point a report can be produced. Thus, a convenient way of stopping the simulation is to schedule at the desired point in the future a special 'end simulation' event, whose event routine will clear the event list.

The principal 'simulation-oriented' statements in SIMSCRIPT are:

(*a*)   Dealing with entities

> *CREATE* 'entity'
> *DESTROY* 'entity'
> *FILE* 'entity' *IN* 'set'
> *REMOVE FIRST* [or *LAST*] 'entity' *FROM* 'set' (it is also possible
> > to search a set for an entity with a given attribute value)

(b)   Dealing with events

> *SCHEDULE* 'event notice' *IN* [or *AT*] 'time'
> *CANCEL* 'event notice'
> *DESTROY* 'event notice'

These operations are self-explanatory. In addition, SIMSCRIPT provides very comprehensive statistics collecting and computing facilities (e.g. means, standard deviations, sums of squares, etc.). There are 10 streams of pseudo-random numbers; the default sequences which they produce may be changed by altering the seeds (for more details on random number generation see chapter 4).

GPSS

The General Purpose Simulation System (Gordon [19, 20]) is basically an IBM product, although it has also been implemented on machines of different manufacture. The latest version of the language is GPSS V.

The design philosophy of GPSS is that of block diagrams. Temporary entities, or 'transactions', are created, follow a path through the diagram and are destroyed on exit. The exact route for each transaction and the manner of traversing it, is determined by the blocks comprising the diagram. Some blocks are passed instantaneously; others may delay a transaction for a period of time whose distribution is given; still others may involve delays that depend on the number and state of the other transactions in the system.

To illustrate these ideas on a simple example, consider a system such as a counter in a bank, where customers arrive, queue, are served one at a time by a single server and depart. A block diagram for that system, and the corresponding GPSS statements, are illustrated in figure 2.12.

To turn the statements in the right-hand side of figure 2.12 into an executable GPSS program, they should be supplied with operands, or data fields: the *GENERATE* and *ADVANCE* statements should specify the distributions of the interarrival periods and service times, respectively (these are the only GPSS blocks that involve timing, and hence scheduling of future events); the *QUEUE* and *DEPART*, and the *SEIZE* and *RELEASE* statements identify the queue and the service facility, respectively; the *TERMINATE* statement carries an increment which is added to a count every time a transaction is destroyed; when that count reaches a value specified by the START statement, the simulation stops.

Note that there may be many transactions held up at the *QUEUE* block and, in principle, many transactions passing simultaneously through the *ADVANCE* block, but only one transaction at a time can *SEIZE* the serving facility, which then remains seized until the same transaction passes through the *RELEASE* block. It is that mechanism that ensures sequential servicing.

GPSS provides also storages, chains, groups, conditional branching, testing and a number of other simulation features, always in keeping with the concept of transactions following paths through a network of blocks. Statistics on passage times and occupancies can be collected and standard reports on them are produced by the system. The language does not include general facilities for numerical computation and therefore one cannot use it to manipulate and analyse the data that is collected.

Figure 2.12. The GPSS view of a single-server queue.

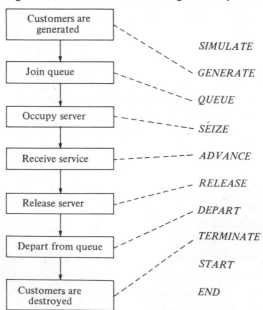

SIMULA

A reasonably detailed description of SIMULA is presented in appendix 1. Here it suffices to make a few general remarks.

Although originally intended as a special purpose simulation language, SIMULA (or SIMULA 67, as it is sometimes referred to) is now a very powerful general purpose language (Dahl & Nygaard [9]; Birtwistle *et al.* [3]), containing a slightly modified ALGOL 60 as a subset. A major new development is that of the **class** concept. Using classes one can construct complex hierarchical data and program structures, and thus extend the language facilities. Two such extensions that have been built into the system are **class** *SIMSET* and **class** *SIMULATION*. The former supplies entity and set manipulation facilities and the latter parallel processes, timing and scheduling primitives. Various random number generation procedures are also provided.

A simulation program can be a block prefixed by *SIMULATION*:

> *SIMULATION* **begin**
>> 'declarations, including those of processes';
>> 'initialise; create and activate instances of the appropriate processes';
>> 'wait until simulation is complete';
>> 'produce report';
>
> **end**;

Alternatively, one can define other classes, using the existing facilities and providing further ones of one's own. A block prefixed by such a class can use both the old and the new facilities. An example of a development based on this extension mechanism is the language DEMOS (Birtwistle [2]).

Comparative evaluation

Some comments on the relative merits and demerits of the three languages mentioned here are in order. We shall group these under the following broad headings: Generality, Convenience and Efficiency.

Being tied to the concept of block diagrams imposes significant constraints on the generality of GPSS. There are, for instance, certain state-dependent operations that do not lend themselves readily to description by block diagrams: e.g. multiserver queues with preemptive priorities or breakdowns, or processor-shared systems where the rate at which individual transactions progress through their service depends on the number of transactions competing for service. Such systems are difficult or impossible to simulate in GPSS. The inability to implement arbitrary numerical algorithms is also a significant disadvantage. SIMSCRIPT and SIMULA are completely general, both from the simulation and from the numerical point of view.

On the other hand, GPSS is the easiest of the three languages to learn and use. Programs written in it tend to be shorter and easier to debug. The production of reports is automatic, albeit inflexible. SIMULA is perhaps more difficult than SIMSCRIPT to learn, but once learnt it is easy to use. A point in SIMULA's favour is that its philosophy supports and encourages the use of structured programming and top-down design techniques; this is a valuable feature when one has to write large and complicated programs. A point in SIMSCRIPT's favour is that its statistics collection facilities are more comprehensive. SIMSCRIPT is also more widely available than SIMULA and its compiler is cheaper.

The run-time efficiency of a simulation language depends, among other things, on the simulation approach adopted, on the algorithms for handling entity and event lists, and on the particular compiler implementation. Some comparative studies (e.g. Virjo [41], Tognetti & Brett [39]) have indicated that GPSS programs tend to be slower than SIMSCRIPT ones, which, in turn, tend to be slower than SIMULA programs. We should point out that the GPSS 360 and SIMSCRIPT II versions (rather than GPSS V and SIMSCRIPT II.5) were used in the comparisons.

2.5   Debugging a simulation program

A chapter dealing with the construction and programming of simulation models would be incomplete without some mention of the many possible errors that might be made, and the methods for detecting them. One can err at all stages of a simulation exercise; for the purpose of this discussion we shall distinguish between 'programming errors', 'logic errors' and, for lack of a better name, 'errors of judgment'.

Programming errors have to do with failing to get the source program accepted by the compiler and the object program executed. The detection and correction of these errors is a fairly straightforward task, which may be rendered more or less painful depending on the quality of the compiler and run-time diagnostics. In particular, it is desirable that the run-time system should relate its error messages to the source program in a meaningful way. Thus 'Line 17: Array subscripts out of range' is much more informative than 'Program interrupt: Addressing exception'.

Having got the program to run, one still has to face the possibility that there are errors in its logic, i.e. that it is not doing what the programmer intended. Logic errors have to be exposed and hunted down by means of various test runs. Of course, it would be much better to be able to prove formally that the program is correct. That, however, is not a practical approach at present (although it may be in the future, when formal proof methods are developed further).

A rough indication of the program's correctness is obtained by running it for special cases where the answers are known (or can be guessed) in advance. Often this involves choosing extreme parameter values: very high or very low arrival rates, very large or very small variances, etc. Sometimes a special case of the model will have an analytical solution which can be compared with the

40

simulation. Another, more detailed but also more laborious verification method consists of producing and inspecting traces of simulation runs. A trace is a complete list of all events that occurred during the run, together with all changes in the system state that took place: a full report on the operation path generated by that particular run. By examining the trace one can check whether the actions taken by the program are those prescribed by the model or not.

Finally, there are questions hanging over the model itself. Is it an adequate representation of the real system? Are the assumptions reasonable? Are the simulation runs appropriate? Has the right data been collected? Is it analysed properly? What confidence should be placed in the performance estimates obtained? Failure to answer these questions correctly is likely to result in the simulation being misused – a regrettable outcome which is, unfortunately, not uncommon. It is all too easy to write a correct simulation program and then draw incorrect conclusions from the output that it produces.

Questions relating to the running of simulation programs and the analysis of their outputs will be addressed in chapters 5, 6 and 7. Knowing how to obtain good estimates of performance measures, and knowing how far to believe those estimates, goes some way towards being able to validate the model: simulation results can be compared with observations of the real system and various hypotheses can be tested (provided, of course, that the 'real system' exists and measurements can be taken from it). There are no general rules concerning the validation of a simulation model; much depends on the object of the study, the nature of the system being simulated, the accuracy desired and other factors.

Exercises

1. Consider the task of simulating the Brownian motion of a small particle immersed in gas or liquid. The particle is bombarded by molecules from all directions at a high rate. Would a fixed time increment or a variable time increment simulator be more appropriate?

2. Each customer joining the queue at a bank counter sets himself a limit on his waiting time: if his service has not begun when that limit is reached, he leaves the queue and does not come back. Outline an event-oriented simulation for this system; the performance measures of interest are the average response time of the customers who stay until they receive service and the probability that a customer will depart without receiving service.

3. A data structure that can be used for implementing event lists is the binary search tree: the event notice at each node of the tree has an event time following that of the left son and preceding that of the right son (thus the current event notice is at the leftmost node without a left son). Devise algorithms for implementing actions (a)–(d) of section 2.3. How does this structure compare with a heap?

3.   SIMULATION EXAMPLES

In this chapter, we shall go through the steps of constructing simulation programs for a few simple, yet non-trivial systems. The language chosen for the purpose is SIMULA (a SIMULA primer can be found in appendix 1), so that these programs will illustrate the process-oriented approach to simulation. Only the mechanics of generating operation sequences will be of interest to us here; the collection of statistics will be kept to a minimum and the analysis of the output will be ignored completely (those questions will be addressed in chapters 5, 6 and 7). SIMULA provides a number of random number procedures; some of these will be used without comment, leaving the discussion of random number generation and use to chapter 4. The report sections of the programs will also be minimal.

3.1   A versatile warehouse model

Consider a storage and removal system, e.g. a warehouse like the one illustrated in figure 3.1. A total of M units of storage is available. Varying batches of unit-sized items are brought into the warehouse from time to time; a batch is accepted if there is enough free storage to accommodate all its items, otherwise it leaves the system and is lost for ever. When the warehouse is not empty, items are removed from it at intervals, according to the *FIFO, LIFO*, or some other rule, and again in batches of varying size. In order to define the model completely, one has to make specific assumptions about the distributions of (i) the intervals between consecutive arrival instants, (ii) the sizes of incoming batches, (iii) the intervals between consecutive removals and (iv) the sizes of removed batches.

Figure 3.1. A warehouse of size M.

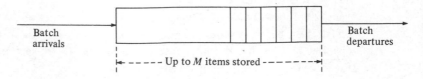

One can think of many systems that lend themselves to representation by this warehouse model. For instance, the car washing station of chapter 1 is obtained as a special case by interpreting the warehouse as a car park, the items as cars (all batches being of size 1) and the intervals between removals as the times taken to wash cars. Other possible applications include bus and air terminals, cargo depots, message buffers for computer communications, etc.

For the purpose of our simulation program, we shall assume that

(i)   the intervals between consecutive batch arrival instants are distributed exponentially with mean $1/ARR$;

(ii)   the number of items in an input batch is equally likely to take any value in the range $IN1$ to $IN2$, inclusive;

(iii) while there are items in the warehouse, the intervals between consecutive removal instants are distributed exponentially with mean $1/REM$; if after a removal instant the warehouse is empty, the next input batch is awaited before generating the interval until the next removal instant;

(iv)   the size of an output batch is equally likely to be any integer in the range $OUT1$ to $OUT2$, inclusive; the actual number of items removed is equal to either that size, or the number of items in the warehouse, whichever is the smaller.

To keep the program simple, we shall concentrate on aspects of the system that are independent of the order in which items are removed from the warehouse. There will be two performance measures of interest: the proportion of incoming batches that are turned away because of insufficient storage space and the average number of items in the warehouse. The first can be estimated by collecting two counts, say $ARRIVED$ and $REJECTED$, recording the total number of batches that arrived during the simulation, and those that were turned away, respectively. For the second performance measure, one needs to collect the item-hours integral accumulated during the simulation (denote it by $IHAREA$) and divide it by the simulation time. If $N(t)$ is the number of items in the warehouse at time t then the value of $IHAREA$ over the interval $(0, T)$ is

$$IHAREA = \int_0^T N(t)\, dt,$$

and $IHAREA/T$ is an estimate of the average number of items during that interval. Since $N(t)$ is a step function (it jumps up at arrival instants and down at removal instants), $IHAREA$ need only be updated at selected moments in time (immediately before $N(t)$ changes value). Thus the only state variables that have to be maintained are the above counts and, for the integral, the number of items currently in the warehouse, N, and the time when that number last changed, $LASTEVENT$.

The activities and events that take place in this system can be assigned in a natural way to two processes — let us call them $ARRIVALS$ and $REMOVALS$

respectively. The first is concerned with the incoming batches and the appropriate state changes, and the second with the outgoing batches and the appropriate state changes. The actions of these processes can be described informally as follows:

> *ARRIVALS*:
> repeat the following actions endlessly:
> {generate interval until next arrival instant and wait for that interval;
>   increment *ARRIVED* by 1;
>   generate number of items in batch;
>   if there is not enough room, increment *REJECTED* by 1,
>   otherwise {update *IHAREA*;
>   set *LASTEVENT* to the current time;
>   update *N*;
>   if the removal process is passive (because the warehouse was
>   empty), activate it}};

Note that it is quite all right to define and set in action a potentially infinite process. Termination can be ensured by the main program at the end of the simulation period. Note also that 'the removal process' mentioned above must be a reference to an existing instance of process *REMOVALS*. As with all SIMULA classes, a process declaration is just a template from which process instances can be created.

> *REMOVALS*:
> repeat the following actions endlessly:
> {repeat while there are items present:
>   {generate interval until next removal instant and wait for that
>   interval;
>   update *IHAREA*;
>   set *LASTEVENT* to the current time;
>   generate size of outgoing batch and set the number of removed
>   items to the smaller of that size and *N*; update *N*};
> passivate (since the warehouse is now empty)};

The actions of the main program (which in SIMULA is treated as a process, and is referred to as *MAIN*) are:

> *MAIN*:
> initialise global variables;
> create an instance of process *ARRIVALS* and activate it;
> create an instance of process *REMOVALS*, together with a reference –
>   say *WORKER* (for use by the arrivals process) – and activate it;
> wait for the simulation period;
> produce report and stop;

44

Two of the SIMULA random number generation procedures will be used in the program. In common with all such procedures, they take as one of their parameters an integer which is modified by the SIMULA random number generator at every procedure invocation. Thus a single integer variable – call it *SEED* – can be supplied as the actual parameter to all procedures. The initial value of *SEED* will determine the sequence of random integers and hence the sequence of all random values generated during the simulation. Different operation sequences for the system are obtained by giving different initial values to *SEED*.

The real procedure *NEGEXP(A,X)* produces a random value distributed exponentially with mean $1/A$ $(A > 0)$; X is the integer mentioned above. That procedure will generate the intervals between consecutive arrival instants and between consecutive removal instants. The integer procedure *RANDINT (A,B,X)* produces random integers equally likely to take any of the values $A, A + 1, \ldots, B$ $(A$ and B must be integers satisfying $A \leqslant B)$; it will generate the sizes of incoming and outgoing batches.

We are now ready to write the complete program:

```
SIMULATION
    begin comment process declarations;
    PROCESS class ARRIVALS;
    begin comment declare local integer for number of items in batch
        and enter infinite loop;
        integer NUMBER;
        while true do
        begin HOLD(NEGEXP(ARR,SEED));
            ARRIVED:=ARRIVED+1;
            NUMBER:=RANDINT(IN1,IN2,SEED);
            if NUMBER>M—N then
                REJECTED:=REJECTED+1 else
            begin IHAREA:=IHAREA+N * (TIME—LASTEVENT);
                LASTEVENT:=TIME;
                N:=N+NUMBER;
                if WORKER.IDLE then activate WORKER;
            end;
        end;
    end of class ARRIVALS;
    PROCESS class REMOVALS;
    begin comment declare local integers for size of outgoing batch and
            number removed, and enter infinite loop;
        integer SIZE,NUMBER;
        while true do
```

```
          begin while N>0 do
                 begin HOLD(NEGEXP(REM,SEED));
                        IHAREA:=IHAREA+N*(TIME−LASTEVENT);
                        LASTEVENT:=TIME;
                        SIZE:=RANDINT(OUT1,OUT2,SEED);
                        NUMBER:=if SIZE<N then SIZE else N;
                        N:=N−NUMBER
                 end;
                 comment warehouse is now enpty;
                 PASSIVATE;
          end;
      end of class REMOVALS;
      comment declarations of global variables;
      real ARR,REM,IHAREA,LASTEVENT,SIMPERIOD;
      integer ARRIVED,REJECTED,IN1,IN2,OUT1,OUT2,N,M,SEED;
      ref(REMOVALS)WORKER;
      comment main program actions start here;
      ARR:=INREAL; REM:=INREAL; SIMPERIOD:=INREAL;
      IN1:=ININT; IN2:=ININT; OUT1:=ININT; OUT2:=ININT;
      M:=ININT; SEED:=ININT;
      activate new ARRIVALS;
      WORKER:−new REMOVALS;
      activate WORKER;
      HOLD(SIMPERIOD);
      OUTTEXT("THE PROPORTION OF REJECTED BATCHES IS");
      OUTFIX(REJECTED/ARRIVED,3,10); OUTIMAGE;
      OUTTEXT("AVERAGE NO. OF ITEMS IN WAREHOUSE=");
      OUTFIX(IHAREA/SIMPERIOD,3,10); OUTIMAGE;
   end of program;
```

Each run of this program produces two lines of output, containing the two performance measure estimates obtained from that run. The system configuration is defined by the values of the parameters ARR, REM, $IN1$, $IN2$, $OUT1$, $OUT2$ and M. The duration of the simulation run is controlled by the value of $SIMPERIOD$. The integer read into $SEED$, which determines the sequence of random numbers, must be odd. It would be possible, of course, to have a separate stream of random numbers for each of the random number procedures by supplying them with different parameters in place of $SEED$.

3.2 The machine interference model

This is a classic example which provides a good framework for introducing set manipulation. A factory contains M identical machines, all working on similar tasks independently of each other. Each machine breaks down from time to time; when that happens, it remains inoperative until it is repaired. We shall assume that the time necessary to repair a broken down machine is distributed exponentially with mean $1/REP$, and that the intervals of uninterrupted operation for a machine are distributed exponentially with mean $1/BRK$. There are R identical repairmen ($R \leqslant M$), each of whom can attend to one broken down machine at a time. If a machine breaks down when all the repairmen are busy, its repair cannot be started immediately; broken down machines form a queue which is served by the repairmen on a First-In-First-Out basis.

The object of simulating such a system might be to determine the optimal number of repairmen to employ. Either the average number of inoperative machines, or the average length of time that machines remain inoperative after breaking down, could be adopted as a measure of performance (both those quantities decrease with R and are, in fact, closely related; the repairmen's wage bill, on the other hand, increases with R). We shall choose the second. To estimate it, the program should accumulate all inoperative periods for all machines (call that total *DOWNTIME*) and divide it by the total number of breakdowns (call it *BREAKS*). Thus whenever a machine breaks down, the time of that event should be recorded, so that the length of the ensuing inoperative period can eventually be calculated and added to *DOWNTIME*.

It is very convenient to think of this system as a collection of processes – M machines and R repairmen – going through their actions in parallel. Since all machines are identical, it suffices to declare one process, *MACHINE*, and then create M instances of it. Similarly, a process *REPAIRMAN* can be declared and R instances of it created.

At any moment in time, a machine can be either operative or broken down, and a repairman can be either busy repairing a machine or idle (if there is no broken down machine for him to repair). The transitions into and out of those states can be programmed in a simple and elegant way by defining two sets, *BROKEN* and *AVAILABLE*, which will contain the broken down machines and the idle repairmen, respectively. In SIMULA sets are implemented by doubly linked lists, so that a First-In-First-Out ordering of the elements is easily realised.

The following is an outline of the actions of machines and repairmen:

> *MACHINE*:
> repeat endlessly:
> {generate interval until next breakdown instant and wait for that
>   interval;
>   join the set *BROKEN* (at the end of the line);
>   note the current time in a local variable, *LASTBREAK*;
>   if there are repairmen in *AVAILABLE*, activate the first of them;
>   passivate (until repair is complete);
>   increment *BREAKS* by one;

calculate length of inoperative period and add it to *DOWNTIME*};
REPAIRMAN:
repeat endlessly:
{leave the set *AVAILABLE*;
  repeat while there are machines in the set *BROKEN*;
    {remove the first machine from *BROKEN*;
    generate a repair interval and wait for it;
    activate the repaired machine};
  join the set *AVAILABLE* (at the end of the line);
  passivate (until activated by a machine)};

Note how the interaction between machines and repairmen is achieved via the activation statements. When a process does not know when its next action should be executed, it passivates itself. At the appropriate time, another process activates it.

The *NEGEXP* procedure will be used to generate the operative and repair intervals. As in the previous example, the sequence of random numbers generated during the simulation will depend on a single integer, *SEED*, whose initial value should be odd.

Assuming that the simulation starts with all machines operative and all repairmen available (this need not be the case), the actions of the main program are:

MAIN:
initialise global variables;
create *M* instances of *MACHINE* and activate them;
create *R* instances of *REPAIRMAN* and activate them;
wait for the simulation period;
produce report and stop;

If it desired to start the simulation with, say, *J* of the *M* machines broken down, then the main program should create and activate *J* machines, wait for a sufficiently long interval so that they all join the set *BROKEN* (this must happen eventually, since there are no available repairmen), and after that create and activate the rest of the machines and all the repairmen. The simulation period should be considered to start at the latter instant.

The above outline is easily translated into a program:

SIMULATION
    begin comment process declarations;
        PROCESS **class** *MACHINE*;
            begin comment declare local variable and enter infinite loop;
                real *LASTBREAK*;
                while true do
                begin *HOLD(NEGEXP(BRK,SEED))*;

```
                    INTO(BROKEN);
                    LASTBREAK:=TIME;
                    if not AVAILABLE.EMPTY then
                          activate AVAILABLE.FIRST;
                    PASSIVATE;
                    BREAKS:=BREAKS+1;
                    DOWNTIME:=DOWNTIME+TIME−LASTBREAK;
              end;
        end of class MACHINE;
        PROCESS class REPAIRMAN;
        begin comment declare local variable and enter infinite loop;
              ref(MACHINE)MACH;
              while true do
              begin OUT;
                    while not BROKEN.EMPTY do
                    begin MACH:−BROKEN.FIRST;
                          MACH.OUT;
                          HOLD(NEGEXP(REP,SEED));
                          activate MACH;
                    end;
                    INTO(AVAILABLE);
                    PASSIVATE;
              end;
        end of class REPAIRMAN;
        comment declarations of global variables;
        real BRK,REP,DOWNTIME,SIMTIME;
        integer M,R,BREAKS,SEED,I;
        ref(HEAD)BROKEN,AVAILABLE;
        comment main program actions;
        BRK:=INREAL; REP:=INREAL; SIMTIME:=INREAL;
        M:=ININT; R:=ININT; SEED:=ININT;
        BROKEN:−new HEAD;
        AVAILABLE:−new HEAD;
        for I:=1 step 1 until M do
              activate new MACHINE;
        for I:=1 step 1 until R do
              activate new REPAIRMAN;
        HOLD(SIMTIME);
        OUTTEXT("THE AVERAGE INOPERATIVE PERIOD IS");
        OUTFIX(DOWNTIME/BREAKS,3,10); OUTIMAGE;
end of program;
```

Small modifications of the program would allow one to obtain other performance measures too. For example, the average number of broken down machines can be estimated by accumulating the broken down machine-hours integral (similar to the item-hours integral of section 3.1) and dividing it by the simulation period. That integral should be updated every time a machine is about to join, or is about to leave, the *BROKEN* set (the number of machines in the set is given by *BROKEN.CARDINAL*); a global variable recording the time of the last such event would have to be maintained.

3.3   A system with priorities

There are many real-life systems where customers are scheduled for service according to some priority rule. Examples of such systems include surgical wards in hospitals, road junctions, large computers. The customer population is divided into classes, or types, which may or may not have different arrival patterns and service requirements. Each customer type is assigned a priority (typically a positive integer), which is used by the scheduling algorithm in selecting customers for service.

Consider the simulation of a priority system with K customer types and C servers ($K, C \geqslant 1$), such as the one illustrated in figure 3.2. The numbering of the customer types is such that type 1 has the highest priority, type 2 the second highest, ..., type K the lowest. There is a separate queue for each type where customers of that type are placed in order of arrival. The C servers are identical. Each of them can serve one customer at a time, which means that there can be at most C customers in service at any one time. Customers of different types may have different arrival characteristics and different service demands.

If interruptions of service are not allowed, i.e. if customers are always served to completion, then the scheduling algorithm is said to be 'non-preemptive'. Whenever a server completes a service, it goes on to the non-empty queue with

Figure 3.2

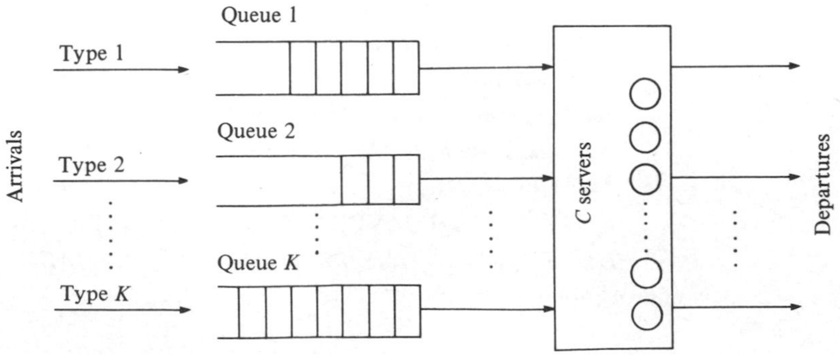

the lowest index (highest priority) and services the first customer in that queue. If, on the other hand, higher priority customers may interrupt the service of lower priority ones, then the algorithm is 'preemptive'. With a preemptive priority discipline, a customer of type i ($i = 2, 3, \ldots, K$) may be in service only when the total number of customers of types $1, 2, \ldots, i - 1$ in the system is less than C. Preempted customers re-join their respective queues (at the head); when eventually a server becomes available to them, they can either continue their service from the point of interruption (preemptive-resume discipline) or start it again from the beginning (preemptive-repeat discipline).

We shall tackle first the system with non-preemptive priorities. Assume that the intervals between consecutive arrivals of type i customers are exponentially distributed with mean $1/ARR_i$ and that the required service times for type i customers are exponentially distributed with mean $1/SER_i$ ($i = 1, 2, \ldots, K$). These parameters may be held in global arrays, or they may be local to the processes generating customer arrivals (there will be one of those for each type). The performance measures of interest will be the average sojourn times (intervals between arrival and departure) for customers of different types. Each customer will record the time of his arrival into the system and, just before departing, will add his sojourn time to a total for that type.

The principal components of the program will be (i) processes which generate customer arrivals (*ARRIVALS*; one declaration, K instances), (ii) an array *QUEUE* of K sets, (iii) processes which serve customers (*SERVER*; one declaration, C instances), (iv) a set *AVAILABLE* containing the servers that are not busy, (v) customer processes (*CUSTOMER*; one declaration, instances created at arrivals and destroyed at departures) and (vi) arrays of K elements *SOJOURN* and *NUMTHROUGH* for accumulating sojourn times and numbers of customers through the system respectively. The processes that generate customers, and those representing the customers themselves will have an integer parameter denoting the customer type. The priority scheduling algorithm, will be implemented by maintaining an integer variable, *TOP*, containing the index of the last queue attended by a server. If there are non-empty queues, *TOP* will be equal to the highest priority among them (lowest index), otherwise it will be equal to K.

We shall now proceed to outline the customer generation, service and customer processes.

ARRIVALS (taking the customer type as parameter):
initialise arrival and service rates for this type;
repeat endlessly:
{generate interval until next arrival and wait for that interval;
  generate a service requirement, create and activate a customer of this
    type and with this service requirement};

SERVER:
repeat endlessly:
{leave the set *AVAILABLE* (if in it);
  repeat while the *TOP* queue is not empty:
    {remove the first customer from the *TOP* queue;
    wait for that customer's required service time;
    activate the customer (it is time for him to leave)};
  if *TOP* is less than *K*, increase *TOP* by one (try the next queue), other-
    wise rejoin the set *AVAILABLE* and passivate (until activated by a
    customer)};

CUSTOMER (type and required service time are parameters):
note time of arrival in a local variable;
join the queue for this type;
if type is less than *TOP* (i.e. this customer has higher priority than that
  of the *TOP* queue), set *TOP* to type;
if the set *AVAILABLE* is not empty, activate the first server in it;
passivate (until activated by a server);
update *SOJOURN* and *NUMTHROUGH* for this type;

Note that the loop 'while the *TOP* queue is not empty' does not bind a server
to a particular queue. A server process is held in suspension during a customer's
service; in the meantime, the value of *TOP* may be changed, either by another
server (if there are no more customers in that queue) or by an incoming
customer (if his priority is greater). Thus the next customer that the server picks
may be from a different queue.

The actions of the main program are:

MAIN:
initialise variables;
create the *K* queues and the *K* customer generation processes, and
  activate the latter;
create the set *AVAILABLE*;
create and activate the *C* server processes;
wait for the simulation period;
produce report and stop.

There is a slight problem with the array declarations. In order to declare an
array of *K* elements, *K* must have been initialised, which implies that the array
declarations must be in an inner block with respect to *K*. But if *K* is declared in
the simulation block, and the arrays in an inner one, then they would not be
accessible to the process in the simulation block. The solution is to declare and
initialise *K* (and, perhaps, *C*) in an outer block with respect to the simulation
one. Here is the complete program:

```
begin comment outer block;
        integer K,C;
        K:=ININT; C:=ININT;
        SIMULATION
        begin comment process declarations;
        PROCESS class ARRIVALS(TYPE); integer TYPE;
        begin real ARR,SER;
                ARR:=INREAL; SER:=INREAL;
                comment infinite loop;
                while true do
                begin HOLD(NEGEXP(ARR,SEED));
                        activate new CUSTOMER(TYPE,NEGEXP(SER,
                            SEED));
                end;
        end of ARRIVALS;
        PROCESS class SERVER;
        begin ref(CUSTOMER)CUST;
                comment infinite loop;
                while true do
                begin OUT;
                        while not QUEUE(TOP).EMPTY do
                        begin CUST:-QUEUE(TOP).FIRST;
                            CUST.OUT;
                            HOLD(CUST.SERTIME);
                            activate CUST;
                        end the TOP queue is now empty;
                        if TOP<K then TOP:=TOP+1 else
                        begin INTO(AVAILABLE);
                            PASSIVATE;
                        end;
                end;
        end of SERVER;

        PROCESS class CUSTOMER(TYPE,SERTIME);
                        integer TYPE; real SERTIME;
        begin real ARRTIME;
            ARRTIME:=TIME;
            INTO(QUEUE(TYPE));
            if TYPE<TOP then TOP:=TYPE;
            if not AVAILABLE.EMPTY then
                    activate AVAILABLE.FIRST;
            PASSIVATE;
            SOJOURN(TYPE):=SOJOURN(TYPE)+TIME-ARRTIME;
```

$$NUMTHROUGH(TYPE):=NUMTHROUGH(TYPE)+1;$$

  end of *CUSTOMER*;

  comment other global declarations;
  integer *SEED,TOP,I*; **real** *SIMTIME*;
  integer array *NUMTHROUGH*(1:*K*);
  real array *SOJOURN*(1:*K*);
  ref(*HEAD*)*AVAILABLE*;
  ref(*HEAD*)**array** *QUEUE*(1:*K*);

  comment main program actions;
  SEED:=*ININT*; *SIMTIME*:=*INREAL*; *TOP*:=1;
  for *I*:=1 **step** 1 **until** *K* **do**
  begin *QUEUE*(*I*):—**new** *HEAD*;
        ACTIVATE **new** *ARRIVALS*(*I*);
  end;
  AVAILABLE:—**new** *HEAD*;
  for *I*:=1 **step** 1 **until** *C* **do**
        activate new *SERVER*;
  HOLD(*SIMTIME*);
  for *I*:=1 **step** 1 **until** *K* **do**
  begin *OUTTEXT*("THE AVERAGE SOJOURN FOR TYPE");
        OUTINT(*I*,3); *OUTTEXT*("CUSTOMERS IS");
        OUTFIX(*SOJOURN*(*I*)/*NUMTHROUGH*(*I*),3,10);
        OUTIMAGE;
  end;
  end of *SIMULATION* block;
  end of program;

The input to this program should appear in the order *K,C,SEED,SIMTIME,* $ARR_1,SER_1,ARR_2,SER_2,\ldots,ARR_K,SER_K$. As written, the simulation starts with an empty system. Immediately after the servers are activated, they enter the set *AVAILABLE* and passivate, leaving *TOP* with the value *K*. However, if desired, the main program could create varying numbers of customers of different types prior to activating the *ARRIVALS* processes. It would then have to initialise *TOP* appropriately.

Suppose now that the priority discipline is preemptive-resume. A customer who finds on arrival that some servers are busy with customers of lower priority than his own, is allowed to interrupt one of them and start his service immediately. The interrupted service is the one with the lowest priority, and if there are several services of that priority in progress, the one that started most recently. The displaced customer is returned to the head of his queue and eventually continues his service from the point of interruption.

54

This preemptive priority system can be simulated by a program that is slightly more complicated, but has basically the same structure as the one given above. The changes concern mainly the *SERVER* and *CUSTOMER* processes. There should be some mechanism for determining which servers are engaged with which priority customers, and which among them started service most recently. We have chosen to use for this purpose an array of K sets, $BUSY_1$, $BUSY_2, \ldots, BUSY_K$. When a server is about to start servicing a customer of type i, he joins at the end of set $BUSY_i$ and remains there for the duration of the service, or until he is interrupted. In order that a server may decide whether he emerges from a service (i.e. from the *HOLD* statement) as a result of normal completion or as a result of an interruption, a local boolean variable, *INTERRUPTED*, is maintained. In addition, the time of starting a service should be recorded by the server in another local variable, *BEGANSERVICE*, so that in the event of an interruption the remaining service time of the interrupted customer can be computed.

Any customer who does not find, on arrival, other customers of his type already waiting, should attempt to get a server. If the set *AVAILABLE* is not empty, then the first server in it is activated. Otherwise, the sets $BUSY_K$, $BUSY_{K-1}, \ldots, BUSY_{TYPE+1}$ are examined, in that order (they are the ones that may contain servers serving lower priority customers). If and when one of those sets is found to be non-empty, the last server in it is preempted (i.e. **reactivate**-d). In addition to those changes, another local variable, *REMSERVICE*, should be included in class *CUSTOMER*, to keep track of the remaining service time. That variable starts by being equal to the service time, and is updated after every interruption of the customer's service.

The new declarations of processes *SERVER* and *CUSTOMER* are as follows:

```
PROCESS class SERVER;
begin ref(CUSTOMER)CUST;
        boolean INTERRUPTED; real BEGANSERVICE;
        while true do
        begin comment get busy;
                while not QUEUE(TOP).EMPTY do
                begin CUST:−QUEUE(TOP).FIRST;
                        INTO(BUSY(CUST.TYPE));
                        CUST.OUT;
                        BEGANSERVICE:=TIME;
                        INTERRUPTED:=false;
                        HOLD(CUST.REMSERVICE);
                        if not INTERRUPTED then activate CUST else
                        begin if QUEUE(CUST.TYPE).EMPTY
                                then CUST.INTO(QUEUE(CUST.TYPE))
```

```
                              else CUST.PRECEDE(QUEUE(CUST.TYPE).
                              FIRST);
                              CUST.REMSERVICE:=CUST.REMSERVICE-
                              (TIME-BEGANSERVICE);
                end;
           end;
           if TOP<K then TOP:=TOP+1 else
           begin INTO(AVAILABLE);
                PASSIVATE;
           end;
       end;
   end of SERVER;

PROCESS class CUSTOMER(TYPE,SERTIME);
                   integer TYPE; real SERTIME;
begin real ARRTIME,REMSERVICE; integer I;
     ARRTIME:=TIME; REMSERVICE:=SERTIME;
     INTO(QUEUE(TYPE));
     if QUEUE(TYPE).CARDINAL=1 then
     begin if TYPE<TOP then TOP:=TYPE;
             if not AVAILABLE.EMPTY then
                    activate AVAILABLE.FIRST else
             begin I:=K;
                    while I>TYPE and BUSY(I).EMPTY do
                          I:=I-1;
                    if I>TYPE then
                    begin BUSY(I).LAST qua SERVER.
                          INTERRUPTED:=true;
                          reactivate BUSY(I).LAST;
                    end;
             end;
     end;
     PASSIVATE;
     SOJOURN(TYPE):=SOJOURN(TYPE)+TIME-ARRTIME;
     NUMTHROUGH(TYPE):=NUMTHROUGH(TYPE)+1;
   end of CUSTOMER;
```

The introduction of the sets BUSY necessitates two more program modifications. The global set array declaration should now read

```
     ref(HEAD)array QUEUE,BUSY(1:K);
```

and the 'for' statement in the main program which initialises the array QUEUE and the ARRIVALS processes should include

```
     BUSY(I):-new HEAD;
```

It should be pointed out, perhaps, that both the non-preemptive and the preemptive priority simulations can be simplified (the latter quite considerably) if there is only one server ($C = 1$). Then one does not have to worry about several customers, maybe with different priorities, being in service at the same time; the necessity for the sets *AVAILABLE* and *BUSY*, and for the reference *CUST*, disappears.

3.4   A queueing network model

There are many systems – among them job shops, department stores and large computers – that can be modelled by using queueing networks. Such systems consist of a number of interconnected service stations (nodes), each providing a different type of service and having a separate queue where customers may wait. The customers, or 'jobs', as they are usually called, may enter the system at one or more nodes, go from node to node demanding services, and may leave the system from one or more nodes. An example of a network with six nodes is illustrated in figure 3.3.

To define a queueing network model one has to specify (*a*) the number of nodes, (*b*) the number of servers at each node, (*c*) the scheduling discipline at each node, (*d*) the maximum queue size at each node and (*e*) the characteristics of job behaviour (arrivals, routing from node to node, required service at different nodes, action taken if refused admission into a queue). We shall make the following assumptions;

There are N nodes, with a single server at each node, service in order of arrival (*FIFO* scheduling), and no limit to the number of waiting jobs. All jobs are statistically identical. The intervals between consecutive external arrivals into the network are distributed exponentially with mean $1/ARR$. A newly arriving job joins node i with probability $q_{0,i}$ ($i = 1, 2, \ldots, N$), or decides to leave immediately with probability $q_{0,0}$; these probabilities satisfy

$$\sum_{i=0}^{N} q_{0,i} = 1.$$

Figure 3.3. A queueing network.

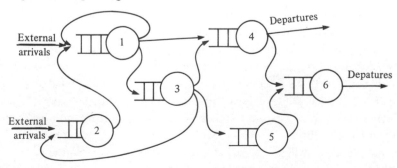

57

A job that has just completed service at node i, goes to node j with probability $q_{i,j}$ ($i, j = 1, 2, \ldots, N$), or leaves the system altogether with probability $q_{i,0}$; these probabilities also sum up to 1 for all i:

$$\sum_{j=0}^{N} q_{i,j} = 1, \quad i = 1, 2, \ldots, N.$$

The required service times at node i are distributed exponentially with mean $1/SER_i$ ($i = 1, 2, \ldots, N$).

Clearly, there is more than one way of programming the simulation of such a system. The central feature of our approach will be a SIMULA class, *STATION*, containing the attributes and actions associated with a node of the network. More precisely, class *STATION* will have the following structure:

> *STATION*:
> declarations: a real, *SER* (service rate);
> an array, *Q* (routing probabilities $q_{i,j}$, for a given i);
> a set, *QUEUE*;
> a reference to process *SERVER* called *DEVICE*;
> actions: initialise *SER*;
> initialise *Q*;
> create a *QUEUE*;
> create a *SERVER*, assign it to *DEVICE* and activate it;

The N nodes of the queueing network can thus be represented by an array, *NODE*, whose elements are *STATION*s. A process, *ARRIVALS*, will generate the jobs coming into the network from outside. Each job will be represented by a SIMULA class, *JOB*, containing a procedure for moving the job from node to node and a variable recording the time of arrival (in this program the jobs will be passive entities, not processes). To carry out the servicing and dispatching of jobs, a global process, *SERVER*, will be declared and an instance of it (referred to as *DEVICE*) will be created in each *STATION*. In order that process *SERVER* may access attributes local to class *STATION* (such as *QUEUE*), it takes a reference to *STATION* as a parameter.

We shall assume that the only performance measure of interest is the average total sojourn time, i.e. the average interval between the arrival of a job into the network and its departure from the network.

Every time a job arrives from outside, or completes service at a node, a random selection from a set of alternatives has to be made, according to a set of probabilities. It will be convenient, therefore, to declare a global procedure, *CHOICE*, which will take as parameters an integer N and an array A whose elements $a_0, a_1, \ldots, a_N$ are non-negative and sum up to 1, and which will return 0 with probability a_0, 1 with probability $a_1, \ldots$, and N with probability a_N. That procedure will be invoked at arrival and service completion instants, using the appropriate routing probabilities. The idea behind it is to divide the interval

58

(0, 1) into $N+1$ subintervals of lengths $a_0, a_1, \ldots, a_N$ respectively, then generate a random number distributed uniformly on (0, 1) and return the index of the subinterval into which it falls (the algorithm is described and discussed in more detail in section 4.2).

Let us give in outline the declarations of processes *ARRIVALS* and *SERVER*, and that of class *JOB*.

ARRIVALS:

declarations: a real, *ARR* (arrival rate);

an array, *Q* (routing probabilities $q_{0,i}$);

a reference to *JOB*, *NEWJOB*;

actions: initialise *ARR*;

initialise *Q*;

repeat endlessly;

{generate interval until next arrival instant and wait for that interval;

create a new *JOB*, *NEWJOB*;

set the *ARRTIME* of *NEWJOB* to the current time;

send *NEWJOB* on its way by invoking its procedure *MOVE*, passing it *N* and *Q* as parameters};

SERVER (this process takes a reference to class *STATION* as a parameter and accesses the local attributes *SER*, *Q* and *QUEUE* via that reference):

repeat endlessly:

{repeat while *QUEUE* is not empty:

{generate a service interval and wait for it;

send the first *JOB* in *QUEUE* on its way, by invoking its procedure *MOVE*, passing it *N* and *Q* as parameters};

passivate};

JOB (this class is prefixed by *LINK*, since it needs to join and leave sets):

declarations: a real, *ARRTIME* (time of arrival);

procedure *MOVE* (taking an integer, *N*, and an array, *A*, as parameters):

{invoke *CHOICE*, passing it *N* and *A*;

if the result, *i*, is greater than zero, then

{join the *QUEUE* at the *i*th node;

if the *DEVICE* there is idle, activate it},

otherwise

{calculate the sojourn time of this job and add it to the global *SOJOURN*;

increment the global *NUMTHROUGH* by one;

leave the system}};

The SIMULA random number generation procedures *NEGEXP* and *UNIFORM* will be used, the resulting sequences depending on a global integer, *SEED*. The actions of the main program are simple:

> *MAIN*:
> initialise variables;
> create the *N* elements of the array *NODE*;
> create and activate an *ARRIVALS* process;
> wait for the simulation period;
> produce report and stop.

We are now ready to write the complete program. As in the previous example, the simulation block will be enclosed in an outer block where the number of nodes, *N*, will be declared and initialised.

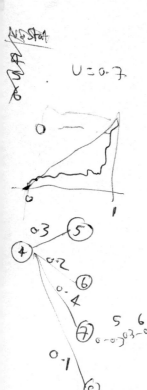

```
begin comment outer block;
    integer N; N:=ININT;
    SIMULATION
    begin comment declare the global objects;
        comment for an explanation and discussion of the following
            procedure, see section 4.2;
        integer procedure CHOICE(N,A); integer N; real array A;
        begin integer I; real F,U;
            F:=A(0);
            U:=UNIFORM(0,1,SEED);
            while U⩾F do
            begin I:=I+1;
                F:=F+A(I);
            end;
            CHOICE:=I;
        end of procedure CHOICE;
        comment a class describing a node in the network;
        class STATION;
        begin comment declarations;
            real SER;
            real array Q(0:N);
            ref(HEAD)QUEUE;
            ref(SERVER)DEVICE;
            integer J;
            comment actions;
            SER:=INREAL;
            for J:=0 step 1 until N do Q(J):=INREAL;
            QUEUE:—new HEAD;
            DEVICE:—new SERVER(this STATION);
            activate DEVICE;
```

```
          end of class STATION;
          comment a universal service process;
          PROCESS class SERVER(S); ref(STATION)S;
          begin ref(JOB)J;
                while true do
                begin while not S.QUEUE.EMPTY do
                        begin J:—S.QUEUE.FIRST;
                              HOLD(NEGEXP(S.SER,SEED));
                              J.MOVE(N,S.Q);
                        end;
                        PASSIVATE;
                end;
          end of process SERVER;
          comment here are the N nodes;
          ref(STATION)array NODE(1:N);
          comment the job is an object without actions;
          LINK class JOB;
          begin real ARRTIME;
                procedure MOVE(N,A); integer N; real array A;
                begin integer I;
                      I:=CHOICE(N,A);
                      if I>0 then
                      begin INTO(NODE(I).QUEUE);
                            if NODE(I).DEVICE.IDLE then activate
                              NODE(I).DEVICE;
                      end else
                      begin SOJOURN:=SOJOURN+TIME—
                            ARRTIME;
                            NUMTHROUGH:=NUMTHROUGH+1;
                            OUT;
                      end;
                end of procedure MOVE;
          end of class JOB;
          comment the process that brings jobs into the system;
          PROCESS class ARRIVALS;
          begin comment declarations;
                real ARR;
                real array Q(0:N);
                ref(JOB)NEWJOB;
                integer J;
                comment actions;
                ARR:=INREAL;
                for J:=0 step 1 until N do Q(J):=INREAL;
```

```
                        while true do
                        begin HOLD(NEGEXP(ARR,SEED));
                              NEWJOB:—new JOB;
                              NEWJOB.ARRTIME:=TIME;
                              NEWJOB.MOVE(N,Q);
                        end;
                  end of process ARRIVALS;
                  comment global variables;
                  integer SEED,NUMTHROUGH,I;
                  real SOJOURN,SIMTIME;
                  comment actions of main program;
                  SEED:=ININT; SIMTIME:=INREAL;
                  for I:=1 step 1 until N do NODE(I):—new STATION;
                  activate new ARRIVALS;
                  HOLD(SIMPERIOD);
                  OUTTEXT("THE AVERAGE SOJOURN TIME IS");
                  OUTFIX(SOJOURN/NUMTHROUGH,3,10); OUTIMAGE;
            end of SIMULATION block;
      end of program;
```

The program's input should appear in the following order: N, $SEED$, $SIMTIME$, SER_1, $q_{1,j}$ ($j = 0, 1, \ldots, N$), SER_2, $q_{2,j}$ ($j = 0, 1, \ldots, N$), $\ldots$, SER_N, $q_{N,j}$ ($j = 0, 1, \ldots, N$), ARR, $q_{0,j}$ ($j = 0, 1, \ldots, N$).

There are several ways in which the model described here can be generalised. Obviously, the exponential distributions for the interarrival and service times can easily be replaced by other distributions: instead of invoking the $NEGEXP$ procedure, one could declare, in class $STATION$ and in the $ARRIVALS$ process, different random number generation procedures and use them. The jobs need not be statistically identical. There may be a number of job types with different characteristics. Moreover, jobs may change type as they move from node to node. Priority scheduling disciplines may be in force at some, or all nodes. There may be different numbers of servers at different nodes.

All these generalisations can be implemented by the techniques introduced in this and the previous sections. Of course, if nodes differ by more than the values of some parameters, then the corresponding $STATION$ classes may have to be declared and created separately. When there are multiple job types, class $STATION$ would have to contain a rectangular, or higher dimensional array of routing probabilities. For example, if jobs can change type during their sojourn in the network, one needs the probabilities $p_{i,r,j,s}$ that a job of type r completing service at node i will go to node j as a job of type s. The procedures $CHOICE$ and $MOVE$ would have to be modified accordingly. More complicated routing behaviour can also be handled by means of 'artificial' types. For instance, if the node a job visits next depends not only on the node at which it is currently, but also on the node it visited last, then the index of the last node can be used as a current type descriptor.

Some network systems are 'closed', in the sense that there are no external arrivals or departures; a fixed number of jobs circulate in the network for ever. A simulation of such a system would not need *ARRIVALS* processes. The main program would create the required number of jobs and enter them into the appropriate queues. A network may also be 'mixed', i.e. open with respect to some job types and closed with respect to others. Examples of mixed networks frequently occur in the modelling of computer systems (e.g. a multiprogrammed computer may have a fixed number of terminal users and at the same time deal with a stream of batch jobs). Obviously, in a closed network it does not make sense to talk about average total sojourn times. One may be interested in the sojourn times at particular nodes, or in the intervals between consecutive visits by the same job to a given node, or in the numbers of jobs at a given node or nodes, etc.

Exercises

1. Simulate the evolution of a certain population of cells. Each cell lives for an exponentially distributed interval of time, at the end of which it either divides into two new cells (with probability q), or dies (with probability $1 - q$). The initial population size is K cells.

2. Implement the simulation of the single-server system subject to break-downs which was described in section 2.1.

3. A taxi company plans to install two ranks, $R1$ and $R2$, with $K1$ and $K2$ cars, respectively. Customers arrive at the two ranks in independent streams, with exponentially distributed interarrival times (means $1/ARR1$ and $1/ARR2$ respectively). The positions of the ranks are such that the $R1$ customers who find that all cars are occupied may be supplied with a taxi from $R2$ (if one is available), but the reverse is not true. Any customer who cannot get a taxi goes away immediately. The trip durations are exponentially distributed with mean $1/SER$. In an effort to determine the optimal values for $K1$ and $K2$, the company wishes to determine the average number of trips completed per unit time (or, alternatively, the average number of customers turned away per unit time). Write a simulation program to evaluate this.

4. Simulate the following multiprogrammed computer system with M pages of main memory. There are two job queues: an inner queue containing the active jobs and an outer queue of jobs for which there is not enough room in memory. Associated with each job is a random integer, uniformly distributed in the range $[M1, M2]$, indicating the number of pages required by the job. The sum of all memory require-

63

ments for the jobs in the inner queue cannot exceed M. Service is provided by a single server, in fixed quanta of size S. After receiving a quantum of service, a job either goes back to the end of the inner queue (with probability q), or leaves the system (with probability $1 - q$), freeing all its memory pages. In the latter case, the outer queue is scanned for a job that can be admitted into memory. New jobs (arriving at exponentially distributed intervals) join the inner queue or the outer queue, depending on whether there is room for their memory requirement or not. The performance measure of interest is the average number of jobs in the system.

5. Design and simulate a queueing network model of a Channel ferry port. Include service stations like 'ticket inspection', 'passport control', 'petrol', 'currency exchange' and 'embarkation'. There might be different types of passengers, e.g. 'on foot', 'in cars', 'in coaches', 'in lorries', taking different paths through the network and having different service requirements. The performance measures could be the average sojourn times for customers of various types.

4. PSEUDO-RANDOM NUMBER SEQUENCES

4.1 Uniform variables

Simulation studies, in common with other Monte Carlo applications, require sources of random numbers. Ideally, such a source ought to produce an endless sequence of numbers – a realisation of a sequence of independent and identically distributed random variables whose distribution function is specified in advance. A moment's reflection convinces us, however, that this is an unattainable ideal. Admittedly, one could generate random integers by physical means: rolling dice, spinning roulette wheels, using special purpose mechanical or electronic devices. Large tables of such integers can be created and stored for future use (the RAND Corporation, for example, produced a famous table of a million random digits). This is clearly unattractive, because of the cost of producing, storing and accessing a table of a useful size. Computers with built-in random number hardware are perfectly feasible, but no manufacturer has constructed one yet. Besides, that solution also has its disadvantages: one could not use the same sequence of numbers more than once.

If physical phenomena are rejected as sources of random numbers, the alternative is to use numerical algorithms. Of course, the idea of using a deterministic algorithm to generate random numbers is a little difficult to swallow: how can they be random if they are fully predictable? The objection is valid; no algorithm can produce a sequence of numbers that would have all the properties of a sequence generated by a 'truly random' source (for an excellent treatment of the subject, see Knuth [30]). However, for a practical application one can be less demanding. As long as the sequence has the appearance of being random, i.e. it passes certain statistical tests of randomness (to which we shall return later), its deterministic nature does not really matter. From now on, we shall be concerned with these algorithmically generated sequences, which are said to be 'pseudo-random'. When there is no danger of ambiguity, we shall continue to use the adjective 'random'.

As we shall see in the next section, the starting point for obtaining random numbers with arbitrary distribution functions is the standard uniform variate. Our first objective, therefore, is to devise methods for generating sequences of real numbers, $\{U_n\}$, uniformly distributed over the interval (0, 1). Obviously, that uniformity will be approximate, since in a computer real numbers are approximated by rational fractions with a finite number of digits. It is easier, in fact, to generate a sequence of integers, $\{X_n\}$, taking values in some wide range $0, 1, \ldots, m-1$ with approximately equal frequencies; the uniform numbers U_n are then obtained as

$$U_n = X_n/m. \tag{4.1}$$

The most commonly used approach is to compute the next number in the sequence $\{X_n\}$ by applying some transformation $f(\cdot)$ to the last one. Thus, starting with a given number X_0, called the 'seed', one obtains the sequence

$$X_0, X_1 = f(X_0), \ldots, X_{n+1} = f(X_n), \ldots. \tag{4.2}$$

The function $f(\cdot)$ must of course be defined over, and take values in, the same range of integers: $0, 1, \ldots, m-1$. This immediately reveals a weakness in the generators of the above type. Since at most m different values can appear in the sequence (4.2), the value of some X_i is certain to reappear after at most m steps. But if $X_{i+n} = X_i$ for some n, then according to (4.2), $X_{i+n+1} = X_{i+1}, X_{i+n+2} = X_{i+2}$, etc. In other words, all generators of type (4.2) are guaranteed to be periodic, and the period lengths do not exceed m. This is yet another reason for choosing large values for m.

A large m is necessary, but certainly not sufficient, to ensure a sequence with a long period. Around the time when both computers and the Monte Carlo methods came into being, John von Neumann suggested the 'middle square' algorithm for generating random numbers. This was of type (4.2) with the transformation $f(\cdot)$ consisting of squaring a k-digit number X_n and then taking the middle k digits of the ($2k$-digit) result as X_{n+1}. Assuming binary arithmetic, the maximum period of a middle square sequence is 2^k. That method subsequently fell into disrepute because, although some sequences produced were quite satisfactory, many were not: they had short periods or degenerated into a string of zeros.

Another, and much more successful family of algorithms (Lehmer; see Knuth [30]) employs a linear congruential transformation $f(\cdot)$:

$$X_{n+1} = (aX_n + c) \bmod m, \tag{4.3}$$

where a and c are non-negative constants and $X \bmod m$ is the remainder of the division of X by m. These algorithms have been extensively studied, both theoretically and empirically, so that their behaviour is by now well understood. In addition, they are simple, easy to implement and economical in their time and memory requirements, which makes them very suitable for computer applications.

The following result (Hull & Dobell [24]) allows one to choose the constants a, c and m so as to achieve the largest possible period:

A sequence generated by (4.3) has a period of length m if, and only if,

(i) c and m have no common factors greater than 1;
(ii) every prime factor of m is also a factor of $a - 1$;
(iii) if 4 is a factor of m then it is also a factor of $a - 1$.

Note that if the period is of length m then all integers $0, 1, \ldots, m-1$ appear in the sequence. Different values of the seed X_0 generate different cyclic permutations of the same basic ordering of those integers; that ordering is determined by a and c.

In binary computers m is usually taken of the form $m = 2^b$, where b is the number of bits (excluding sign) in the machine representation of integers (e.g. $m = 2^{31}$ in IBM 370 computers). This choice greatly facilitates the evaluation of (4.3): reduction modulo m is performed by extracting the b least significant binary digits. However, that convenience is bought at a price: the integers defined by the low-order d bits of the numbers X_n have a period not longer than 2^d. In particular, the last bit of X_n has a period no longer than 2: the numbers X_n are either all even, or all odd, or even and odd numbers alternate strictly (obviously the latter must happen if the sequence $\{X_n\}$ has period m). This phenomenon can be avoided by choosing an m which is prime (e.g. $m = 2^{31} - 1$). Even if it is not avoided, its effect is negligible if the entire numbers X_n are used – as in (4.1).

When $m = 2^b$, conditions (i)-(iii) imply that as long as c is odd and a is of the form $a = 4k + 1$ ($k = 0, 1, \ldots$), the linear congruential algorithm (4.3) has the maximum period m. Now we are faced with the task of choosing those constants so that not only the period is maximised but the sequences generated are sufficiently random. It is not enough that the numbers X_n should be uniformly spread over the range $[0, m - 1]$; they should also appear to be independent of each other. The most immediate symptom of dependency is a significant correlation between successively generated numbers, X_n and X_{n+1}. An analysis of that serial correlation (Coveyou; see Knuth [30]) suggests that in order to minimise it, the multiplier a should be neither too small nor too large - say $m^{1/2} < a < m - m^{1/2}$ (and preferably near the top of that interval) - and the constant c should be

$$c \approx [(3 - \sqrt{3})/6] \, m \approx 0.21m.$$

In a maximum period generator, the presence or absence of undesirable dependencies is also related to the so called 'potency'. The potency is defined as the least integer s such that m is a factor of $(a - 1)^s$. Such an integer exists since every prime factor of m is a factor of $a - 1$. It can be argued (see Knuth [30]) that the generator will not be satisfactory unless its potency is at least 5. When $m = 2^b$, the maximum possible potency is $b/2$ if b is even, $(b + 1)/2$ if b is odd ($b \geqslant 3$); it is achieved by selecting a multiplier of the form $a = 8k + 5$ ($k = 0, 1, \ldots$).

The above guidelines certainly help the construction of acceptable random number generators. However, they alone do not guarantee satisfactory results. Having chosen the constants a, c and m, the resulting generator should be tested for randomness. Some of the more important tests will be described in section 4.3. Failing to pass even one of those tests would be sufficient to reject the generator.

Let us now consider some other algorithms for generating random numbers. A special case of (4.3) deserves attention, as it is quite widely used. This is the 'multiplicative congruential', or 'power residue' generator, obtained by setting $c = 0$:

$$X_{n+1} = (aX_n) \bmod m. \tag{4.4}$$

There are arguments both for and against multiplicative generators. On the positive side, they are obviously simpler and hence faster. Also, for certain values of m, namely when m is prime or is a product of low powers of primes, they have better statistical properties than the linear congruential ones. This is because for such m the potency of the linear congruential generators is necessarily very low. On the negative side, (4.4) violates condition (i) and therefore cannot have period m. When $m = 2^b$ ($b \geqslant 4$), the maximum period of the multiplicative congruential generator is 2^{b-2}. In order to achieve that period, the multiplier must be of the form $a = 8k + 3$ or $a = 8k + 5$ ($k = 0, 1, \ldots$) and the seed X_0 must be odd; all numbers in the sequence generated by (4.4) are then also odd. The random number generator in SIMULA is of this type, although it may well have been better to have chosen a linear congruential one instead. It is doubtful whether the slight increase in speed is an adequate compensation for the loss of three quarters of the maximum period.

If m is prime, then the multiplicative congruential generator can have period $m - 1$. To achieve this, the multiplier a should have the property that the smallest integer s for which $a^s - 1$ is divisible by m is $s = m - 1$. Any seed except zero is admissible. An example of such a generator is the one used in SIMSCRIPT: its modulus and multiplier are $m = 2^{31} - 1$ and $a = 14^{29}$. The trade-offs here are not very obvious; some efficiency is gained by dispensing with the additive constant and some is lost by giving up the convenient modulus $m = 2^{31}$.

A number of algorithms based on more general recurrences than (4.2) have been suggested, in an effort to increase the period and improve randomness. Suppose, for example, that the sequence is constructed by applying a transformation to the last two numbers in order to obtain the next one:

$$X_0, X_1, X_2 = f(X_1, X_0), \ldots, X_{n+1} = f(X_n, X_{n-1}), \ldots . \tag{4.5}$$

If all numbers X_n belong to the set $\{0, 1, \ldots, m - 1\}$, then clearly the maximum period of (4.5) is m^2: that sequence does not begin to repeat until the same two consecutive numbers (X_i, X_{i+1}) have been generated again.

68

A very simple example of the above type is the 'additive congruential' generator producing Fibonacci sequences (mod m):

$$X_{n+1} = (X_n + X_{n-1}) \bmod m. \tag{4.6}$$

Although it occasionally achieves quite long periods, this particular algorithm turns out to be a rather poor source of random numbers. It improves, however, if X_{n-1} in (4.6) is replaced by X_{n-k}, for some reasonably large k (say $k = 16$). A satisfactory additive congruential generator would have, of course, the advantage of speed, since no multiplications are involved.

Very good results are obtained by generators of the type

$$X_{n+1} = (a_0 X_n + a_1 X_{n-1} + \ldots + a_{k-1} X_{n-k+1}) \bmod m, \tag{4.7}$$

where m is a prime number. Then a period of length $m^k - 1$ can be guaranteed provided that the multipliers $a_0, a_1, \ldots, a_{k-1}$ are chosen appropriately, and that the k initial numbers $X_0, X_1, \ldots, X_{k-1}$ are not all equal to zero (for more details, see Knuth [30]). The task of selecting appropriate multipliers is non-trivial.

Perhaps the most promising method was proposed by MacLaren & Marsaglia (see Knuth [30]). The idea is to use two sources of random numbers $\{X_n\}$ and $\{Y_n\}$, and to 'shuffle' one by means of the other. A linear array of k elements contains k numbers from the X sequence (k is fixed in advance; the value $k = 128$ was suggested originally). The next number in the Y sequence is used to generate an index, thus selecting an element of the array. That element is output as the next random number and is then replaced by the next number in the X sequence. This algorithm performs very well indeed, even when the X and Y sequences are not particularly good when taken in isolation.

4.2   Random sampling from different populations

We have discussed the generation of random numbers $U_1, U_2, \ldots$, which appear to be independent and uniformly distributed on the interval $(0, 1)$. Let us assume now that a source of such numbers is available, and consider how they can be used to generate other random quantities with different characteristics. From now on, the symbol U will always denote one of the above uniform random variates:

$$P(U \leqslant x) = \begin{cases} 0 \text{ for } x < 0 \\ x \text{ for } 0 \leqslant x < 1 \\ 1 \text{ for } 1 \leqslant x. \end{cases} \tag{4.8}$$

One of the simplest random experiments that one may wish to simulate is the toss of a (biased) coin: a decision is made between two alternatives, 1 and 2, so that 1 is selected with probability α and 2 with probability $1 - \alpha$ $(0 < \alpha < 1)$. It can be seen immediately from (4.8) that the following procedure accomplishes this task:

> generate U;
>
> if $U < \alpha$ then output 1 else output 2.

A similar procedure can be used to choose among K alternatives, so that 1 is selected with probability α_1, 2 with probability $\alpha_2, \ldots, K$ with probability α_K ($\alpha_i > 0, i = 1, 2, \ldots, K, \alpha_1 + \alpha_2 + \ldots + \alpha_k = 1$). An array F of K elements containing the partial sums $F(i) = \alpha_1 + \alpha_2 + \ldots + \alpha_i$ ($i = 1, 2, \ldots, K$) is made available to the procedure:

> generate U;
>
> set a counter, I, to 1;
>
> while $U \geqslant F(I)$ do
>
> > increment I by 1;
>
> output I;

If all alternatives are equally likely, i.e. if one wishes to generate integers from the set $\{1, 2, \ldots, K\}$ so that each integer appears with probability $1/K$, then it is enough to generate U and output $1 + \lfloor KU \rfloor$, where $\lfloor x \rfloor$ is the largest integer less than or equal to x.

Note that the array F used by the above procedure contains the cumulative distribution function of the discrete random variable I which takes values 1, 2, $\ldots, K$ with probabilities $\alpha_1, \alpha_2, \ldots, \alpha_k$ respectively:

$$F(i) = P(I \leqslant i), \quad i = 1, 2, \ldots, K.$$

The procedure can be said to 'invert' that distribution function: for a given value of U it finds the value of i such that

$$F(i-1) \leqslant U < F(i) \tag{4.9}$$

(this is illustrated in figure 4.1; $F(0)$ is defined as 0).

The same idea applies when the set of values taken by the random variable is infinite. Consider, for example, the generation of a geometrically distributed random variable, I, taking the value i with probability $\alpha^{i-1}(1 - \alpha)$ ($i = 1, 2, \ldots$; $0 < \alpha < 1$). That variable might represent the number of trials until the first

Figure 4.1. Generating a discrete random variable.

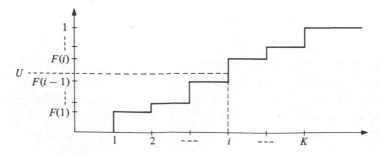

failure, when the probability of success at each trial is α (see appendix 2). The cumulative distribution function is given by

$$F(i) = 1 - \alpha^i, \quad i = 1, 1, 2, \ldots \tag{4.10}$$

For a given value of U, the inequalities (4.9), after substitution of (4.10), can be solved explicitly. They imply

$$i - 1 \leqslant \ln(1 - U)/\ln\alpha < i. \tag{4.11}$$

Thus a geometrically distributed random variable can be generated by the following simple procedure:

generate U;
output $1 + [\ln(1 - U)/\ln\alpha]$.

Remark: $1 - U$ may be replaced by U in the above expression, since both have the same uniform distribution. This is not advisable, however, if U is generated by means of a full period linear congruential algorithm; then the value $U = 0$ will appear eventually, causing the $\ln(\cdot)$ routine to fail. With a multiplicative generator it is safe to replace $1 - U$ by U.

Suppose now that we wish to generate a random variable X whose distribution function $F(x) = P(X \leqslant x)$ is continuous. That distribution function possesses a continuous and monotone increasing inverse $F^{-1}(y)$ satisfying $F^{-1}[F(x)] = x$. From what has been said so far, it should come as no surprise that X can be generated as follows:

generate U;
output $F^{-1}(U)$.

This 'inverse transformation' method is illustrated in figure 4.2.

It is easy to demonstrate that the variable X produced in this way has, indeed, the desired distribution:

$$P(X \leqslant x) = P[F^{-1}(U) \leqslant x] = P[U \leqslant F(x)]$$
$$= F(x).$$

Figure 4.2. Generation of a continuous random variable.

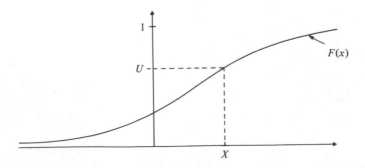

Clearly, the applicability of the inverse transformation method is influenced by the ease with which the inverse of the distribution function can be determined. A classic example of an explicitly invertible distribution function is the exponential one:

$$F(x) = 1 - e^{-\mu x}, \quad x \geqslant 0. \tag{4.12}$$

This is the continuous analogue of the geometric distribution. An exponentially distributed random variable can be thought of as the time until the next occurrence of an event in a process where events occur at random at rate μ per unit time (see appendix 2). It can be immediately verified that the inverse of (4.12) is given by

$$F^{-1}(y) = -(1/\mu) \ln (1-y)$$

Thus, in order to generate an exponentially distributed random variable with mean $1/\mu$, we do the following:

generate U;
output $-(1/\mu) \ln (1-U)$.

The remark following the geometric random variable generator applies here too.

More often than not, finding the inverse of an arbitrary distribution function $F(x)$ is not so straightforward. It is always possible, of course, to approximate $F(x)$ by some simpler function – say a piecewise linear one – and then invert the latter numerically. That is the approach adopted by GPSS in all cases. There are, however, other methods which might be better suited to specific requirements.

If the probability density function $f(x)$ of the desired random variable can be enclosed completely in a rectangle with base (a, b) and height c (as shown in figure 4.3), then one can proceed by 'rejection'.

Figure 4.3. The rejection method.

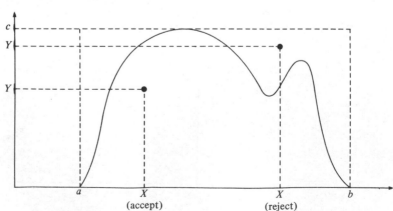

The rejection method employs the following procedure:

1. Generate U_1 and set $X = a + (b-a) U_1$;
2. Generate U_2 and set $Y = cU_2$;
3. If $Y < f(X)$ then output X and stop, otherwise repeat from 1.

In other words, random points (X, Y), uniformly distributed on the rectangle $(a, b) \times (0, c)$ are generated, until one of them falls below the density curve; the X coordinate of that point is then output as the desired random variable. To justify the method, we have to show that

$$P[x \leqslant X < x + dx \,|\, Y < f(X)] = f(x)\, dx, \quad a < x < b. \tag{4.13}$$

Remembering that X is uniform on (a, b) and Y is uniform on $(0, c)$, and using the formula for conditional probabilities, we can rewrite the left-hand side of (4.13) as

$$P[x \leqslant X < x + dx, \, Y < f(X)]/P[Y < f(X)]$$
$$= \{[dx/(b-a)][f(x)/c]\}/\{1/[(b-a)c]\} = f(x)\, dx$$

(the probability that the (X, Y) point falls below the density curve, $P[Y < f(X)]$, is equal to the ratio between the area under the curve, i.e. 1, and that of the whole rectangle).

The execution time of the rejection algorithm is proportional to the number of points generated, which is distributed geometrically with mean $1/P[Y < f(X)] = (b-a)c$. Therefore, that method is efficient only when the area of the enclosing rectangle is not very large, i.e. when there is not much 'empty space' in the rectangle above the density curve.

If the probability density function of the desired random variable can be expressed as a linear combination

$$f(x) = \alpha_1 f_1(x) + \alpha_2 f_2(x) + \ldots + \alpha_K f_K(x), \tag{4.14}$$

where $f_1(x), f_2(x), \ldots, f_K(x)$ are probability density functions and $\alpha_1 + \alpha_2 + \ldots + \alpha_K = 1$ ($\alpha_i > 0, i = 1, 2, \ldots, K$), then one can apply the so called 'composition method'. This can be described as follows:

> generate a random integer, I, taking the value 1 with probability α_1, 2 with probability $\alpha_2, \ldots, K$ with probability α_K;
> generate a random variable having the probability density function $f_I(x)$ and output it as the desired result.

Clearly, the variable produced in this way has the density function $f(x)$ given by (4.14). Equally clearly, in order that the composition method be of practical use, the component density functions $f_i(x)$ – or at least the more probable of them – should be easy to generate. For example, the hyperexponential distribution is tailormade for this method. Its density function is of the form

$$f(x) = \alpha_1 \mu_1\, e^{-\mu_1 x} + \alpha_2 \mu_2\, e^{-\mu_2 x} + \ldots + \alpha_K \mu_K\, e^{-\mu_K x},$$

so that its generation amounts to that of an exponential distribution with parameter μ_i, with probability α_i ($i = 1, 2, \ldots, K$).

Perhaps the most important applications of the composition method have to do with devising efficient procedures for generating random variables with arbitrary distributions. The idea is to partition the area under the target density function into non-overlapping pieces in such a way that most of the area is covered by pieces of very simple shape, say rectangles. The density function can then be expressed in the form (4.14), where α_i and $f_i(x)$ are the area and the density function of the ith piece, respectively ($i = 1, 2, \ldots, K$). An example of such a partition is illustrated in figure 4.4. In this example, the rectangles 1, 2, $\ldots$, 8, with areas $\alpha_1, \alpha_2, \ldots, \alpha_8$, respectively, represent uniform densities $f_1(x)$, $f_2(x), \ldots, f_8(x)$, on the corresponding intervals. The step function $\alpha_1 f_1(x) + \alpha_2 f_2(x) + \ldots + \alpha_8 f_8(x)$ covers most of the area under $f(x)$. The remaining pieces, 9, 10, $\ldots$, 21, with areas $\alpha_9, \ldots, \alpha_{21}$ represent density functions defined by the respective portions of $f(x)$ (each shifted down to the abscissa and scaled appropriately, so as to integrate to one). The composition algorithm would select an index, i, with probability α_i ($i = 1, 2, \ldots, 21$) and then generate a random variate from the density $f_i(x)$. Most of the time (i.e. in a fraction $\alpha_1 + \ldots + \alpha_8$ of all cases) this last step will be almost immediate, since one of the uniform densities will be selected. Occasionally, a variate from a more complex density function will have to be generated, e.g. by the rejection method. Those occurrences will be rare (a fraction $\alpha_9 + \ldots + \alpha_{21}$ of all cases).

A well-known procedure for generating normally distributed random variates by the composition method was proposed by Marsaglia, MacLaren & Bray (see Knuth [30]). That procedure uses a judicious partitioning of the area under the right-hand half of the normal density function into rectangles and wedge-shaped pieces of carefully chosen dimensions, plus a table look-up technique for selecting one of the component density functions. The resulting program is rather difficult to write, but very fast to run.

In addition to the general methods discussed so far, there are a number of special algorithms applicable to particular distributions. We shall mention briefly some of the more important of these.

Figure 4.4. Applying the composition method to an arbitrary density function.

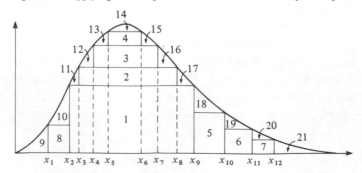

Normal distribution (mean zero and standard deviation one; see appendix 2). An ingenious algorithm based on generating the polar coordinates of a point on the plane was discovered by Box, Muller & Marsaglia (see Knuth [30]):

> generate U_1 and U_2;
> output $X = (-2 \ln U_1)^{1/2} \cos (2\pi U_2)$.

One can calculate $Y = (-2 \ln U_1)^{1/2} \sin (2\pi U_2)$ as well; that random variable is also normally distributed and is independent of X. To justify this algorithm we note that the point (X, Y) has polar coordinates R (distance from the origin) and V (angle), given by

$$R = (-2 \ln U_1)^{1/2}; \quad V = 2\pi U_2.$$

Moreover, since U_1 and U_2 are independent and uniformly distributed on $(0, 1)$, the joint probability density function of R and V is

$$f(r, v) = \frac{1}{2\pi} [\exp (-r^2/2)] \, r.$$

Hence, we can write

$$P(x \leqslant X < x + dx, \ y \leqslant Y < y + dy)$$

$$= \frac{1}{2\pi} e^{-(r^2/2)} r \left| \frac{\partial(r, v)}{\partial(x, y)} \right| dx \, dy,$$

where r and v are such that $x = r \cos (v)$ and $y = r \sin (v)$, and

$$\frac{\partial(r, v)}{\partial(x, y)} = \begin{vmatrix} \dfrac{\partial r}{\partial x} & \dfrac{\partial r}{\partial y} \\ \dfrac{\partial v}{\partial x} & \dfrac{\partial v}{\partial y} \end{vmatrix} = \left\{ \begin{vmatrix} \dfrac{\partial x}{\partial r} & \dfrac{\partial x}{\partial v} \\ \dfrac{\partial y}{\partial r} & \dfrac{\partial y}{\partial v} \end{vmatrix} \right\}^{-1} = \frac{1}{r}$$

is the Jacobian determinant of the transformation $(x, y) \to (r, v)$. Therefore, the joint probability density function of X and Y is equal to

$$f(x, y) = \frac{1}{2\pi} e^{-[(x^2 + y^2)/2]} = \left[\frac{1}{(2\pi)^{1/2}} e^{-x^2/2} \right] \left[\frac{1}{(2\pi)^{1/2}} e^{-y^2/2} \right],$$

i.e. X and Y are independent and normally distributed.

Another algorithm for generating variates that are *approximately* normally distributed is based on the central limit theorem. In its simplest form, the latter states that the sum of a large number of independent and identically distributed random variables is approximately normal. Remembering that the mean and variance of the uniform $(0, 1)$ distribution are $\frac{1}{2}$ and $\frac{1}{12}$ respectively, we see that the variate

$$X = \sum_{i=1}^{12} U_i - 6$$

is approximately normally distributed with mean 0 and variance 1. The approximation can be further improved by applying a certain polynomial transformation to X (Teichroew, see Knuth [30]).

Erlang distribution. If the events of a given type occur at random (in a Poisson stream) at a rate μ, i.e. if the intervals between consecutive occurrences are distributed exponentially with mean $1/\mu$, then the interval until the nth event – the sum X_n of n independent and identically distributed exponential random variables – has the n-stage Erlang density function:

$$f(x) = \mu(\mu x)^{n-1} e^{-\mu x}/(n-1)!, \quad x \geqslant 0. \tag{4.15}$$

From this definition, and remembering that when U is uniform, $(-1/\mu)\ln(1-U)$ is distributed exponentially with mean $1/\mu$, we see that an Erlang variate can be obtained by generating n uniform variates $U_1, U_2, \ldots, U_n$ and computing

$$X_n = -\frac{1}{\mu}\sum_{i=1}^{n}\ln(1-U_i) = -\frac{1}{\mu}\ln\left[\prod_{i=1}^{n}(1-U_i)\right]. \tag{4.16}$$

When n is large, the Erlang distribution approaches a normal one, with mean n/μ and variance n/μ^2.

Poisson distribution. Given a Poisson stream of events with rate μ (see appendix 2), the number $N(t)$ of events that occur during an interval of length t has the distribution

$$p_n = P(N(t) = n) = (\mu t)^n e^{-\mu t}/n!, \quad n = 0, 1, \ldots. \tag{4.17}$$

In terms of the Erlang random variable X_n introduced above, the Poisson distribution can be expressed as

$$p_n = P(X_n \leqslant t) - P(X_{n+1} \leqslant t) = P(X_n \leqslant t < X_{n+1}), \quad n = 0, 1, \ldots.$$

This last equation, together with (4.16), suggests the following procedure for generating integers with the Poisson distribution:

set $X = 1$; set $N = 0$;
while $X \geqslant e^{-\mu t}$ do
{generate U; set $X = (1 - U)X$; set $N = N + 1$};
output $N - 1$.

4.3 Statistical tests

All the methods described in the last section relied for their operation on a good source of uniform random numbers. But how can one tell whether a given random number generator – be it linear congruential, multiplicative, or some other sort – produces a good sequence of uniform numbers? The guidelines of section 4.1, while necessary, do not guarantee satisfactory results. It is essential that, before starting to use a random number generator, it should be subjected to a series of tests designed to expose the undesirable properties it might possess.

The first and most basic problem is to test whether the numbers produced have the desired distribution. Given a (finite) sample of numbers, $X_1, X_2, \ldots,$ X_n, and a probability distribution function $F(x)$, one has to accept or reject the hypothesis that this is a sample of independent observations from the given distribution. Moreover, the verdict should be reliable: the probability of rejecting a true hypothesis should be small and (much more difficult to ensure) the probability of accepting a false hypothesis should also be small. This is, of course, a classic problem in statistics and methods of dealing with it have existed for a long time. We shall describe two famous tests.

The χ^2 test

The set of possible values taken by the random variable is divided into d non-intersecting subsets $A_1, A_2, \ldots, A_d$. Let p_j be the probability that an element of the sample belongs to the jth of these subsets, if the hypothesis is true: $p_j = P(X_i \in A_j), i = 1, 2, \ldots, n, j = 1, 2, \ldots, d$. Then the expected number of Xs falling into A_j would be np_j ($j = 1, 2, \ldots, d$). On the other hand, we can count the observed numbers of Xs falling into A_j; let that number be f_j ($j = 1, 2, \ldots, d$). The χ^2 statistic is defined as follows:

$$\chi^2_{d-1} = \sum_{j=1}^{d} \frac{(f_j - np_j)^2}{np_j}. \tag{4.18}$$

It is said to have $d - 1$ degrees of freedom because of the single relation existing between the observed frequencies:

$$\sum_{j=1}^{d} f_j = n.$$

If the hypothesis is true and the expected frequencies are, indeed, equal to np_j ($j = 1, 2, \ldots, d$), then for large values of n the right-hand side of (4.18) has approximately the same distribution as the sum of the squares of $d - 1$ independent normally distributed random variables with mean 0 and variance 1. The probability density function of that distribution is given by

$$h_{d-1}(x) = x^{(d-3)/2} e^{-x/2} / [2^{(d-1)/2} \Gamma((d-1)/2)], \tag{4.19}$$

where $\Gamma((d-1)/2)$ is defined by the recurrence relation

$$\Gamma(x) = (x-1) \Gamma(x-1), \quad x \geqslant 1$$

and by the initial conditions $\Gamma(1) = 1$ and $\Gamma(\tfrac{1}{2}) = \pi^{1/2}$.

Before carrying out the test, a level of significance, α, must be decided upon. That is the probability of rejecting the hypothesis when it is, in fact, true. The value of α should be small, but not too small (say $\alpha = 0.1$ or $\alpha = 0.05$). It must be remembered that when the likelihood of rejecting a true hypothesis decreases, that of accepting a false one increases (hence the term 'level of significance').

Next, from a table of the χ^2 distribution (see Tables), two points x_1 and x_2 are obtained;

$$P(\chi^2_{d-1} \leqslant x_1) = \frac{\alpha}{2} \quad \text{and} \quad P(\chi^2_{d-1} \leqslant x_2) = 1 - \frac{\alpha}{2}.$$

In other words, the value of χ^2 calculated by (4.18) will be inside the interval (x_1, x_2) with probability $1 - \alpha$, if the hypothesis is true. Therefore, if (4.18) yields a value less than x_1 or greater than x_2, then the hypothesis ought to be rejected; the occurrence of an unlikely value argues against the hypothesis.

Let us restate the conditions under which it is appropriate to apply the χ^2 test. First, the observations in the sample must be independent. Second, the size of the sample must be large (in order that the normal approximation applies). An accepted 'rule of thumb' in this respect is that the expected number of observations in each subset should be at least 5, i.e. $np_j \geqslant 5, j = 1, 2, \ldots, d$. The larger the sample size, the less likely it is that a false hypothesis will be accepted (the latter also depends, of course, on how close the 'true' distribution is to the hypothesised one). The number and size of subsets also influence the power of the test. On the whole, the lower the value of d, the easier it is to accept a false hypothesis.

The χ^2 test can be applied to both discrete and continuous distributions (originally it was intended mainly for discrete ones). Suppose, for example, that a sample of integers $X_1, X_2, \ldots, X_n$ is to be tested for being geometrically distributed with mean $1/(1-\beta), 0 < \beta < 1$. The d subsets of possible values can be defined as follows:

$$A_j = \begin{cases} \{j\} \text{ for } j = 1, 2, \ldots, d-1 \\ \{d, d+1, \ldots\} \text{ for } j = d. \end{cases}$$

Then the hypothesised probability of taking a value in the jth subset is

$$p_j = \begin{cases} \beta^{j-1}(1-\beta) & \text{for } j = 1, 2, \ldots, d-1 \\ \beta^{d-1} & \text{for } j = d. \end{cases}$$

These probabilities, together with the observed frequencies f_j $(j = 1, 2, \ldots, d)$ are substituted into (4.18) in order to evaluate the χ^2 statistic and perform the test.

As an example of a continuous distribution, take a sample of real numbers $U_1, U_2, \ldots, U_n$, allegedly distributed uniformly on the interval $(0, 1)$. To test that hypothesis, divide the interval $(0, 1)$ into d subintervals of equal length $1/d$:

$$A_j = \{x | (j-1)d \leqslant x < j/d\}, \quad j = 1, 2, \ldots, d.$$

(if, for example, $d = 64$, then the first six bits of U_i determine the subset into which it falls). The expected frequencies will be equal to $np_j = n/d, j = 1, 2, \ldots, d$.

The Kolmogorov-Smirnov test

The hypothetical distribution function $F(x) = P(X \leqslant x)$ is assumed to be continuous. The sample of observations $X_1, X_2, \ldots, X_n$ defines an empirical distribution function $F_n(x)$:

$$F_n(x) = \text{(number of } X\text{s which are} \leqslant x)/n \qquad (4.20)$$

The agreement between hypothesis and observations is measured by the distance between the functions $F(x)$ and $F_n(x)$ (figure 4.5). Two statistics are computed:

$$\left. \begin{array}{l} K_n^+ = n^{1/2} \max_x [F_n(x) - F(x)] \\[2mm] K_n^- = n^{1/2} \max_x [F(x) - F_n(x)]. \end{array} \right\} \qquad (4.21)$$

If the hypothesis is true then both K_n^+ and K_n^- should have the same distribution function, $K_n(x)$, given by

$$K_n(x) = P(K_n^+ \leqslant x)$$
$$= \frac{x}{n^{1/2}} \sum_{k=0}^{m} \binom{n}{k} \left(\frac{k}{n} - \frac{x}{n^{1/2}} \right)^k \left(\frac{x}{n^{1/2}} - \frac{k}{n} + 1 \right)^{n-k-1}, \qquad (4.22)$$

where $m = \lfloor xn^{1/2} \rfloor$. This distribution is exact for every n; there is no approximation involved here. When n is large, e.g. $n > 500$, (4.22) is approximated by

$$K_\infty(x) = 1 - e^{-2x^2}, \quad x \geqslant 0. \qquad (4.23)$$

As with the χ^2 test, a level of significance, α, is decided upon. From a table of the K_n distribution (see Tables), two values, x_1 and x_2 are obtained, such that

$$K_n(x_1) = \alpha/2 \quad \text{and} \quad K_n(x_2) = 1 - (\alpha/2).$$

If either of the statistics K_n^+ and K_n^- defined by (4.21) turns out to be outside the interval (x_1, x_2), the hypothesis is rejected. The evaluation of those statistics is simplified by the fact that the maxima involved are necessarily achieved at one of the sample points X_i $(i = 1, 2, \ldots, n)$. If the sample is arranged in increasing

Figure 4.5. Hypothetical and empirical distribution functions.

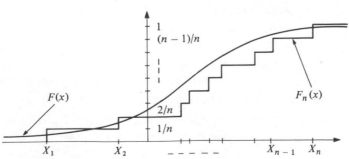

79

order, so that $X_1 \leqslant X_2 \leqslant \ldots \leqslant X_n$, then (4.21) can be written as

$$
\begin{aligned}
K_n^+ &= n^{1/2} \max_{1 \leqslant i \leqslant n} \left[\frac{i}{n} - F(X_i) \right] \\
K_n^- &= n^{1/2} \max_{1 \leqslant i \leqslant n} \left[F(X_i) - \frac{i-1}{n} \right].
\end{aligned} \tag{4.24}
$$

To summarise, the idea behind both the χ^2 and the Kolmogorov–Smirnov tests is that the observed behaviour of a sample is compared with its hypothesised behaviour. If the agreement is suspiciously good (evaluated statistic $< x_1$) or suspiciously poor (evaluated statistic $> x_2$), then the hypothesis is rejected; otherwise it is accepted. The likelihood of accepting a false hypothesis decreases as the sample size is increased. Often it is advisable to test several samples from different parts of the sequence; local departures from the hypothesis may thus be exposed.

Applications to random number sequences

Let us return now to the problem of testing a random number generator which produces a sequence $U_1, U_2, \ldots$ of supposedly independent and uniformly distributed numbers between 0 and 1. We have seen how either the χ^2 or the Kolmogorov–Smirnov test can be used to check for uniformity. However, neither test, as described so far, will establish independence; in fact, they both assume it. Of course, we can never convince ourselves that all numbers in the sequence are mutually independent. What can be done is to test for certain weaker properties that the sequence would possess if the numbers were independent. Some of these we shall now proceed to outline.

If consecutive pairs of numbers $(U_1, U_2), (U_3, U_4), \ldots$ are considered as points on the two-dimensional plane, then those points should be uniformly distributed on the unit square $(0, 1) \times (0, 1)$. That hypothesis can be tested by dividing the unit square into d^2 sub-squares of area $1/d^2$ each and applying the χ^2 test to a sample of n pairs; the expected frequencies would be $np_j = n/d^2$, $j = 1, 2, \ldots, d^2$. This is known as the *serial test*. Similarly, consecutive triples $(U_1, U_2, U_3), (U_4, U_5, U_6), \ldots$ should be uniformly distributed on the unit cube. Again this can be tested by dividing the cube into d^3 sub-cubes and applying the χ^2 test to a sample of n triples, and so on. (Note that passing one of these tests does not in the least imply passing the next.) It is obvious, however, that one cannot go far along this road: the number of subsets and hence the necessary sample sizes become prohibitively large, or else d has to be chosen as very small, which reduces the power of the test. The randomness of k-tuples ($k \geqslant 4$) and other groups of numbers has to be tested by cruder means.

Selected characteristics of consecutive k-tuples $(U_1, U_2, \ldots, U_k), (U_{k+1}, U_{k+2}, \ldots, U_{2k}), \ldots$ can be examined. Consider, for example, the sequence $X_1, X_2, \ldots$, where X_j is the largest number in the jth k-tuple. If the Us are independent and uniformly distributed on $(0, 1)$, then the distribution function of X_j is

$$F(x) = P(X_j \leqslant x) = x^k, \quad 0 \leqslant x \leqslant 1, \tag{4.25}$$

since in order that X_j does not exceed x, all numbers in the jth k-tuple must be less than or equal to x. That hypothesis can be tested by applying, say, the Kolmogorov–Smirnov test to a sample $X_1, X_2, \ldots, X_n$ obtained from n k-tuples. This is referred to as the *maximum of k test*.

Other categorisations of k-tuples are obtained by converting the uniform real numbers U_i to uniform integers, $Y_i = \lfloor mU_i \rfloor$, on some range $[0, m-1]$ (m should not be very large, e.g. $m = 13$). The well-known *poker test* was originally designed for 5-tuples: seven subsets of 5-tuples are defined, somewhat like the poker hand combinations:

A_1: All five integers are different $(v\,w\,x\,y\,z)$;
A_2: One pair $(v\,v\,w\,x\,y)$;
A_3: Two pairs $(vv\,ww\,x)$;
A_4: Three of a kind $(vvv\,w\,x)$;
A_5: Full house $(vvv\,ww)$;
A_6: Four of a kind $(vvvv\,w)$;
A_7: Five of a kind $(vvvv v)$.

The probability p_j that a 5-tuple belongs to subset A_j ($j = 1, 2, \ldots, 7$) can be easily computed, given independence and uniformity. A χ^2 test is then applied to a sample of n 5-tuples.

The test for uniformity examines how often, on the average, numbers from the sequence $U_1, U_2, \ldots$ fall into subintervals of the interval $(0, 1)$. However, the distributions of those occurrences are just as important as the averages. Let (a, b), $0 \leqslant a < b \leqslant 1$, be a subinterval of the interval $(0, 1)$. If, for some i and k, $U_i \in (a, b)$, $U_{i+k} \in (a, b)$ but $U_j \notin (a, b)$ for $j = i + 1, i + 2, \ldots, i + k - 1$, then we say that there is a 'gap' of length k. The gap lengths should be distributed geometrically:

$$P(\text{gap length} = k) = \beta^{k-1}(1 - \beta), \quad \text{where } \beta = 1 - (b - a). \tag{4.26}$$

The hypothesis (4.26) can be tested by applying the χ^2 test to a sample of n consecutive gaps. This is the *gap test*. The subinterval (a, b) is often taken as $(0, \frac{1}{2})$ or $(\frac{1}{2}, 1)$.

A particular measure of the dependency between U_i and U_{i+1} is provided by the serial correlation coefficient (appendix 2):

$$r = \left[\sum_{i=1}^{n} U_i U_{i+1} - n\bar{U}^2 \right] \bigg/ \left[\sum_{i=1}^{n} U_i^2 - n\bar{U}^2 \right], \tag{4.27}$$

where U_{n+1} is replaced by U_1 and $\bar{U} = (U_1 + U_2 + \ldots + U_n)/n$. The correlation coefficient lies between -1 and 1. A value of r close to 1 or to -1 implies an almost linear dependence between U_i and U_{i+1}. Values close to 0 tend to indicate that U_i and U_{i+1} are uncorrelated (it should be remembered, however, that two random variables may be uncorrelated and yet dependent). The exact distribution of r is unknown but for large values of n (e.g. $n > 500$), if U_i and U_{i+1} are uncorrelated, the statistic evaluated by (4.27) should satisfy

$$-2/n^{1/2} < r < 2/n^{1/2} \qquad\qquad (4.28)$$

with probability ≈ 0.95. The hypothesis of serial non-correlation ought to be rejected if the observed value of r violates (4.28).

A random number generator which passes all of the above tests will probably be satisfactory for the majority of simulation experiments. However, there may still be applications for which the sequences produced will be insufficiently random. Other, more elaborate and more powerful tests are available (e.g. see Knuth [30]); those tests should also be applied if the generator is intended for general use (e.g. if it is to be incorporated into a simulation language or package).

4.4   When to use what distribution

Having addressed the question of *how* to generate and test various random number sequences, it is appropriate now to consider *which* random number sequences should be generated under different circumstances. Suppose, for example, that prior to a simulation, an empirical distribution of a random variable is obtained by observing the real system in operation. Should that empirical distribution be used in the simulation as it stands, or should one attempt to approximate it with a distribution function from some well-known family? If the latter, what kind of distribution function should be selected?

The answers to these questions depend on how much information is available about the random variable of interest. If it is possible to decide beforehand what the general form of the distribution is, then the problem is reduced to estimating the necessary parameters. Even when that cannot be done, it is probably better to fit a curve from some parameterised family to the sample of observations, than to use the empirical distribution directly. As a general principle, the fewer the quantities that have to be estimated, the better. Thus, having to estimate a mean is better than having to estimate a mean and a variance, which is better than having to estimate three moments, etc. Using an empirical distribution function is equivalent to estimating all the moments of a random variable from a given sample of observations.

The physical nature of a random variable will often suggest the form of its distribution function. For example, if in order to execute a certain task, a large number of elementary operations of about the same size have to be carried out one after the other, then the distribution function of the task execution time will be close to normal. This is a consequence of the central limit theorem: the sum of a large number of independent random variables is approximately normally distributed. The normal distribution has two parameters: μ (mean) and σ (standard deviation). Having estimated these, one can generate the random variable by the methods of section 4.2 (if X is distributed normally with mean 0 and standard deviation 1, then $\mu + \sigma X$ is distributed normally with mean μ and standard deviation σ).

Another very useful limit theorem states that if a large number of independent event streams are merged together, and if the events in each stream occur at a very low rate, then the resulting stream is approximately Poisson. Since the intervals between consecutive events in a Poisson stream are distributed exponentially (appendix 2), that result can also be interpreted as follows: if a large number of independent activities are in progress, and if the expected duration of each activity is very large, then the interval until the first completion of an activity is distributed approximately exponentially. Let us demonstrate this in one special case (the validity of the result is not, of course, restricted to that case). Suppose that n independent activities, with durations $X_1, X_2, \ldots, X_n$ distributed uniformly between 0 and n/μ ($\mu > 0$), are started simultaneously. The interval until the first completion of an activity is $Y_n = \min(X_1, X_2, \ldots, X_n)$; its distribution function is given by

$$F_n(y) = P(Y_n \leqslant y) = P[\min(X_1, X_2, \ldots, X_n) \leqslant y]$$

$$= 1 - P[\min(X_1, X_2, \ldots, X_n) > y]$$

$$= 1 - \prod_{i=1}^{n} P(X_i > y)$$

$$= 1 - \left(1 - \frac{\mu y}{n}\right)^n.$$

If we let $n \to \infty$ in this last expression, we see that

$$\lim_{n \to \infty} F_n(y) = 1 - e^{-\mu y},$$

i.e. the limiting distribution of Y_n is exponential, with mean $1/\mu$.

Poisson streams are commonly used to model the arrivals of customers, or jobs, to a service facility. This is because, if the customer population is large and if each customer visits the facility rarely, then the above result applies: the overall arrival stream is Poisson and the intervals between consecutive arrivals are distributed exponentially. Only one parameter has to be estimated: the average interarrival interval (or its reciprocal, the average number of arrivals per unit time).

Other random variables for which it may be argued that their distribution is exponential are: the operative period of a complicated machine (the time until the first of a large number of components breaks down); the lifetime of an organism (death may be caused by a large number of factors); the residence of a customer at a facility (if that residence can be terminated for a large number of reasons). However, one should verify the assumptions in each special case before arriving at a conclusion; the result may not hold if there are dependencies, or if one type of event occurs much more frequently than the others.

Suppose now that the available information is insufficient to decide the form of the distribution of a random variable. An empirical distribution has been obtained from gathering statistics, and it is desired to approximate that empirical distribution with a 'smooth' one. To do this, it would be nice to have a parameterised family of distribution functions, such that any given distribution function can be approximated arbitrarily closely by functions from the family. We shall describe one such family.

Consider a network of service stages such as the one illustrated in figure 4.6. A job enters server 1 and receives an exponentially distributed service with mean $1/\mu_1$; it then either goes to server 2 (with probability α_1) or leaves the network (with probability $1 - \alpha_1$); in the former case, the job receives from server 2 an exponentially distributed service with mean $1/\mu_2$ and then either goes to server 3 (probability α_2) or leaves the network (probability $1 - \alpha_2$), etc; after server k the job leaves the network. This is referred to as a Coxian network of service stages. The distribution of the time a job spends in the network is a Coxian distribution (see Cox [6]).

It is easily seen that the exponential, hyperexponential and Erlang distributions are Coxian. Moreover, any linear combination of Coxian distributions is also Coxian. It turns out, in fact, that any distribution that can be represented by an arbitrary network of exponential stages can also be represented by a Coxian network. The Coxian family of distributions is 'dense', in the sense that an arbitrary distribution can be approximated as closely as desired by Coxian distributions.

A Coxian distribution with k stages is determined by $2k - 1$ parameters: the average service times $1/\mu_i$ $(i = 1, 2, \ldots, k)$ and the branching probabilities α_i $(i = 1, 2, \ldots, k - 1)$. By choosing k and those parameters appropriately, any distribution functions can be approximated to any accuracy. In general, the higher the desired accuracy, the more stages are required.

To generate a Coxian random variable, X, one can use the composition method (section 4.2): with probability $\alpha_0, \alpha_1 \ldots \alpha_{i-1}(1 - \alpha_i)$ $(i = 1, 3, \ldots, k;$ $\alpha_0 = 1, \alpha_k = 0)$, X is equal to the sum of i exponentially distributed random variables with means $1/\mu_1, 1/\mu_2, \ldots, 1/\mu_i$ respectively.

Figure 4.6. A Coxian network of service stages.

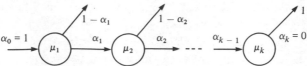

Exercises

1. The sequence $X_1, X_2, \ldots$ of integers in the range $[0, m-1]$ is produced by a linear congruential generator with modulus $m = 2^d$. The following two methods are suggested for using that sequence in order to generate random directions N, S, E, W (with equal probabilities):

   (a) divide X_i by 4 and use the remainder to indicate the direction;
   (b) use $\lfloor 4(X_i/m) \rfloor$ to indicate the direction.

   Are both methods equally acceptable?

2. Given a source $U_1, U_2, \ldots$ of uniformly distributed random numbers on the interval $(0, 1)$, it is desired to generate random points uniformly spread over the circle of unit radius centred at the origin. The following two methods are suggested:

   (a) generate $X = 2U_i - 1$ and $Y = 2U_{i+1} - 1$ (the point (X, Y) is uniform on the square $(-1, 1) \times (-1, 1)$); if $X^2 + Y^2 \leqslant 1$ then output (X, Y), otherwise repeat;
   (b) generate $R = U_i$ and $\varphi = 2\pi U_{i+1}$ (R is a random distance from the origin and φ is a random angle); output the point with coordinates $R \cos \varphi$ and $R \sin \varphi$.

   Are both methods equally acceptable?

3. Let U_1, U_2 and U_3 be three independent, uniformly distributed random variables on the interval $(0, 1)$. Show that $X = \max(U_1, U_2)$ and $Y = U_3^{1/2}$ have the same distribution.

4. Under the conditions of question 3, what is the distribution of the random variable $Z = -\ln(U_1 U_2 U_3)$?

5. Given a source of uniform random numbers, generate a random variable whose probability density function is given by

   (a) $f(x) = 2/(1+x)^3, \quad x \geqslant 0$;
   (b) $f(x) = 1/[\pi(1+x^2)]; \quad -\infty < x < \infty \quad$ (Cauchy distribution);
   (c) $f(x) = (\alpha/\beta^\alpha) x^{\alpha-1} e^{-(x/\beta)^\alpha}, \quad x \geqslant 0 \quad$ (Weibull distribution).

5.   COLLECTION AND ANALYSIS OF SIMULATION DATA

So far we have concentrated on the mechanics of simulating a system. The object has been to produce, by means of a computer program, operation paths whose behaviour is statistically identical to that of the real system. Now the time has come to tackle the equally important problem of how to use the operation paths generated by the program in order to obtain reliable estimates of system performance measures at a reasonable cost. What information should be collected? How much of it should be collected? What should be done with it? These questions are the subject of the remaining three chapters.

There is an unfortunate tendency among simulation practitioners to relax after writing a satisfactory simulator (thinking that the job is almost done then) and not pay sufficient attention to the gathering and analysis of data. That tendency accounts for a large number of failed simulation studies (and perhaps an even larger number of apparent successes which should have been regarded as failures). It is very easy to draw the wrong conclusions from a simulation, not because the program is incorrect, but because its output is incorrectly interpreted.

5.1   Estimation of parameters

The performance measures that interest us are, typically, the values of certain parameters, e.g. the probability of finding a waiting room full, the average number of broken down machines, the average sojourn time in a network, etc. (Occasionally, one wishes to determine an entire distribution; we shall leave that case until the end of this chapter.) Let α be the (unknown) value of the desired quantity and suppose that it is a parameter of the random variable X, defined over a given period of system operation (in the preceding examples, X can be taken, respectively, as the total amount of time that the waiting room was full, the total amount of machine down-time, the total amount of time spent in the network by a given number of jobs). The value of X obtained from a single run (or perhaps a portion of a run) of the simulation program is called an 'observation'. Our task is to estimate α, given a sample of observations $X_1, X_2, \ldots, X_n$ ($n \geq 1$).

It is customary to distinguish between 'point' and 'interval' estimation. A point estimate is a single number, A, which is a function of the sample and which is in some sense representative of α. An interval estimate is a pair of numbers, (A_1, A_2), both of which are functions of the sample, such that α lies between A_1 and A_2 with a given probability. For a simulation result to be meaningful, it is essential that both point and interval estimates be obtained: the former may be used in applications but its accuracy is judged by the width of the latter. Ideally, one would like the interval estimate (or the confidence interval, as it is usually called) to be narrow and to contain the desired quantity with a high probability. We shall discuss confidence intervals in the next section.

Let $A = A(X_1, X_2, \ldots, X_n)$ be a point estimate for α. Since each of the observations in the sample is a random variable (being the outcome of a simulation run), A is a random variable too. If A is equal to α on the average, i.e. if for all n

$$E[A] = \alpha, \tag{5.1}$$

then A is said to be 'unbiased'. If A approaches α, in probability, as n increases, i.e. if for every $\epsilon > 0$,

$$P(|A - \alpha| < \epsilon) \to 1 \quad \text{when } n \to \infty, \tag{5.2}$$

then A is said to be 'consistent'.

Clearly, being unbiased and being consistent are two very desirable properties of an estimate (there are others: e.g. see Freeman [15]). If should be emphasised, however, that even an estimate which possesses those properties can be widely off the mark on a particular sample. Sometimes it is advisable to choose an estimation method that leads to consistent but biased point estimates, if the corresponding confidence intervals are better. A weaker property than lack of bias, which is often acceptable, is that A approaches α, on the average, when the sample size increases:

$$E[A] \to \alpha \quad \text{when } n \to \infty. \tag{5.3}$$

An estimate satisfying (5.3) is said to be asymptotically unbiased.

If the desired parameter, α, is the expectation of the random variable X, and if one is given a sample of *independent* observations $X_1, X_2, \ldots, X_n$, then an unbiased and consistent point estimate for α is the arithmetic mean

$$\bar{X} = \frac{1}{n} \sum_{i=1}^{n} X_i. \tag{5.4}$$

That $\bar{X}$ is unbiased can be seen immediately by taking expectations in (5.4), noting that $E[X_i] = \alpha$ for all i. The consistency of $\bar{X}$ follows from the fact that its variance, given by

$$\text{Var}[\bar{X}] = \frac{1}{n^2} \sum_{i=1}^{n} \text{Var}[X_i] = \text{Var}[X]/n, \tag{5.5}$$

87

tends to zero as n tends to infinity. Without going into the details of the proof, it is intuitively obvious that the lower the variability of an estimate, the more likely it is to take a value close to its mean, which in this case is the desired parameter.

As an example, consider the problem of estimating the average sojourn time, w, of customers in a certain system which is in equilibrium (i.e. the system behaviour is statistically invariant with time; in particular, all customers have the same average sojourn time). Leaving aside for the moment the question of how to simulate a system in equilibrium, suppose that such a simulation has been run until exactly k customers went through the system and that the total sojourn time, B_1, of those k customers was accumulated. Then, taking $X_1 = B_1/k$ as the observation corresponding to that run, it is clear that $E[X_1] = w$. Another such simulation run, with a different random number stream (but again until k customers go through) will yield another total, B_2, and another observation, X_2, still with $E[X_2] = w$. Repeating this process n times would produce a sample $X_1, X_2, \ldots, X_n$, from which to obtain an unbiased and consistent point estimate $\bar{X}$ as in (5.4).

Why go to the trouble of running the simulation n times? Why not make just one run, taking the sojourn times of successive customers as the observations in the sample (each of those sojourn times is, on the average, equal to w) and use $X_1 = B_1/k$ as the point estimate? The reason is that the sojourn times of successive customers are not, in general, independent. A customer with a long sojourn time is likely to have encountered long queues, and therefore his successor is also likely to encounter them and have a long sojourn time. While X_1 is still an unbiased estimate, and is even consistent (as $k \to \infty$), its variance is not easy to estimate. We shall see in the next section that it is important to be able to estimate the variance of an estimate, in order to determine a confidence interval for it.

Why run the simulation until k customers have gone through the system, instead of running it for a fixed period of time, T? In the latter case one would collect the total sojourn time, B, and the number of customers that go through, K, and take $X = B/K$ as the corresponding observation. Then, however, both B and K would be random variables and it would be no longer true that $E[X] = w$ (the expectation of a ratio is generally not equal to the ratio of expectations). Hence, the point estimate would be biased, although it would be asymptotically unbiased. If the simulation period is reasonably large, the bias will be acceptably small (most of the simulation examples in chapter 3 suffered from this defect, for the sake of simplicity).

The average sojourn time is an example of a 'customer-oriented' performance measure. To obtain an observation for a customer-oriented performance measure, the progress of individual customers – a certain number of them – has to be monitored. On the other hand, a 'system-oriented' performance measure is a function of some global state descriptor where customers lose their individuality. That state descriptor is usually an integer, or a vector of integers. For example, in a single-server system with C types of customers ($C \geqslant 1$) and non-preemptive priorities, the system state might be described by a vector of $C + 1$ integers $\mathbf{V} = (I, N_1, N_2, \ldots, N_C)$, where I indicates the type of the customer receiving service and N_j ($j = 1, 2, \ldots, C$) is the number of type j customers waiting in the queue (the vector $\mathbf{V} = (0, 0, \ldots, 0)$ corresponds to an empty system).

A system-oriented performance measure is generally of the form $\alpha = E[f(\mathbf{V})]$, where $\mathbf{V}$ is the vector describing the system state and $f(\cdot)$ is some real-valued function of it. In the above priority system, that function might be, for instance,

(a) $\quad f(\mathbf{V}) = \begin{cases} 1 \text{ if } I = i \\ 0 \text{ if } I \neq i \end{cases}$, $\quad$ for a given $i = 1, 2, \ldots, C$;

(b) $\quad f(\mathbf{V}) = N_j$, $\quad$ for a given $j = 1, 2, \ldots, C$;

(c) $\quad f(\mathbf{V}) = (N_1 + N_2 + \ldots + N_C)^k$, $\quad k = 1, 2, \ldots$.

In the case (a), the performance measure $\alpha = E[f(\mathbf{V})]$ is the probability that a customer of type i is being served; in case (b) it is the average number of type j customers waiting; in case (c) it is the kth moment of the total number of customers waiting.

The system state vector is, in general, a function of time, $\mathbf{V}(t)$. If, however, the system is in equilibrium, the distribution of $\mathbf{V}(t)$ is invariant with time: $\mathbf{V}(t)$ and $\mathbf{V}(t')$ have the same distribution for all t and t' (this is not to say, of course, that the states themselves are the same in any given operation path). In particular, any performance measure $\alpha = E[f(\mathbf{V}(t))]$ is then independent of t. If the system is simulated over a period of fixed length, T, an observation X_1 for that performance measure is provided by

$$X_1 = \frac{1}{T} \int_0^T f(\mathbf{V}(t)) \, dt. \tag{5.6}$$

It is readily seen that X_1 is unbiased: taking expectations in (5.6) yields

$$E[X_1] = \frac{1}{T} E\left[\int_0^T f(\mathbf{V}(t)) \, dt \right] = \frac{1}{T} \int_0^T E[f(\mathbf{V}(t))] \, dt = \frac{1}{T} \int_0^T \alpha \, dt = \alpha.$$

Hence, repeating the experiment n times, with different random number streams, one would obtain a sample of independent observations $X_1, X_2, \ldots, X_n$; the sample mean $\bar{X}$, given by (5.4), will be an unbiased and consistent point estimate for α.

The integral in the right-hand side of (5.6) can be accumulated quite easily as the simulation progresses, since $\mathbf{V}(t)$ changes only at selected points in time, when events occur. For example, in the case (b) above, $f(\mathbf{V}(t))$ is the step function $N_j(t)$ indicating the number of type j customers waiting at time t. A possible realisation of $N_j(t)$ is illustrated in figure 5.1; the moments $t_1, t_2, \ldots$

are the consecutive event times when $N_j(t)$ jumps either up by one or down by one.

The desired integral is the area under the step function, in the interval $(0, T)$. To calculate it, the simulation program should maintain a global variable, $AREA$, and should keep track of the last event time, t_{i-1}, as well as the current one, t_i. Then, just before the state variable $N_j(t)$ is changed, i.e. at time t_i^-, the value of $AREA$ is increased by $(t_i - t_{i-1}) N_j(t_i^-)$.

Returning to equation (5.6), note that $Y_1 = f(\mathbf{V}(T))$ is also an unbiased observation for α. One could, in principle, avoid the trouble of accumulating the integral and simply take the value of the performance measure observed at the end of the simulation period. That, however, would be a false saving, since the accuracy of an estimate derived from a sample of such observations, $Y_1, Y_2, \ldots,$ Y_n, is likely to be much poorer. When the simulation period is large, each observation obtained according to (5.6) is close to α with a high probability (in fact, the right-hand side of (5.6) tends to α, as $T \to \infty$, with probability one). No such property holds for the observations Y_i.

We have seen that, depending on the nature of the performance measure to be estimated, different rules for stopping the simulation have to be employed in order to ensure lack of bias. In the case of customer-oriented measures the rule is 'a fixed number of customers through the system', whereas for system-oriented ones it is 'a fixed simulation period'. Obviously, these rules are not always compatible. If one is interested in both customer-oriented and system-oriented performance measures, some of the estimates may have to be biased. In general, the longer the simulation run, the lower the bias of an observation derived from it.

Before leaving the topic of point estimates, we shall give a relationship between a customer-oriented and a system-oriented performance measure, valid in almost any system in equilibrium. This relationship, known as 'Little's result', makes it possible to obtain the estimates of two performance measures at the price of one.

Figure 5.1. A realisation of $N_j(t)$.

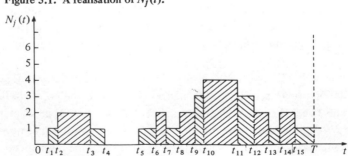

Let Ξ be an arbitrary system where some entities - which we call customers - arrive from the outside, remain for varying intervals of time and then depart. It is assumed that Ξ is in equilibrium. Let m be the expected number of customers in Ξ, w the expected time that customers spend in Ξ (the expected sojourn time) and λ the rate at which customers arrive into Ξ (the average number of arrivals per unit time). Little's result states that

$$m = \lambda w. \tag{5.7}$$

Thus, given the arrival rate λ, an estimate for w yields one for m and vice versa. Note that the definition of the system Ξ is very flexible. If, for example, one is dealing with a network of service stations, Ξ could refer to the whole network or to a selected node or nodes; the customers may include all the jobs or a selected type or types. Against that generality, the result is valid only for means; there is not a similar simple relationship between the higher moments of the number of customers in the system and of the sojourn time. A simple proof of Little's result (there are several) may be found in Gelenbe & Mitrani [17].

Some consequences of relation (5.7) are worth mentioning. Consider a system with C parallel identical servers ($C \geqslant 1$) and a common queue of customers. Let q be the expected time that a customer spends waiting in the queue and $1/\mu$ be the expected service time. Clearly, the expected time that a customer spends in the system is $w = q + (1/\mu)$ and (5.7) can be rewritten as

$$m = \lambda q + (\lambda/\mu).$$

Now define 'the system' as consisting of the queue only; let m' be the average number of customers waiting. Applying Little's result to this redefined system yields

$$m' = \lambda q.$$

Subtracting the last equation from the previous one we get

$$m - m' = \lambda/\mu. \tag{5.8}$$

In other words, the average number of customers being served, which is the same as the average number of busy servers, is equal to the quantity λ/μ when the system is in equilibrium. This is true no matter what are the distributions of the interarrival times and service times; they may even be dependent. Note that λ/μ is the average amount of work brought into the system per unit time. Obviously, the average number of busy servers cannot be greater than the total number of servers. Thus if $(\lambda/\mu) > C$ the system cannot possibly reach a state of equilibrium (it cannot, in general, even if $\lambda/\mu = C$); after a long time of operation one would observe ever growing queues.

Equation (5.8) generalises easily to systems with several different job types: if the arrival rate and average service time for type i customers are λ_i and $1/\mu_i$ respectively, then the average number of servers occupied by type i customers is λ_i/μ_i, regardless of the scheduling rule. If the system is to reach equilibrium with respect to all customer types, the condition

$$\sum_i (\lambda_i/\mu_i) < C$$

must be satisfied. In the special case of a single server, the average number of busy servers (or servers busy with type i customers) is the probability that the server is busy (or busy with a type i customer).

It is useful to be aware of these facts. The effort of rediscovering them through simulations can be saved, or they can be used to check that a simulation behaves as it should.

5.2 Confidence intervals

Assume that we are given a sample of independent and identically distributed observations, $\mathbf{X} = (X_1, X_2, \ldots, X_n)$, and wish to obtain from it a confidence interval for an unknown parameter, α. In what follows, we shall concentrate on the case when α is the mean of the underlying distribution. This case is not overly restrictive, since various quantities of interest can be treated as means of appropriately defined functions of the system state variables (see section 5.1). We know already that the sample mean, $\bar{X} = (X_1 + X_2 + \ldots + X_n)/n$ is an unbiased and consistent point estimate for α.

The confidence interval is defined by two real-valued functions of the sample, $A_1(\mathbf{X})$ and $A_2(\mathbf{X})$, such that no matter what the true value of α is,

$$P\{A_1(\mathbf{X}) < \alpha \leqslant A_2(\mathbf{X})\} = 1 - \beta, \quad 0 < \beta < 1. \tag{5.9}$$

The probabilistic statement in (5.9) should be interpreted to mean that if a large number of confidence intervals were computed according to the functions A_1 and A_2, a proportion $1 - \beta$ of them would contain the true value of α. The probability $1 - \beta$ is often referred to as the 'confidence coefficient', or simply 'confidence', of the confidence interval.

The general approach to finding confidence intervals is based on the existence of a random variable, $Z(\mathbf{X}, \alpha)$, a function of the sample and of the unknown parameter, whose distribution is fixed and known. Given such a random variable, one can find two numbers, z_1 and z_2, such that

$$P(z_1 < Z(\mathbf{X}, \alpha) \leqslant z_2) = 1 - \beta, \quad 0 < \beta < 1. \tag{5.10}$$

The inequalities involving $Z(\mathbf{X}, \alpha)$ can then be solved with respect to α, to transform (5.10) into (5.9).

The observations X_i arising from simulation runs tend to be approximately normally distributed. We saw in the last section that, both for customer-oriented and for system-oriented performance measures, the accumulation of X_i involved the addition of many small contributions (either from customers or from events). By invoking the central limit theorem (appendix 2) it is possible to claim that each observation in the sample is normally distributed with mean α and variance σ^2 (both unknown).

92

Since the sum of normally distributed random variables is normally distributed, the arithmetic mean $\bar{X}$ is also normally distributed. Its mean is α (it is unbiased) and its variance, given by (5.5), is σ^2/n. Hence, the random variable

$$\tilde{Z}(\mathbf{X}, \alpha) = \frac{\bar{X} - \alpha}{\sigma/n^{1/2}} \tag{5.11}$$

has the standard normal distribution (mean 0 and variance 1).

We are almost in a position to follow the approach outlined above. The distribution of $\tilde{Z}$ is fixed and known. Having chosen a confidence coefficient, $1 - \beta$, a table of the standard normal distribution (see Tables) would yield $\tilde{z}_1$ and $\tilde{z}_2$ satisfying

$$P(\tilde{z}_1 < \tilde{Z} \leqslant \tilde{z}_2) = 1 - \beta. \tag{5.12}$$

It is customary to choose $\tilde{z}$ so that $P(\tilde{Z} \leqslant \tilde{z}) = 1 - (\beta/2)$ and then $\tilde{z}_1 = -\tilde{z}$, $\tilde{z}_2 = \tilde{z}$, as illustrated in figure (5.2). Substituting (5.11) into (5.12) and solving the inequalities for α we obtain something resembling a confidence interval:

$$P\{\bar{X} - (\tilde{z}\sigma/n^{1/2}) < \alpha \leqslant \bar{X} + (\tilde{z}\sigma/n^{1/2})\} = 1 - \beta. \tag{5.13}$$

Unfortunately, the variable $\tilde{Z}$ is a function not only of the sample and of α, but also of another parameter, σ. Everything would be fine if the value of σ were known, but without it the upper and lower limits of the interval in (5.13) cannot be determined.

A natural way to remedy this situation is to estimate σ from the sample of observations. The sample variance, S^2, given by

$$S^2 = \left[\sum_{i=1}^{n} (X_i - \bar{X})^2 \right] / (n - 1), \tag{5.14}$$

is an unbiased estimate for σ^2 (that is true for any underlying distribution). Indeed, taking expectations in (5.14), having added and subtracted α in each

Figure 5.2

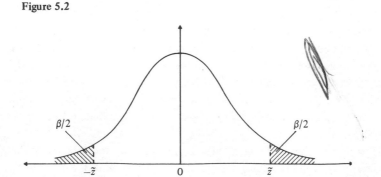

bracketed term, we get

$$E[S^2] = E\left[\sum_{i=1}^{n} (X_i - \alpha + \alpha - \bar{X})^2\right]\bigg/(n-1)$$

$$= \left\{\sum_{i=1}^{n} E[(X_i - \alpha)^2] - nE[(\bar{X} - \alpha)^2]\right\}\bigg/(n-1)$$

$$= [n\sigma^2 - n(\sigma^2/n)]/(n-1)$$

$$= \sigma^2.$$

Moreover, when the observations X_i are normally distributed, the random variable

$$Z(\mathbf{X}, \alpha) = \frac{\bar{X} - \alpha}{S/n^{1/2}} \tag{5.15}$$

has Student's distribution with $n-1$ degrees of freedom, t_{n-1} (see appendix 2).

This time we have a variable which is a function only of the sample of observations and of α, and whose distribution is fixed and known. When $n \geqslant 3$, the t_n density function, like the normal one, is symmetric around the vertical axis (the former approaches the latter as $n \to \infty$). Given the values of n and β one can find a number z (see Tables) such that $P(t_{n-1} \leqslant z) = 1 - (\beta/2)$. Hence,

$$P(-z < Z \leqslant z) = 1 - \beta. \tag{5.16}$$

Substituting (5.15) into (5.16) and solving the inequalities for α yields the confidence interval

$$P\{\bar{X} - (zS/n^{1/2}) < \alpha \leqslant \bar{X} + (zS/n^{1/2})\} = 1 - \beta. \tag{5.17}$$

A few remarks are in order at this point, concerning the implications of interval estimation.

(1) The half-width of the confidence interval, $zS/n^{1/2}$ (corresponding to a given confidence coefficient $1 - \beta$), is a measure of the accuracy of the estimate. Therefore, assuming that z and S do not change very much with n, the accuracy increases in inverse proportion to the square root of the sample size. In other words, in order to double the accuracy, the number of observations has to be increased four times. Suppose, for example, that the following relative accuracy requirement is specified in advance: the half-width of the 95% confidence interval should not exceed 5% of the estimated value of the parameter. An idea of the number of observation points that will be necessary to satisfy that requirement can be obtained from the inequality $(zS/n^{1/2}) \leqslant 0.05\bar{X}$, where z is such that $P(t_{n-1} \leqslant z) = 0.975$. Rough estimates for S and $\bar{X}$ can be obtained from a few observation points; they will give an approximate lower bound on n: $n \geqslant (20zS/\bar{X})^2$.

(2) It is important and worthwhile to try to reduce the variance of the estimate. If, by carefully designing the simulation experiment, the value of S can be

halved, that is equivalent to a four-fold reduction in the amount of work necessary to achieve the same accuracy. Such 'variance reduction' techniques exist and some of them will be described in the next chapter.

(3) The derivation of confidence intervals is closely related to the testing of hypotheses. The random variable Z, given by (5.15), can be used to test the null hypothesis that the unknown parameter is equal to α. That test can be carried out as follows: choose the level of significance, or 'size' of the test, β (the probability of rejecting the hypothesis when it is true); evaluate $Z(\mathbf{X}, \alpha)$; if it falls outside the interval $(-z, z)$ such that $P(-z < t_{n-1} \leqslant z) = 1 - \beta$, then reject the null hypothesis, otherwise accept it. From this formulation it follows immediately that the set of values of α for which $Z(\mathbf{X}, \alpha)$ falls into the acceptance region is precisely the confidence interval corresponding to the sample $\mathbf{X}$. There is thus a duality between a test with level of significance β and a confidence interval with coefficient $1 - \beta$.

(4) In general, the less information used in deriving a confidence interval, the wider that interval will be. Thus, given normally distributed observations with known variance, a confidence interval is provided by (5.13); if the variance is unknown, (5.17) has to be used instead. For the same sample size and confidence coefficient, and assuming that S is close to σ, the (5.17) interval is likely to be wider than the (5.13) one; this is because $\tilde{z} < z$ (the normal distribution has less 'spread' than the t_{n-1} distribution). If the observations cannot be assumed to be normally distributed, then an approximate confidence interval can still be derived from the Chebichev's inequality. This applies to an arbitrary random variable X and states that

$$P\{|X - E[X]| \leqslant (\operatorname{Var}[X]/\beta)^{1/2}\} \geqslant 1 - \beta \qquad (5.18)$$

(see appendix 2). Using the sample mean, $\bar{X}$, as the random variable and approximating $\operatorname{Var}[\bar{X}]$ by S^2/n, (5.18) yields

$$P\{\bar{X} - [S/(n\beta)^{1/2}] \leqslant \alpha < \bar{X} + [S/(n\beta)^{1/2}]\} \geqslant 1 - \beta. \qquad (5.19)$$

As in the case of (5.17), we have an interval whose half-width is proportional to $S/n^{1/2}$. However, the coefficient of proportionality is now $1/\beta^{1/2}$, which causes this last approximate confidence interval, requiring no information about the underlying distribution, to be the widest of all.

5.3 Short-run and long-run performance

So far it has been taken for granted that, when deriving point and interval estimates for a performance measure, a sample of independent observations is available (preferably a large one). This, however, is not always an easy requirement to satisfy. We shall examine here some of the problems involved and some of the solutions that have been proposed.

There are two categories of system performance measures that require radically different approaches:

(*a*) Short-run (transient) performance. One is interested in the evolution of a system during some relative short period of time. The initial conditions (i.e. the state of the system at the beginning of the period) have a significant effect on that evolution and hence on any performance measures over the period.

(*b*) Long-run (steady-state, equilibrium) performance. Of interest is the behaviour of a system that has been running for a long time and has 'settled down'. If $\mathbf{V}(t)$ is the system state vector at time t of its operation and $p(\mathbf{v}, t) = P\{\mathbf{V}(t) = \mathbf{v}\}$ is the probability distribution of that state vector, then the steady-state, or equilibrium distribution is said to exist when the limits

$$p(\mathbf{v}) = \lim_{t \to \infty} p(\mathbf{v}, t)$$

exist, are independent of the initial conditions and sum to 1:

$$\sum_{\mathbf{v}} p(\mathbf{v}) = 1.$$

It is clear from this definition that, although a system may pass through an initial transient phase (which may be long, or even infinite), if and when it approaches equilibrium, the probability of finding it in any given state ceases to vary with time.

The only way to get a sample of independent observations for a short-run performance measure is to run the simulation n times, over the same period and starting with the same initial conditions, but using different random number sequences. Care should be taken to ensure that the random number seeds for the different runs are not related. It is a bad idea, for example, to use as seeds consecutive integers produced by the program's random number generator: the sequences corresponding to such seeds are shifted copies of each other. Since one is dealing with short runs, it is economically feasible to make several of them; the size of the sample will be governed by the required accuracy and by cost constraints. This method of obtaining samples is referred to as the 'independent replications' method.

Long-run performance measures pose two problems, the second of which is more serious. The first problem is that the existence of a transient phase may cause the estimates to be biased. The second is that since the runs are by their nature long, one cannot normally afford to carry out many independent replications. An obvious solution to the first problem is to discard the data collected during the transient part of the run. That, of course, begs the question of how to decide when the system is sufficiently close to equilibrium. One could maintain a current estimate of the probability of a particular system state and examine it at selected points of time; when the difference between consecutive estimates becomes small, equilibrium can be assumed. Alternatively, and more crudely, the transient phase can be said to have ended when the current estimate of some performance measure stops moving in one direction and starts oscillating. Whichever criterion is adopted, one cannot help feeling that it is a waste to simulate

96

the system for some interval of time and then throw away all information that was collected during that interval. The transient period can be reduced considerably by starting the simulation in a state which is close to the average equilibrium one. For example, if there are reasons to believe that in the long run a system will be quite heavily loaded with customers, it is better to start the simulation with a non-empty system than with an empty one. There is also an estimation method (to be described in the next section) which avoids completely the problem of transient phase.

To cope with the high cost of long simulation runs, the generally accepted practice is to make a single long run, divide it into n portions, or sub-runs (after having discarded the transient part) and then work with the sample of observations obtained from those portions. If the performance measure of interest is customer-oriented (see section 5.1), then to ensure lack of bias the portions should be such that a fixed number of customers, k, contribute to the data accumulated in each portion. If, on the other hand, the performance measure is system-oriented, then the estimate will be unbiased if the portions are of fixed length, T. In both cases, this method of dividing the simulation run is referred to as 'batched means'.

A sample of observations, $X_1, X_2, \ldots, X_n$, obtained by the method of batched means, suffers from a serious defect: such observations are not in general independent of each other. Consider, for example, the warehouse model in chapter 3: if during one sub-run the warehouse should fill up with items, it is likely to be quite full during (at least part of) the next sub-run. The sample mean, $\bar{X} = (X_1 + X_2 + \ldots + X_n)/n$, is an unbiased estimate for the underlying expectation, α, despite the dependencies. However, the variance of $\bar{X}$ is now equal to

$$\text{Var}[\bar{X}] = (\sigma^2/n) + \left[2 \sum_{i=1}^{n-1} \sum_{j=i+1}^{n} \text{Cov}(X_i, X_j)\right]/n^2, \tag{5.20}$$

where $\sigma^2 = \text{Var}(X_i), i = 1, 2, \ldots, n$. Replacing, as was done in the transition from (5.13) to (5.17), the standard deviation of $\bar{X}$ by $S/n^{1/2}$, is no longer satisfactory. In fact, since the covariances in (5.20) are likely to be positive, such a substitution will tend to underestimate the variance of $\bar{X}$ and hence lead to unjustifiably narrow confidence intervals.

There are three ways of dealing with the problem of dependent observations. The 'brute force' method is to make each sub-run so large that the dependencies will be negligible. This is essentially equivalent to the independent replications method and is therefore just as expensive. The second way is to try and take the dependencies into account; we shall outline the approach (which falls under the general heading 'time series analysis') in the remainder of this section. The third way is to define the sub-runs in such a manner that the observations become genuinely independent; this will be the subject of the next section.

Since the system is in equilibrium, the sample $X_1, X_2, \ldots, X_n$ is already assumed to satisfy $E[X_i] = \alpha$, $\text{Var}[X_i] = \sigma^2$, for all i. We now add another assumption, namely that

$$\text{Cov}(X_i, X_{i+k}) = E[(X_i - \alpha)(X_{i+k} - \alpha)] = \gamma(k), \quad \text{for all } i, k. \quad (5.21)$$

In other words, the covariance between two observations depends only on their relative distance and not on their position in the sequence. Sequences satisfying (5.21) are said to be 'covariance-stationary' and $\gamma(k)$ is their 'covariance function'. Often the sample is thought of as coming from an infinite sequence, so that $\gamma(k)$ is defined for all values $k = 0, \pm 1, \pm 2, \ldots$. When $k = 0$, we have $\gamma(0) = \sigma^2$; for $k \neq 0$, $\gamma(k) = \gamma(-k)$. In terms of the covariance function, (5.20) can be rewritten as

$$\text{Var}[\bar{X}] = [\gamma(0)/n] + \left[2 \sum_{k=1}^{n-1} (n-k)\,\gamma(k)\right]\bigg/ n^2. \quad (5.22)$$

In most practical cases, given reasonably large sub-runs, it is quite safe to assume that the dependence does not extend over more than m sub-runs, where m is some small integer like 1 or 2; i.e., assume that $\gamma(k) = 0$ for $k = m + 1$, $m + 2, \ldots, n - 1$. Then $\gamma(0), \gamma(1), \ldots, \gamma(m)$ can be estimated from the sample:

$$\tilde{\gamma}(0) = \left[\sum_{i=1}^{n} (X_i - \bar{X})^2\right]\bigg/ (n-1) = S^2$$

$$\tilde{\gamma}(k) = \left[\sum_{i=1}^{n-k} (X_i - \bar{X})(X_{i+k} - \bar{X})\right]\bigg/ (n-k), \quad k = 1, 2, \ldots, m. \quad (5.23)$$

These estimates are not unbiased but, under the assumptions that we have made, they are asymptotically unbiased and consistent. The right-hand side of (5.22) is estimated by the expression

$$[\tilde{\gamma}(0)/n] + \left[2 \sum_{k=1}^{m} (n-k)\,\tilde{\gamma}(k)\right]\bigg/ n^2, \quad (5.24)$$

which, for large n and small m, is approximately equal to

$$\left[\tilde{\gamma}(0) + 2 \sum_{k=1}^{m} \tilde{\gamma}(k)\right]\bigg/ n = \tilde{S}^2/n \quad (5.25)$$

(the contents of the square brackets has been denoted by $\tilde{S}^2$).

Next, the random variable

$$\hat{Z} = (\bar{X} - \alpha)/(\tilde{S}/n^{1/2}) \quad (5.26)$$

can be said to have approximately Student's t distribution with $n - 1$ or, more conservatively, $n - m - 1$ degrees of freedom. This is only an approximation because $\tilde{S}^2$, unlike the S^2 of (5.14), does not have the distribution of a sum of squares of independent normal random variables. The confidence interval for

α which is based on the random variable $\hat{Z}$, with confidence coefficient $1-\beta$, has the form

$$P\{\bar{X}-(z\tilde{S}/n^{1/2}) < \alpha \leq \bar{X}+(z\tilde{S}/n^{1/2}\} = 1-\beta, \tag{5.27}$$

where z is such that $P(t_{n-m-1} \leq z) = 1-(\beta/2)$. Note that the main difference between (5.17) and (5.27) is the replacement of S by $\tilde{S}$. The dependence between observations is taken into account by the addition of the term $2[\tilde{\gamma}(1)+\tilde{\gamma}(2)+\ldots+\tilde{\gamma}(m)]$ in the expression for $\tilde{S}^2$.

Another approach to estimating the variance of $\bar{X}$, which we shall not discuss in detail, relies on the properties of the sample 'spectrum'. For an infinite sequence $\{X_i\}$, $i = 1, 2, \ldots$, with covariance function $\gamma(k)$, $k = 0, \pm 1, \pm 2, \ldots$, the spectral density function, $\varphi(s)$, is defined as the Fourier transform of the covariance function:

$$\varphi(s) = \sum_{k=-\infty}^{\infty} \gamma(k)\,e^{-iks} = \gamma(0) + 2\sum_{k=1}^{\infty} \gamma(k)\cos(ks). \tag{5.28}$$

The problem of estimating the variance of $\bar{X}$ is essentially equivalent to that of estimating $\varphi(0)$. This can be seen by comparing the right-hand side of (5.28), for $s = 0$, with the expression for $\tilde{S}^2$ in (5.25). A procedure which uses the sample of observations in order to estimate the spectral density at $s = 0$ was recently proposed by Heidelberger & Welch [22]; the interested reader is directed to that paper, and to its bibliography for further references.

5.4 The regenerative method

Suppose that in the course of a simulation run one can identify moments in time $t_1, t_2, \ldots$, which have the following properties:

(i)   the lengths of the intervals between consecutive moments, $d_i = t_i - t_{i-1}$, are independent and identically distributed random variables;

(ii)   the system state at time t_i, $\mathbf{V}(t_i)$, is the same for all i;

(iii) the behaviour of the system after time t_i depends only on the state $\mathbf{V}(t_i)$ and not on what happened before t_i $(i = 1, 2, \ldots)$.

Such moments are called 'regeneration points' for the simulation process; the intervals between them are referred to as 'regeneration cycles'. It is clear from these definitions that the portions of an operation path of a regenerative system during consecutive regeneration cycles are independent and identically distributed. Therefore, if the sub-runs of a long simulation run are defined to coincide with consecutive regeneration cycles, the observations collected during those sub-runs will be independent and identically distributed random variables.

A few examples should help to clarify these concepts. Consider the systems that were simulated in chapter 3. For the warehouse model, the moments t_i, just before the arrival of a new batch into an empty warehouse, are regeneration points. To continue the simulation after t_i, one generates the size of the incoming batch, the interval until the next arrival instant, the interval until the next removal instant, etc., all of which is completely independent of anything that happened before t_i. Note that the moments t_i', just before the arrival of a new batch into a warehouse containing, say, k items, are not in general regeneration points: in that case the next removal instant has already been scheduled and its position may depend on the last removal instant, which is before t_i'. However, if the intervals between consecutive removals are distributed exponentially, then the moments t_i' become regeneration points too. The exponential distribution has the 'memoryless property' (appendix 2), which ensures that the interval until the next removal instant is independent of the interval since the last removal instant. Alternatively, if the interremoval intervals are general but the interarrival ones are exponentially distributed, then the moments t_i'', just after the removal of a batch which leaves an empty warehouse, are regeneration points.

For the machine interference model, if the operative periods for all machines are distributed exponentially, then the moments just after a repair completion which leaves all machines operative (and all repairmen idle) are regeneration points. If the repair times are exponentially distributed, then the moments just after a breakdown which leaves all machines broken down (and all repairmen busy) are regeneration points. If neither the operative periods nor the repair times are exponentially distributed, then that system is not regenerative: it never returns to a state which is in all respects equivalent to one visited previously.

In the case of a multiserver queueing system with several customer types, if the interarrival intervals for all types are exponentially distributed, the arrival instants of, say, type 1 customers who find an empty system are regeneration points (if there is only one type of customer, then those instants are regeneration points even when the interarrival intervals are general). Similar remarks apply to (open) networks of service stations.

Even when regeneration points exist, the parameters of a system may be such that it never reaches them. For example in a single-server queueing system where customers arrive at the rate of three per minute and each takes on average a minute to serve, the queue will tend to grow and grow, and there will never be another customer who finds the system empty. Thus it only makes sense to talk about a system being regenerative when an equilibrium regime exists; then the regeneration cycles are certain to be finite.

The regenerative properties of a system can be used to obtain a sample of independent observations for a performance measure. Assume that the performance measure is system-oriented, i.e. it has the form $\alpha = E[f(\mathbf{V})]$, where $\mathbf{V}$ is the system state vector (see section 5.1). We have seen that from a simulation run of fixed length, T, an unbiased estimate for α is obtained by evaluating:

$$X = \frac{1}{T} \int_0^T f[\mathbf{V}(t)] \, dt.$$

To apply the regenerative method, the system is simulated not for a fixed period but for a number of regeneration cycles. The simulation starts and ends at a regeneration point, going through a sequence of $n + 1$ such points: $t_0 = 0, t_1, t_2,$ ..., t_n. Let $d_i = t_i - t_{i-1}$ be the length of the ith regeneration cycle ($i = 1, 2,$ ..., n); these lengths are independent and identically distributed random variables. Denote by Y_i the performance measure integral over the ith regeneration cycle:

$$Y_i = \int_{t_{i-1}}^{t_i} f[V(t)]\, dt.$$

The Y_is are also independent and identically distributed random variables (Y_i and d_i, however, are obviously dependent). The following key result (Crane & Iglehart [7]) relates Y_i and d_i with the desired performance measure:

$$\alpha = E[Y_i]/E[d_i]. \tag{5.29}$$

The problem is thus to derive from the sample of observations (Y_1, d_1), $(Y_2, d_2), \ldots, (Y_n, d_n)$, point and interval estimates for α. The point estimate that immediately suggests itself is

$$A = \frac{1}{t_n} \int_0^{t_n} f[V(t)]\, dt = \left[\sum_{i=1}^{n} Y_i\right]\bigg/\left[\sum_{i=1}^{n} d_i\right] = \bar{Y}/\bar{d}, \tag{5.30}$$

where $\bar{Y}$ and $\bar{d}$ are the sample means of $\{Y_i\}$ and $\{d_i\}$ respectively. That estimate is, regrettably, biased: the expectation of the ratio of two random variables is not equal to the ratio of their expectations, which implies that

$$E[A] = E[\bar{Y}/\bar{d}] \neq E[\bar{Y}]/E[\bar{d}] = E[Y_i]/E[d_i] = \alpha.$$

The bias tends to 0 as $n \to \infty$ but for small n it may be considerable. This is the price one pays for eliminating the dependencies between observations. Several other estimates have been suggested, aimed at reducing the bias of (5.30) (see, for example, Iglehart [25]). Perhaps the most notable of these is the 'jackknife estimate', $\bar{\theta}$, defined as follows:

$$\bar{\theta} = \frac{1}{n}\sum_{i=1}^{n} \theta_i, \tag{5.31}$$

where $\theta_i = n(\bar{Y}/\bar{d}) - (n-1)(n\bar{Y} - Y_i)/(n\bar{d} - d_i), i = 1, 2, \ldots, n$. Both A and θ are consistent estimates, so the difference $A - \bar{\theta}$ tends to 0 as n increases.

To derive a confidence interval for α, centred on the estimate A, consider the independent and identically distributed random variables $X_i = Y_i - \alpha d_i$ ($i = 1, 2, \ldots, n$). According to (5.29), $E[X_i] = 0$. Denoting $\mathrm{Var}(X_i) = \sigma_X^2$, $\mathrm{Var}(Y_i) = \sigma_Y^2$, $\mathrm{Var}(d_i) = \sigma_d^2$ and $\mathrm{Cov}(Y_i, d_i) = \sigma_{Y,d}$, we can write

$$\sigma_X^2 = \sigma_Y^2 - 2\alpha\sigma_{Y,d} + \alpha^2\sigma_d^2. \tag{5.32}$$

101

Next, by the central limit theorem, the random variable

$$\left[\sum_{i=1}^{n} X_i\right] \bigg/ (n\sigma_X^2)^{1/2} = n(\bar{Y} - \alpha\bar{d})/(n\sigma_X^2)^{1/2} = \bar{d}n^{1/2}(A - \alpha)/\sigma_X, \qquad (5.33)$$

is approximately normally distributed with mean 0 and variance 1. This should yield a confidence interval for α, but before that the unknown variance σ_X^2 has to be estimated from the sample. Unbiased estimates for σ_Y^2, σ_d^2 and $\sigma_{Y,d}$, respectively, are provided by

$$S_Y^2 = \frac{1}{n-1} \sum_{i=1}^{n} (Y_i - \bar{Y})^2,$$

$$S_d^2 = \frac{1}{n-1} \sum_{i=1}^{n} (d_i - \bar{d})^2$$

and

$$S_{Y,d} = \frac{1}{n-1} \sum_{i=1}^{n} (Y_i - \bar{Y})(d_i - \bar{d}).$$

Substituting these into (5.32) and using A instead of α leads to the following estimate for σ_X^2:

$$S_X^2 = S_Y^2 - 2AS_{Y,d} + A^2 S_d^2. \qquad (5.34)$$

Now the random variable $\bar{d}n^{1/2}(A - \alpha)/S_X$ has approximately Student's t distribution with $n - 1$ degrees of freedom, which gives a confidence interval of the form

$$P\{A - [zS_X/(\bar{d}n^{1/2})] < \alpha \leqslant A + [zS_X/(\bar{d}n^{1/2})]\} = 1 - \beta, \qquad (5.35)$$

where z is such that $P(t_{n-1} \leqslant z) = 1 - (\beta/2)$.

A confidence interval centred on the jackknife estimate, $\bar{\theta}$, is obtained by remarking that the random variable

$$(\bar{\theta} - \alpha)/(S_\theta/n^{1/2}),$$

where

$$S_\theta^2 = \frac{1}{n-1} \sum_{i=1}^{n} (\theta_i - \bar{\theta})^2,$$

has approximately the distribution t_{n-1}. The corresponding confidence interval is

$$P\{\bar{\theta} - (zS_\theta/n^{1/2}) < \alpha \leqslant \bar{\theta} + (zS_\theta/n^{1/2})\} = 1 - \beta, \qquad (5.36)$$

with z having the same meaning as in (5.35).

Some comparisons between the estimates A and $\bar{\theta}$, and the confidence intervals associated with them (see Iglehart [25], where other estimates are also discussed), indicate that when the number of cycles is not large, estimation

102

based on $\bar{\theta}$ is superior to that based on A; when n is large, there is not much to choose between the two. On the other hand, the jackknife method requires much more storage to implement, since all the values Y_i and d_i have to be kept until the end.

Let us sum up the relative advantages and disadvantages of the batched means and regeneration methods for long-run simulations. Dividing the simulation run into sub-runs of fixed size has the merit of leading to unbiased point estimates. The observations in the sample are in general dependent and those dependencies have to be taken into account when deriving confidence intervals. That, however, is quite easily done, assuming that only observations that are close to each other in the sample are correlated. The sub-runs should start when the system is close to equilibrium, after the transient portion of the run has been discarded.

Dividing the simulation run into regeneration cycles (if possible), eliminates two problems: that of dependencies between observations and that of the transient portion (the first cycle is statistically identical to all the others, so the question does not arise). On the negative side, the point estimates are biased, which may cause the associated confidence intervals not to cover the desired performance measures (this may happen, of course, with any interval estimate but a biased midpoint certainly aggravates the situation). Also, it is very difficult to apply the regenerative method to customer-oriented performance measures.

5.5   Estimating distributions

Sometimes it is important to examine the distribution of a certain quantity of interest, and not just selected characteristics (like mean or variance). This should not be confused with the distribution of a statistic that is collected for the purpose of estimating a performance measure. For example, in order to estimate the mean sojourn time of customers in a system, the total sojourn time, B, of all customers during a simulation run (or sub-run) is collected and is divided by the number of customers, k (section 5.1). The distribution of the statistic B/k is approximately normal – a fact which is used in deriving a confidence interval for the mean. However, the distribution of individual sojourn times can be completely different, and it might be of interest to establish what it is.

One way of determining the distribution of a random variable, ξ, is to determine all its moments: $m_i = E[\xi^i]$, $i = 1, 2, \ldots$. In practice, of course, this means estimating the first M moments, for some finite M. The methods discussed in the previous sections can be used for this purpose. If ξ is a customer-oriented quantity, taking value ξ_j for the jth customer, then the appropriate statistic for estimating its ith moment is

$$\frac{1}{k} \sum_{j=1}^{k} \xi_j^i, \quad i = 1, 2, \ldots, M,$$

where k is the number of customers that passed through the system during the simulation run. If ξ is system-oriented then the statistic is of the form

$$\frac{1}{T}\int_0^T [\xi(t)]^i \, dt, \quad i = 1, 2, \ldots, M,$$

where T is the length of the run (if the regeneration method is applied, then the integrals and the lengths of the cycles are kept separate.

If the form of the desired distribution is known in advance, then the problem reduces to one of estimating a certain number of parameters. Thus, an exponential distribution is completely determined by its mean; a normal one by its mean and variance; etc. In general, if a distribution depends on r parameters, then knowledge of the first r moments is sufficient to determine them. Consider, for example, the hyperexponential distribution, whose density function is given by

$$f(x) = \sum_{j=1}^n \alpha_j \mu_j \, e^{-\mu_j x}; \quad \sum_{j=1}^n \alpha_j = 1.$$

This distribution is specified by $2n - 1$ parameters: $\mu_1, \mu_2, \ldots, \mu_n$ and $\alpha_1, \alpha_2, \ldots, \alpha_{n-1}$ (since the αs sum up to one). Its ith moment is expressed in terms of these parameters as follows:

$$m_i = \sum_{j=1}^n \alpha_j (i!/\mu_j^i), \quad i = 1, 2, \ldots.$$

Conversely, if $m_1, m_2, \ldots, m_{2n-1}$ are known (or have been estimated), then the above system of simultaneous (non-linear) equations can be solved for μ_j and α_j.

When the form of the distribution is not known in advance, the moments can still provide a good approximation. The family of Coxian distributions (section 4.4) is particularly useful in this respect. A Coxian distribution with n exponential stages has $2n - 1$ parameters (the means of the n stages and the probabilities of finishing after stages $1, 2, \ldots, n - 1$). Since an arbitrary distribution can be approximated as closely as desired by a Coxian one (given a sufficient number of stages), an acceptable approach would be to choose n, estimate the first $2n - 1$ moments and then solve a system of equations to find the corresponding n-stage Coxian distribution.

Alternatively, one could estimate directly the probability density function of a random variable by collecting in an array a frequency histogram of its occurrences. For example, if the random variable is the sojourn time of customers in the system, the positive real axis is split into intervals $(0, h), (h, 2h), \ldots,$ $((n - 1)h, nh), (nh, \infty)$, for some $h > 0$; the ith element of the histogram array will contain the proportion of customers whose response times fell into the ith interval ($i = 1, 2, \ldots, n + 1$). In the case of system-oriented quantities 'proportion of customers' should be replaced by 'proportion of time'.

Frequency histograms are visually appealing and for that reason are usually included in the simulation output. They should not, however, be used as a substitute for point and interval estimates.

Exercises

1. In a queueing system with C types of customers, what statistics should be collected in order to estimate

    (a) The variance of the number of type j customers in the system;

    (b) The variance of the sojourn time for type j customers;

    (c) The average length of a type j busy period (i.e. the period between the arrival of a type j customer who finds no other type j customers in the system, and the next departure of a type j customer who leaves no other type j customers behind)?

2. Instead of estimating the variance of the observations in a sample by S^2 in (5.14), one could obtain a variance estimate within each run of the simulation and then average those estimates. What would be wrong with such a procedure?

3. Identify a sequence of regeneration points for the following system: A fixed number, N, of customers are circulating forever between two service stations; after receiving service at station 1 a customer goes to station 2 and vice versa. The service times at the two stations are independent and their distributions can be arbitrary.

4. The density function of the Erlang distribution (see appendix 2) is given by

    $$f(x) = \lambda(\lambda x)^{n-1} e^{-\lambda x}/(n-1)!,$$

    where λ is a positive real number and n is an integer $\geqslant 1$. Assuming that a performance measure has the Erlang distribution how can the parameters of that distribution be estimated?

5. Answer the same question as above, this time assuming that the performance measure is distributed uniformly on some interval (a, b).

6.   VARIANCE REDUCTION METHODS

Obtaining accurate estimates by simulation, or by any other statistical procedure for that matter, tends to be expensive. The main reason for this is the variability of observed performance, which is in turn caused by random phenomena. Different observations of the same system yield different values for a given performance measure, thus making its exact determination impossible. Intuition tells us that these differences will 'average out' over a large number of observations, but making a large number of observations is precisely what causes the experiment to become expensive. Moreover, the greater the variability among the observed values, the more observations are necessary in order to achieve the desired accuracy. Indeed, we saw in the last chapter that, no matter what estimation method is adopted, the half-width of the confidence interval (which is the accepted measure of accuracy) is proportional to the sample standard deviation; it is also inversely proportional to the square root of the sample size. If, therefore, one manages somehow to obtain a sample with a lower variance, the accuracy of the estimate will be improved (or, alternatively, the same accuracy will be achieved with fewer observations).

The subject of variance reduction has received considerable attention and a number of methods have been developed (e.g. see Kleijnen [29]). Some of these do not apply readily to simulations, since they were designed with different applications in mind. There are, however, a few techniques that help to increase the efficiency of simulations, sometimes substantially, by producing less variable observations. This chapter is devoted to them.

6.1   Common random number streams

Suppose that it is desired to compare the performance of a system under two different operating policies, A and B. For example, in a machine repair shop, A and B might be two scheduling rules for servicing the queue of broken down machines; in a virtual memory computer system, they might be two page replacement algorithms or two procedures for controlling the degree of multiprogramming. Of interest is not the absolute system performance under the two policies but the relative difference between them. That is, if the performance

106

measure which is chosen as a basis for comparison takes values α_A and α_B under A and B respectively, the object is to estimate the quantity $\alpha_A - \alpha_B$.

The 'classic' way to approach this problem is to obtain, by one of the methods described in the last chapter, a sample of n observations under policy A, $X_1^A, X_2^A, \ldots, X_n^A$, and an independent sample of n observations under policy B, $X_1^B, X_2^B, \ldots, X_n^B$. The sample A mean and variance are given by

$$\bar{X}_A = \frac{1}{n} \sum_{i=1}^{n} X_i^A; \quad S_A^2 = \frac{1}{n-1} \sum_{i=1}^{n} (X_i^A - \bar{X}_A)^2.$$

Similarly, sample B yields mean $\bar{X}_B$ and variance S_B^2. Then the point estimate for $\alpha_A - \alpha_B$ is $\bar{X}_A - \bar{X}_B$ and the latter's variance estimate is $(S_A^2 + S_B^2)/n$. The confidence interval for $\alpha_A - \alpha_B$, with level of confidence $1 - \beta$, is centred on $\bar{X}_A - \bar{X}_B$ and its half-width is approximately equal to $z(S_A^2 + S_B^2)^{1/2}/n^{1/2}$, where z is such that $P(t_{2n-2} \leqslant z) = 1 - (\beta/2)$; Student's distribution with $2n - 2$ degrees of freedom is appropriate here.

Now consider what would happen if sample B, instead of being independent of sample A, is obtained under identical conditions. More precisely, the same sequence of random numbers (i.e. the same seed or seeds) that was used to produce X_1^A is also used for X_1^B; similarly for X_2^A and X_2^B, etc. Within sample A and within sample B the observations are just as independent as before, but there is a positive correlation between the corresponding observations of the two samples (e.g. if a burst of arrivals causes a long queue to develop under policy A, the same burst will occur under policy B with presumably the same effect).

The difference $\bar{X}_A - \bar{X}_B$ is still an unbiased estimate for $\alpha_A - \alpha_B$. However, the variance of that difference is now equal to

$$\text{Var}[\bar{X}_A] + \text{Var}[\bar{X}_B] - 2\,\text{Cov}[\bar{X}_A, \bar{X}_B]$$

and is estimated by

$$(S_A^2 + S_B^2 - 2S_{AB})/n,$$

where

$$S_{AB} = \frac{1}{n-1} \sum_{i=1}^{n} (X_i^A - \bar{X}_A)(X_i^B - \bar{X}_B).$$

Clearly, a variance reduction has been achieved: when the samples are positively correlated, $S_A^2 + S_B^2 - 2S_{AB} < S_A^2 + S_B^2$. Moreover, the higher the correlation, the greater the reduction. The half-width of the new confidence interval is $z(S_A^2 + S_B^2 - 2S_{AB})^{1/2}/n^{1/2}$.

Note that, in the trivial special case when A and B are the same policy, an experiment using common random number streams would lead to a point estimate $\bar{X}_A - \bar{X}_B = 0$ and to a confidence interval of length zero (since $S_{AB} = S_A^2 = S_B^2$), for any level of confidence, arbitrarily close to one. In other words, the experiment would demonstrate with certainty that there is no difference between the policies. Independent samples, on the other hand, are likely to produce a non-zero estimate for the difference and a non-zero confidence interval.

It is thus to be recommended that, when estimating performance differences, the alternative system configurations should be simulated under as nearly identical conditions as possible. The simulation effort is then expended more efficiently. This is one of several instances (others will be encountered later) when correlation between observations is beneficial and should be actively encouraged. It must be remembered, however, that the correlation here is across samples, not within a sample.

The structure of a simulation program may sometimes be influenced by the desire to run different policies under identical conditions. Consider, for example, the simulation of a single-server queueing system such as a counter in a bank. The random variables that are generated are the customer interarrival times and their required service times. As far as estimating a given performance measure is concerned, it obviously does not matter whether a customer's required service time is generated at the moment of arrival (and is assigned to that customer as an attribute), or whether it is generated when the customer is about to be served. However, if two scheduling policies are to be compared (e.g. First-Come-First-Served and Last-Come-First-Served), it is better to generate the service times on arrival: using the same stream of random numbers will then ensure that customers who arrive at the same time under the two policies will require the same amount of service.

6.2   Replacing random variables by their expectations

More often than not, the gathering of statistics during a simulation run amounts to adding up a series of quantities of similar type. These could be customer sojourn times, intervals during which a queue is empty, portions of an item–hour integral, etc. The observations produced by such simulation runs are thus sums of random variables. The number of variables that are summed is, in general, also random.

Sometimes the expectations of those random variables are known. In those cases, the variance of the observations can be reduced by adding up, not the quantities that occur in the simulation runs, but their expectations. Consider, for example, the simulation of a telephone exchange with a certain number of lines. The performance measure of interest is the average number of calls that are lost, per unit time, because they find all the lines engaged. The straightforward way of obtaining an observation for that performance measure is to simulate the system over a period of time T, count the number of calls, V, that are lost and return V/T as the observed value.

Bearing in mind that calls are lost only when all lines are engaged, the number V can be written as a sum

$$V = \sum_{i=1}^{N} Y_i,$$

where Y_i is the number of calls that arrived during the ith interval when all lines were engaged, and N is the number of such intervals (if $N = 0$ then the sum is defined as zero). If the length, B_i, of the ith 'engaged' interval is known, and if calls arrive into the system in a Poisson stream at a rate λ, then the expected value of Y_i is λB_i ($i = 1, 2, \ldots, N$). Thus, instead of counting the number of lost calls, one could accumulate the intervals when all lines are engaged. The observed value of the performance measure, V/T, would then be replaced by $\tilde{V}/T$, where $\tilde{V}$ is the number of calls that could be expected to arrive during the observed engaged intervals:

$$\tilde{V} = \lambda \sum_{i=1}^{N} B_i.$$

This replacement does not introduce bias, since $E[V] = E[\tilde{V}]$; however, the variance of the observation is reduced, since $\mathrm{Var}[\lambda B_i] = \lambda^2 \mathrm{Var}[B_i] < \lambda^2 \mathrm{Var}[B_i] + \lambda E[B_i] = \mathrm{Var}[Y_i]$ (for the last equality, see appendix 2). Intuitively, the reduction is brought about because one source of variability – the random arrivals during the engaged intervals – is eliminated; only the variability due to the engaged intervals themselves is left.

Another example which might be instructive is provided by the estimation of average sojourn times in a single-server queueing system with exponentially distributed service times and First-Come-First-Served queueing discipline. To obtain an observation, one would normally simulate the system until k customers have been served; if the sojourn time of the jth customer is Y_j and the total sojourn time is

$$W = \sum_{j=1}^{k} Y_j,$$

then the value returned would be W/k.

On the other hand, a customer who finds, on arrival, m customers in the system, has an expected sojourn time of $(m + 1)/\mu$, where $1/\mu$ is the average service time; this is because of the memoryless property of the exponential distribution (see appendix 2): the expected remaining service time of the customer in service, if any, is the same as the expected service time, i.e. $1/\mu$. Thus, instead of accumulating the sojourn times Y_j, one could accumulate the statistic

$$\tilde{W} = \sum_{j=1}^{k} (m_j + 1)/\mu,$$

where m_j is the number of customers found in the system by the jth customer. The value returned for the observation would then be $\widetilde{W}/k$.

Again, the expectations of W and $\widetilde{W}$ are the same, but the latter has a lower variance than the former. Intuitively, some of the variation caused by the random service times has been eliminated. In the special case when the arrival stream is Poisson with rate λ and the system is in equilibrium, it is known from queueing theory (see appendix 2), that $\mathrm{Var}\,[m_j/\mu] = \lambda/[\mu(\mu-\lambda)^2] < 1/(\mu-\lambda)^2 = \mathrm{Var}\,[Y_j]$. The variances of the sums W and $\widetilde{W}$ are very difficult to determine because the consecutive Y_js (and the consecutive m_js) are correlated.

It should be clear from these examples that replacing, whenever possible, random variables by their expectations leads to a reduction in the variance of observations and hence to a more efficient use of simulation time. In general, the amount of the reduction can only be estimated experimentally. For a theoretical evaluation, some simplifying assumptions have to be made. Suppose, for instance, that the statistic of interest, V, is a sum of independent and identically distributed random variables,

$$V = \sum_{i=1}^{N} Y_i \tag{6.1}$$

where the number of terms, N, is also a random variable. By conditioning upon the value of N, we obtain the expectation of V as

$$E[V] = \sum_{n=0}^{\infty} \{P(N=n)\,E[V\,|\,N=n]\}$$

$$= \sum_{n=0}^{\infty} P(N=n)\,nE[Y] = E[N]\,E[Y], \tag{6.2}$$

where $E[Y]$ is the common expectation of the variables Y_i. The second moment of V is derived in a similar way:

$$E[V^2] = \sum_{n=0}^{\infty} \{P(N=n)\,E[V^2\,|\,N=n]\}$$

$$= \sum_{n=0}^{\infty} \{P(N=n)[nE[Y^2] + n(n-1)(E[Y])^2]\}$$

$$= E[N]\,E[Y^2] + (E[N^2] - E[N])(E[Y])^2] \tag{6.3}$$

$$= E[N]\,\mathrm{Var}\,[Y] + E[N^2](E[Y])^2.$$

Equations (6.2) and (6.3) yield the variance of V:

$$\mathrm{Var}\,[V] = E[V^2] - (E[V])^2$$

$$= E[N]\,\mathrm{Var}\,[Y] + (E[Y])^2\,\mathrm{Var}\,[N]. \tag{6.4}$$

110

On the other hand, if in (6.1) the random variables Y_i are replaced by their
expectation, one would have the statistic

$$\tilde{V} = NE[Y].\tag{6.5}$$

The expectation of $\tilde{V}$, $E[N]\,E[Y]$, is the same as that of V. Its variance, however, is lower:

$$\text{Var}[\tilde{V}] = (E[Y])^2\,\text{Var}[N].\tag{6.6}$$

Eliminating the variability caused by the randomness of Y_i has, in this case,
led to a variance reduction amounting to $E[N]\,\text{Var}[Y]$.

6.3   Antithetic variates

An observation, X, obtained from a simulation run can be thought of as
a function of the random numbers generated during that run. In other words,
the simulation program can be said to transform a finite sequence of standard
uniform variates, $\mathbf{U} = (U_1, U_2, \ldots, U_K)$, into an observation X (we saw in
chapter 4 that the random numbers distributed uniformly between 0 and 1 are
the basis for all other random numbers that may be required). We shall empha-
sise this functional dependency by writing $X = X(\mathbf{U})$. Different observations are
obtained by using different random number sequences, thus $X_1 = X(\mathbf{U}_1)$,
$X_2 = X(\mathbf{U}_2)$, $\ldots$.

In many cases it is possible to reduce the variance of a sample mean by choosing appropriately the random number sequences employed. Assume that there is
an even number, $2n$, of observations in the sample: n of these observations, X_1,
$X_2, \ldots, X_n$, correspond to independent random number sequences $\mathbf{U}_1, \mathbf{U}_2, \ldots,$
$\mathbf{U}_n$; the other n observations, $X_1^*, X_2^*, \ldots, X_n^*$, also correspond to independent
sequences $\mathbf{U}_1^*, \mathbf{U}_2^*, \ldots, \mathbf{U}_n^*$, but $\mathbf{U}_1$ and $\mathbf{U}_1^*$ are dependent, as are $\mathbf{U}_2$ and $\mathbf{U}_2^*, \ldots,$
$\mathbf{U}_n$ and $\mathbf{U}_n^*$. Let $\bar{X}$ and $\bar{X}^*$ be the sample means of the Xs and the X^*s respec-
tively:

$$\bar{X} = \frac{1}{n}\sum_{i=1}^{n} X_i; \quad \bar{X}^* = \frac{1}{n}\sum_{i=1}^{n} X_i^*.$$

Then $\bar{Y} = (\bar{X} + \bar{X}^*)/2$ is an unbiased estimate for $E[X_i] = E[X_i^*]$. The variance
of $\bar{Y}$ is given by

$$\begin{aligned}
\text{Var}[\bar{Y}] &= \tfrac{1}{4}\{\text{Var}[\bar{X}] + \text{Var}[\bar{X}^*] + 2\,\text{Cov}[\bar{X}, \bar{X}^*]\} \\
&= \tfrac{1}{2}\{\text{Var}[\bar{X}] + \text{Cov}[\bar{X}, \bar{X}^*]\}.
\end{aligned}\tag{6.7}$$

Now, if there was no dependence between $\mathbf{U}_i$ and $\mathbf{U}_i^*$ ($i = 1, 2, \ldots, n$), the
covariance between $\bar{X}$ and $\bar{X}^*$ would be zero and the variance of $\bar{Y}$ would be
equal to $\text{Var}[\bar{X}]/2$. If the sequences $\mathbf{U}_i^*$ can be chosen in such a way that $\bar{X}$ and
$\bar{X}^*$ are negatively correlated then the variance of $\bar{Y}$ will be reduced. Variates
that achieve such negative correlation, and hence variance reduction, are called
'antithetic variates' (Page [35]).

111

When looking for antithetic variates, the general idea is to arrange things in such a way that, where a sequence **U** causes certain events to occur frequently, the corresponding sequence **U*** causes those events to occur rarely, and vice versa. Consider, for example, the simulation of a machine repair shop: if, under a random number sequence **U**, the machine operative periods are short and their repair times are long, the load on the repairmen will be high, most of them will be busy and there may be a queue of broken down machines. An antithetic sequence **U*** would be one that would lead to long operative periods and short repair times, and hence to few broken down machines and most repairmen idle. Then the observations corresponding to **U** and **U*** would be negatively correlated. Intuitively, the desired result is obtained if the random numbers from the sequence **U**, used to generate operative periods, are used under **U*** to generate repair times and vice versa. The program could use two random number seeds, one for the operative periods and one for the repair times. The values assigned to those seeds would be interchanged in the antithetic run.

In almost any system where customers arrive at service stations to be served, an antithetic random number sequence can be obtained by some sort of interchange of seeds corresponding to interarrival and service intervals. The effectiveness of the approach – i.e. the degree of negative correlation achieved – will of course depend on the system being simulated. One should bear in mind, however, that even if the variance of the estimate has not been reduced by much, very little has been lost since the cost of using antithetic variates is negligible.

Another possible way of transforming a sequence **U** into an antithetic sequence **U*** is to take $\mathbf{U}^* = 1 - \mathbf{U}$. This can be done with any system. One may reasonably hope that replacing the small random numbers in the sequence **U** with large ones in the sequence **U*** (and vice versa) will produce the desired negative correlation. Again, the effectiveness of the approach is difficult to assess but its cost is minimal. (It may be inadvisable to use this transformation in cases when linear congruential generators are later used to generate exponentially distributed variates; see section 4.2.)

An estimate for the right-hand side of (6.7) is given by

$$S^2 = (S_u^2 + S_{u,u*})/(2n),$$

where

$$S_u^2 = \frac{1}{n-1} \sum_{i=1}^{n} (X_i - \bar{X})^2$$

and

$$S_{u,u*} = \frac{1}{n-1} \sum_{i=1}^{n} (X_i - \bar{X})(X_i^* - \bar{X}^*).$$

Thus the half-width of the confidence interval centred on $\bar{Y}$, with level of

112

confidence $1 - \beta$, is approximately equal to

$$z(S_u^2 + S_{u,u*})^{1/2}/(2n)^{1/2},$$

where z is such that $P(t_{n-1} \leqslant z) = 1 - (\beta/2)$.

6.4   Control variables

There is a general idea underlying most variance reduction methods: it is to utilise any available information about the system being simulated in order to extract less variable observations from the simulation runs. Sometimes that information has a direct bearing on the observations returned (as when random variables are replaced by their expectations), sometimes it acts via appropriately modified simulation runs of the same system (as in the case of antithetic variates) and sometimes it involves simulating a different, but related system (e.g. comparison of alternatives). The method we are about to describe illustrates the use of additional information very clearly.

Assume that a sample of n independent and identically distributed observations, $X_1, X_2, \ldots, X_n$, has been obtained with the object of estimating the performance measure $\alpha = E[X_i]$. The straightforward estimate is, of course, the arithmetic mean, $\bar{X}$; the half-width of the confidence interval is proportional to $S/n^{1/2}$, where S^2 is the sample variance. Suppose, however, that in addition to the Xs, another sample of n independent and identically distributed observations, $Y_1, Y_2, \ldots, Y_n$, has somehow been made available, and that it has the following properties:

    (i)   there is a strong positive correlation between X_i and Y_i;
   (ii)   the expectation $\beta = E[Y_i]$ is known.

This additional information can then be used to construct an estimate with a lower variance. Consider, for instance,

$$V = \bar{X} + \beta - \bar{Y}, \tag{6.8}$$

where $\bar{Y}$ is the mean of the second sample. Clearly, V is an unbiased estimate for α: $E[V] = E[\bar{X}] + \beta - E[\bar{Y}] = \alpha + \beta - \beta = \alpha$. The variance of V is equal to

$$\mathrm{Var}[V] = \mathrm{Var}[\bar{X}] + \mathrm{Var}[\bar{Y}] - 2\,\mathrm{Cov}[\bar{X}, \bar{Y}] \tag{6.9}$$

and it will be lower than $\mathrm{Var}[\bar{X}]$ as long as $\mathrm{Cov}[\bar{X}, \bar{Y}] > \frac{1}{2}\mathrm{Var}[\bar{Y}]$.

The quantity that gives rise to the sample $Y_1, Y_2, \ldots, Y_n$ is referred to as the 'control variable'. In order that it may satisfy the two properties (i) and (ii) above, the control variable should be closely related to the performance measure of interest, and yet be sufficiently simple to enable a direct computation of its expectation.

One possibility is to use as a control variable a performance measure similar to the desired one but in a simplified model of the system. For example, suppose that one is simulating a single-server queueing system (such as a post office counter), where the interarrival intervals and the required service times have nonexponential distributions, and where some complicated scheduling strategy is operated. The object is to estimate the average sojourn time of customers in the system. The control variable could be the average sojourn time in a simpler system, with exponential interarrival and service times and First-Come-First-Served scheduling. In this last case, it is known (see appendix 2) that the expected sojourn time in equilibrium is equal to $\beta = 1/(\mu - \lambda)$, where $1/\lambda$ and $1/\mu$ are the expected interarrival and service time respectively. The X and Y samples are obtained from n simulation runs of the complex and the simple system respectively; moreover, the X_i run and the Y_i run ($i = 1, 2, \ldots, n$) use the same sequence of random numbers so that they are correlated (those sequences vary, of course, with i).

Although often very effective, control variables of the above type have two drawbacks: first, a certain acquaintance with queueing theory is required in order to make the weakest set of simplifying assumptions that will allow an analytical solution; second, any gain deriving from the variance reduction has to be balanced against the additional work expended in simulating the simple system. An alternative approach, which largely avoids these drawbacks, is to choose as a control variable an appropriate quantity from the system that is being studied. Such control variables are called 'concomitant'. In the above single-server queueing system example, a reasonable concomitant variable would be the total amount of time, Y, that the server was busy. It is intuitively obvious that the total customer sojourn time and the total server busy time are correlated. Also if the system is simulated until k customers have been served, then the expectation of Y is equal to k/μ, where $1/\mu$ is the average service time. Thus, n simulation runs would produce both the sample of observed average sojourn times $X_1, X_2, \ldots, X_n$ and the concomitant sample of observed server busy times $Y_1, Y_2, \ldots, Y_n$.

The right-hand side of (6.9) is estimated from the samples in the usual way:

$$S_{\tilde{v}}^2 = (S_x^2 + S_y^2 - 2S_{x,y})/n,$$

where

$$S_x^2 = \frac{1}{n-1} \sum_{i=1}^{n} (X_i - \bar{X})^2; \quad S_y^2 = \frac{1}{n-1} \sum_{i=1}^{n} (Y_i - \bar{Y})^2;$$

$$S_{x,y} = \frac{1}{n-1} \sum_{i=1}^{n} (X_i - \bar{X})(Y_i - \bar{Y}).$$

The half-width of the confidence interval centred on V, with level of confidence $1 - \beta$, is approximately equal to

$$z(S_x^2 + S_y^2 - 2S_{x,y})^{1/2}/n^{1/2}$$

where z is such that $P(t_{n-1} \leqslant z) = 1 - (\beta/2)$.

A greater reduction of the variance may be achieved by attaching a suitable weight to the control variable contribution. The estimate (6.8) is replaced by

$$\tilde{V} = \bar{X} + \xi(\beta - \bar{Y}), \tag{6.10}$$

and the value of ξ is chosen so as to minimise the variance of $\tilde{V}$. We have

$$\text{Var}[\tilde{V}] = \text{Var}[\bar{X}] + \xi^2 \text{Var}[\bar{Y}] - 2\xi\,\text{Cov}[\bar{X},\bar{Y}]. \qquad (6.11)$$

The right-hand side of (6.11), which is quadratic in ξ, is minimised for $\xi = \text{Cov}[\bar{X}, \bar{Y}]/\text{Var}[\bar{Y}]$. The corresponding value of the variance of $\tilde{V}$ is

$$\text{Var}[\tilde{V}] = \text{Var}[\bar{X}] - (\text{Cov}[\bar{X}, \bar{Y}])^2/\text{Var}[\bar{Y}]$$
$$= \text{Var}[\bar{X}](1 - r_{\bar{x},\bar{y}}^2),$$

where $r_{\bar{x},\bar{y}}$ is the correlation coefficient between $\bar{X}$ and $\bar{Y}$ (see appendix 2). Note that the variance of $\tilde{V}$ is never greater than that of $\bar{X}$; the higher the correlation between the two samples, the greater the variance reduction. In practice, of course, the optimal value of ξ can only be estimated from the sample.

In conclusion we should perhaps point out that while the control variable method is usually more difficult to implement than the other variance reduction techniques discussed in this chapter, it also tends to be more effective. There are cases reported in the literature (e.g. Gaver & Shedler [16]), where this method has achieved variance reduction by up to a factor of 12.

Exercises

1. The customers arriving (in a Poisson stream) into a service station are discouraged by long queues: a new arrival who finds n customers in front of him joins the queue with probability $1/(n + 1)$. The performance measure of interest is the average number of customers who depart without joining the queue, per unit time. Having simulated the system, the obvious way to obtain an observation for that performance measure is to count the customers who do not join and divide by the simulation time. Devise a method for obtaining an observation with lower variance. (Hint: replace certain random variables by their expectations.)

2. Indicate a good way of generating an antithetic random number sequence for the system in exercise 5.3 (a fixed number of jobs circulating among two service stations).

3. Discuss the possibilities for applying the control variable (or variables) method, in each of the systems described in chapter 3. What program changes and/or additions will be required?

7. DESIGN AND ANALYSIS OF SIMULATION EXPERIMENTS

So far, we have directed our attention towards various aspects of the simulation of a *given* system. That is, the object has been to estimate, through simulation, the performance of a system for a given setting of its parameters. The next stage of an investigation is frequently concerned with questions of possible trends and causal relationships among variables. One asks, for example, 'Is the average passage time through a network affected by the scheduling strategies at certain nodes?', or 'How does that passage time depend on the speed of certain processors?' To answer questions of this type, it is necessary to obtain samples of observations corresponding to different parameter settings, and draw statistical inferences from them. The general problems in this area have to do with the collection and analysis of data derived from (possibly) different populations. We shall describe two techniques, 'analysis of variance' and 'linear regression', which were originally developed in connection with laboratory and agricultural experiments, but which apply equally well to simulations.

7.1 Analysis of variance

Consider a system whose performance may, conceivably, be influenced by a number of 'factors' (such as scheduling strategies, number and speed of processors, pricing and investment policies, etc.). There is a choice of settings, or 'levels' for each factor; a particular combination of settings is usually referred to as a 'treatment'. The problem is to decide whether the effect of these factors, acting either independently or jointly, is significant.

Each treatment gives rise to a sample of observations (in the case of a simulation experiment, these are obtained either by making a number of independent runs, or by partitioning one long run – see chapter 5). It is assumed that these observations are distributed normally (we saw in chapter 5 that this is usually the case, at least approximately) and that their variance is the same for all treatments (this, too, is not unreasonable). Only the means can therefore be influenced by the different treatments, which reduces the problem to one of testing for equality of the means of several normal populations.

Let us examine first the case of a single factor which can be set at k possible levels. These may or may not be quantitative (e.g. k possible values of a numeric parameter, or k different scheduling strategies, etc.). A sample of n observations is obtained for each of the k treatments (it is not essential that these samples be of equal size but we shall assume that they are for simplicity; see figure 7.1).

We wish to test the null hypothesis, H_0, that the given factor has no effect on performance, i.e. that all observations come from the same normal population with mean μ and variance σ^2 (both unknown).

Under the null hypothesis, the random variables $(X_{ij} - \mu)/\sigma$ have the standard normal distribution, $N(0, 1)$ and therefore the sum of squares

$$SS = \sum_{i=1}^{k} \sum_{j=1}^{n} [(X_{ij} - \mu)^2/\sigma^2] \tag{7.1}$$

has the χ^2 distribution with kn degrees of freedom (see appendix 2). Introducing the overall sample mean

$$\bar{X} = \frac{1}{k} \sum_{i=1}^{k} \bar{X}_i, \tag{7.2}$$

the sum of squares (7.1) can be broken up into three components:

$$SS = \sum_{i=1}^{k} \sum_{j=1}^{n} [(X_{ij} - \bar{X}_i)^2/\sigma^2] + n \sum_{i=1}^{k} [(\bar{X}_i - \bar{X})^2/\sigma^2] + kn(\bar{X} - \mu)^2/\sigma^2$$
$$= SS2 + SS1 + SS0. \tag{7.3}$$

The validity of (7.3) is established by adding and subtracting $\bar{X}$ inside the parentheses in the right-hand side of (7.1), expanding the square terms, then adding and subtracting $\bar{X}_i$ and expanding the square terms again. Various cross-products vanish because of the identities

$$\sum_{j=1}^{n} (X_{ij} - \bar{X}_i) = 0, \quad i = 1, 2, \ldots, k. \tag{7.4}$$

Figure 7.1

Treatment	Sample	Sample mean
1	$X_{11}, X_{12}, \ldots, X_{1n}$	$\bar{X}_1$
2	$X_{21}, X_{22}, \ldots, X_{2n}$	$\bar{X}_2$
$\vdots$	$\vdots$	$\vdots$
k	$X_{k1}, X_{k2}, \ldots, X_{kn}$	$\bar{X}_k$

With each sum of squares of linear combinations of standard normal random variables is associated an integer called the 'degrees of freedom'. This is equal to the number of terms in the sum minus the number of linear relations among those terms. The degrees of freedom of $SS2, SS1$ and $SS0$ on the right-hand side of (7.3) are $k(n-1), k-1$ and 1 respectively, due to (7.4) and (7.2). Those degrees of freedom sum up to kn, which is exactly the degrees of freedom of the left-hand side, SS. Under these conditions, one can invoke a result known as 'Cochran's decomposition theorem' (e.g. see Lindgren [34]), which can be stated as follows:

Let $Z_1, Z_2, \ldots, Z_m$ be independent standard normal random variables (mean 0 and variance 1). Suppose that

$$\sum_{i=1}^{m} Z_i^2 = Q_1 + Q_2 + \ldots + Q_r,$$

where Q_j is a sum of squares of linear combinations of the Z_is, with d_j degrees of freedom $(j = 1, 2, \ldots, r)$. If these degrees of freedom satisfy

$$d_1 + d_2 + \ldots + d_r = m$$

then the random variables $Q_1, Q_2, \ldots, Q_r$ are independent and have the χ^2 distribution with $d_1, d_2, \ldots, d_r$ degrees of freedom respectively.

This result implies, in our case, that $SS2, SS1$ and $SS0$ are independent random variables having the χ^2 distribution with $k(n-1), k-1$ and 1 degrees of freedom respectively. (This is not an obvious assertion; at first glance those random variables would appear to be dependent.)

Hence, the ratio

$$F_{k-1,k(n-1)} = [SS1/(k-1)]/[SS2/k(n-1)]$$

$$= \frac{kn(n-1)}{k-1}\left[\sum_{i=1}^{k}(\bar{X}_i - \bar{X})^2\right]\bigg/\left[\sum_{i=1}^{k}\sum_{j=1}^{n}(X_{ij} - \bar{X}_i)^2\right], \quad (7.5)$$

has the F distribution with parameters $k-1$ and $k(n-1)$ (see appendix 2). To test the null hypothesis, at a confidence level $1-\beta$, one finds from a table of the F distribution (see Tables), a number α such that

$$P(F_{k-1,k(n-1)} \leqslant \alpha) = 1-\beta.$$

The right-hand side of (7.5) is then evaluated and if its value is greater than α, the hypothesis is rejected.

The sum of squares $SS2$ is a measure of the deviations of the observations from their means 'within the samples', whereas $SS1$ is a measure of the deviations from the mean 'between the samples'. Intuitively, a large value of $SS1$ with respect to $SS2$ is indicative of a wide spread between the samples, which in turn makes it plausible that the underlying means are different and should lead to the rejection of the null hypothesis.

118

The above model can be presented in the following way:

$$X_{ij} = \mu + a_i + Z_{ij}, \quad i = 1, 2, \ldots, k, \quad j = 1, 2, \ldots, n, \qquad (7.6)$$

where μ is the overall mean, a_i is the contribution of the ith treatment (these contributions are assumed to sum to zero) and Z_{ij} is a normally distributed random variable with mean 0 and variance σ^2. The null hypothesis is

$$H_0: a_1 = a_2 = \ldots = a_k = 0.$$

A similar approach can be applied to more general situations. Suppose that one wishes to study the effects of two factors, A and B, which can be set at p and q levels respectively. There are therefore pq possible treatments; a sample of n observations is obtained for each treatment. Denoting these observations by X_{ijs} (i is the level of factor A, j is the level of factor B and s is the index within the corresponding sample), we assume a model along the lines of (7.6):

$$X_{ijs} = \mu + a_i + b_j + ab_{ij} + Z_{ijs}, \quad i = 1, 2, \ldots, p, \quad j = 1, 2, \ldots, q,$$
$$s = 1, 2, \ldots, n \qquad (7.7)$$

Here, μ is the overall mean, a_i is the contribution of factor A at level i, b_j is the contribution of factor B at level j, ab_{ij} is the contribution of the interaction of the two factors at levels i and j respectively, and Z_{ijs} is a normally distributed random variable with mean 0 and variance σ^2 (both the individual and the interaction contributions are assumed to sum to 0).

One could test three null hypotheses, any of which may be accepted or rejected regardless of the action taken on the other two:

$A_0:$ $a_1 = a_2 = \ldots = a_p = 0$ (factor A has no effect on its own);

$B_0:$ $b_1 = b_2 = \ldots = b_q = 0$ (factor B has no effect on its own);

$AB_0:$ $ab_{11} = ab_{12} = \ldots = ab_{pq} = 0$ (the interaction of factors A and B has no effect).

The following notation will be needed:

$\mu_{ij} = \mu + a_i + b_j + ab_{ij}$ is the population mean corresponding to treatment (i, j);

$$\bar{X} = \left[\sum_{i=1}^{p} \sum_{j=1}^{q} \sum_{s=1}^{n} X_{ijs} \right] \Big/ pqn \quad \text{is the overall sample mean;}$$

$$\bar{X}_{i..} = \left[\sum_{j=1}^{q} \sum_{s=1}^{n} X_{ijs} \right] \Big/ qn \quad \text{is the factor } A \text{ (level } i\text{) sample mean;}$$

$$\bar{X}_{.j.} = \left[\sum_{i=1}^{p} \sum_{s=1}^{n} X_{ijs} \right] \Big/ pn \quad \text{is the factor } B \text{ (level } j\text{) sample mean;}$$

$$\bar{X}_{ij.} = \left[\sum_{s=1}^{n} X_{ijs} \right] \Big/ n \quad \text{is the treatment } (i, j) \text{ sample mean.}$$

The tests are based on the following partitioning of the sum of squares of deviations from the overall population mean:

$$SS = \sum_{i=1}^{p} \sum_{j=1}^{q} \sum_{s=1}^{n} (X_{ijs} - \mu_{ij})^2$$

$$= \sum_{i=1}^{p} \sum_{j=1}^{q} \sum_{s=1}^{n} (X_{ijs} - \bar{X}_{ij.})^2$$

$$+ n \sum_{i=1}^{p} \sum_{j=1}^{q} (\bar{X}_{ij.} - \bar{X}_{i..} - \bar{X}_{.j.} + \bar{X} - ab_{ij})^2$$

$$+ qn \sum_{i=1}^{p} (\bar{X}_{i..} - \bar{X} - a_i)^2$$

$$+ pn \sum_{j=1}^{q} (\bar{X}_{.j.} - \bar{X} - b_j)^2$$

$$+ pqn(\bar{X} - \mu)^2$$

$$= SS3 + SS2 + SS1_1 + SS1_2 + SS0 \qquad (7.8)$$

(the notations for the terms on the right-hand side are self-evident). The sum of squares on the left-hand side of (7.8) has pqn degrees of freedom. Those on the right-hand side have, respectively, $pq(n-1), pq - p - q + 1, p - 1, q - 1$ and 1 degree of freedom. Hence (again according to Cochran's decomposition theorem), the random variables $SS3/\sigma^2, SS2/\sigma^2, SS1_1/\sigma^2$ and $SS1_2/\sigma^2$ are independent and have the χ^2 distribution with $pq(n-1), (p-1)(q-1), p-1$ and $q - 1$ degrees of freedom, respectively.

It follows, therefore, that under the null hypothesis A_0, the ratio

$$F^A_{p-1, pq(n-1)} = [SS1_1/(p-1)]/[SS3/pq(n-1)]$$

$$= \frac{pq^2 n(n-1)}{p-1} \left[\sum_{i=1}^{p} (X_{i..} - \bar{X})^2 \right]$$

$$\left[\left[\sum_{i=1}^{p} \sum_{j=1}^{q} \sum_{s=1}^{n} (X_{ijs} - \bar{X}_{ij.})^2 \right] \right. \qquad (7.9)$$

has the F distribution with parameters $p - 1$ and $pq(n-1)$. This statistic can thus be used to test A_0: the hypothesis is rejected, at confidence level $1 - \beta$, if the evaluated right-hand side of (7.9) exceeds the $(1 - \beta)$-percentile of the appropriate F distribution.

120

Similarly, under the null hypothesis B_0, the ratio

$$F^B_{q-1,pq(n-1)} = [SS1_2/(q-1)]/[SS3/pq(n-1)]$$

$$= \frac{p^2 qn(n-1)}{q-1} \left[\sum_{j=1}^{q} (\bar{X}_{.j.} - \bar{X})^2 \right]$$

$$\bigg/ \left[\sum_{i=1}^{p} \sum_{j=1}^{q} \sum_{s=1}^{n} (X_{ijs} - \bar{X}_{ij.})^2 \right] \tag{7.10}$$

has the F distribution with parameters $q-1$ and $pq(n-1)$. The null hypothesis B_0 is rejected, at confidence level $1-\beta$, if the evaluated right-hand side of (7.10) exceeds the $(1-\beta)$-percentile of that F distribution.

Finally, under the null hypothesis AB_0, the ratio

$$F^{AB}_{(p-1)(q-1),pq(n-1)} = [SS2/(p-1)(q-1)]/[SS3/pq(n-1)]$$

$$= \frac{pqn(n-1)}{(p-1)(q-1)} \left[\sum_{i=1}^{p} \sum_{j=1}^{q} (\bar{X}_{ij.} - \bar{X}_{i..} - \bar{X}_{.j.} + \bar{X})^2 \right]$$

$$\bigg/ \left[\sum_{i=1}^{p} \sum_{j=1}^{q} \sum_{s=1}^{n} (X_{ijs} - \bar{X}_{ij.})^2 \right] \tag{7.11}$$

has the F distribution with parameters $(p-1)(q-1)$ and $pq(n-1)$. This statistic can be used to test the null hypothesis AB_0.

Note that in each of the three tests, the denominator contains the sum of squares measuring deviations within treatments, whereas the numerator contains the sum of squares of deviations between treatments (corresponding to the effect being tested). Large deviations between treatments, relative to those within treatments, lead to the rejection of the corresponding null hypothesis.

It is, of course, possible to study simultaneous effects of more than two factors by the above methods. For example, with three factors there would be three individual effects, three two-way interaction effects and one three-way interaction effect. However, such procedures are rarely carried out in practice, both because of the large amounts of data required and because the significance of multiple interactions is quickly lost. Instead, it is usually possible to design the experiments so as to reduce the number of observations required, at the expense of the higher-order interaction effects. For three and four factors, these designs are sometimes referred to as 'Latin squares' and 'Greco-Latin squares' respectively (e.g. see Cochran & Cox [5]).

7.2   Linear regression

If one only wishes to know whether a factor does or does not influence system performance, then the answer can be obtained by analysis of variance methods. Often, however, the nature of the dependency is of interest. Some sort of functional relationship between the factor level and the resulting performance is desirable, so that one can predict what the performance will be at levels that have not been tried. In this context, instead of talking about a factor, we use the term 'controlled variable'. For example, in a model of a car factory, the controlled variable might be the length of the morning tea-break; the object of an investigation could be to establish a relationship between that variable and the average number of cars produced per day.

Suppose that a set of pairs $(x_1, Y_1), (x_2, Y_2), \ldots, (x_n, Y_n)$ is given, where x_i is the ith value of the controlled variable and Y_i is the corresponding value of the performance measure $(i = 1, 2, \ldots, n)$. These observations are typically obtained from independent simulation runs. It is assumed that x_i and Y_i are related:

$$Y_i = g(x_i) + Z_i, \quad i = 1, 2, \ldots, n, \tag{7.12}$$

where $g(x)$ is a (deterministic) function and the Z_is are independent normally distributed random variables with mean 0 and variance σ^2 (unknown). The primary task is to estimate the function $g(x)$, referred to as the 'regression function'. To make that task possible, a certain parameterised form of the regression function is assumed, and then the parameters are estimated from the available data. For example, $g(x)$ may be taken to be a polynomial of degree m:

$$g(x) = a_0 x^m + a_1 x^{m-1} + \ldots + a_m. \tag{7.13}$$

The problem would then be to estimate the $m + 1$ parameters $a_0, a_1, \ldots, a_m$.

The regression function (7.13) has the advantage of being linear in the unknown parameters. The simplest and most commonly used special case of a polynomial regression function is the linear one of the form

$$g(x) = ax + b. \tag{7.14}$$

We shall concentrate on the analysis of this, 'linear regression', model.

Let us introduce, alongside the observed performance measures Y_i, their expected values μ_i:

$$\mu_i = E[Y_i] = ax_i + b, \quad i = 1, 2, \ldots, n. \tag{7.15}$$

Also, let $\hat{Y}_i$ be the 'regression-derived' performance measures. These are given by the estimated regression line; if $\hat{\alpha}$ and $\hat{\beta}$ are the estimates for the unknown parameters a and b, then

$$\hat{Y}_i = \hat{\alpha} x_i + \hat{\beta}, \quad i = 1, 2, \ldots, n. \tag{7.16}$$

The estimated regression line is chosen so as to minimise the sum of squares of deviations between observed and regression-derived performance measures. In other words, $\hat{\alpha}$ and $\hat{\beta}$ are chosen so as to minimise

$$S(\alpha, \beta) = \sum_{i=1}^{n} (Y_i - \alpha x_i - \beta)^2. \tag{7.17}$$

These 'least squares' estimates are therefore obtained by solving the two simultaneous equations

$$\frac{\partial S(\alpha, \beta)}{\partial \alpha} = 0 = -2 \sum_{i=1}^{n} x_i (Y_i - \alpha x_i - \beta),$$

$$\frac{\partial S(\alpha, \beta)}{\partial \beta} = 0 = -2 \sum_{i=1}^{n} (Y_i - \alpha x_i - \beta). \tag{7.18}$$

These equations yield, after some algebra,

$$\hat{\alpha} = \left[\sum_{i=1}^{n} Y_i (x_i - \bar{x}) \right] \bigg/ \left[\sum_{i=1}^{n} (x_i - \bar{x})^2 \right], \tag{7.19}$$

and

$$\hat{\beta} = \bar{Y} - \hat{\alpha} \bar{x}, \tag{7.20}$$

where

$$\bar{x} = \frac{1}{n} \sum_{i=1}^{n} x_i, \qquad \bar{Y} = \frac{1}{n} \sum_{i=1}^{n} Y_i.$$

Having derived point estimates for the unknown parameters, it is possible, in principle, to use the resulting regression line for prediction purposes. However, such an approach would be unsatisfactory unless it is supported by some additional statistical information. One should have confidence intervals for the parameters as well as point estimates. The hypothesis that the regression line is horizontal, i.e. that the performance measure is independent of the controlled variable, should be tested. If the estimated regression line is used for prediction, then confidence intervals, as well as point estimates for the performance measure should be derived. The initial assumption – that the regression function is linear – may also be questioned.

These problems can be tackled by analysis of variance methods. Consider the following decomposition of the total sum of squares of deviations of observations from their means:

$$SS = \sum_{i=1}^{n} (Y_i - \mu_i)^2 = \sum_{i=1}^{n} (Y_i - ax_i - b)^2$$

$$= \sum_{i=1}^{n} (Y_i - \hat{\alpha} x_i - \hat{\beta})^2 + (\hat{\alpha} - a)^2 \sum_{i=1}^{n} (x_i - \bar{x})^2 + n(\bar{Y} - \mu)^2$$

$$= S1 + (\hat{\alpha} - a)^2 S_x + n(\bar{Y} - \mu)^2, \tag{7.21}$$

where $S1$ is the sum of squares of deviations of the observed from the regression-derived values, S_x is the sum of squares of controlled variable deviations from their mean (it should be remembered that the controlled variable is not a random variable) and $\mu = a\bar{x} + b$ is the overall population mean.

Now, the random variables $Y_i - \mu_i$ are independent and normally distributed with mean 0 and variance σ^2. Hence, the left-hand side of (7.21), divided by σ^2, has the χ^2 distribution with n degrees of freedom. The degrees of freedom of the terms on the right-hand side sum up to n: $n - 2$ for $S1$ (because of the two linear equations for $\hat{\alpha}$ and $\hat{\beta}$), 1 for $(\hat{\alpha} - a)^2$ and 1 for $(\bar{Y} - \mu)^2$. It follows from Cochran's theorem (see section 7.1), that $S1/\sigma^2$, $(\hat{\alpha} - a)^2/(\sigma^2/S_x)$ and $(\bar{Y} - \mu)^2/(\sigma^2/n)$ are independent random variables having the χ^2 distribution with $n - 2$, 1 and 1 degree of freedom respectively.

As a consequence of the above results, the ratio

$$F^a_{1,n-2} = (\hat{\alpha} - a)^2 S_x/[S1/(n-2)] \tag{7.22}$$

has the F distribution with parameters 1 and $n - 2$. This fact can be used both to derive a confidence interval for a and to test the null hypothesis, A_0, that the regression line is horizontal (i.e. that $a = 0$). For a given confidence level, $1 - \delta$, we find from the tables of the F distribution a number γ such that

$$P(F_{1,n-2} \leqslant \gamma) = 1 - \delta$$

Then, from (7.22), we have

$$P[(\hat{\alpha} - a)^2(n - 2) S_x/S1 \leqslant \gamma] = 1 - \delta$$

which yields the following confidence interval for a:

$$P(\hat{\alpha} - \{\gamma S1/[(n - 2) S_x]\}^{1/2} \leqslant a < \hat{\alpha} + \{\gamma S1/[(n - 2) S_x]\}^{1/2}) = 1 - \delta. \tag{7.23}$$

Under the null hypothesis, A_0, the statistic $\hat{\alpha}^2(n - 2) S_x/S1$ has the F distribution with parameters 1 and $n - 2$. Therefore, the hypothesis should be rejected, at confidence level $1 - \delta$, if

$$\hat{\alpha}^2 > \gamma S1/[(n - 2) S_x].$$

In view of (7.23), this is equivalent to saying that the hypothesis $a = 0$ should be rejected if the confidence interval for a does not include the point 0.

Another ratio which has the same F distribution is

$$F^\mu_{1,n-2} = (\bar{Y} - \mu)^2 n/[S1/(n - 2)]. \tag{7.24}$$

It can be used to derive a confidence interval for $\mu = a\bar{x} + b$ and (should the question be raised) to test the null hypothesis $a\bar{x} + b = 0$.

Consider the problem of predicting the value Y of the performance measure corresponding to some new value, x, of the controlled variable. The best one can do with the available information is to take as point estimate the regression-derived value

$$\hat{Y} = \hat{\alpha}x + \hat{\beta}.$$

How good is such a prediction? The difference between $\hat{Y}$ and Y can be expressed as

$$d = \hat{Y} - Y = \hat{\alpha}x + \hat{\beta} - ax - b - Z$$
$$= \hat{\alpha}(x - \bar{x}) + \bar{Y} - ax - b - Z, \tag{7.25}$$

where Z is a normally distributed random variable with mean 0 and variance σ^2. From (7.19) and (7.20) it follows that the random variable d is also normally distributed, with mean 0 and variance given by

$$\text{Var}[d] = (x - \bar{x})^2 \, \text{Var}[\hat{\alpha}] + \text{Var}[\bar{Y}] + \text{Var}[Z]$$
$$= (x - \bar{x})^2 (\sigma^2/S_x) + (\sigma^2/n) + \sigma^2.$$

Unfortunately, σ^2 is unknown. We have already seen, however, that the statistic

$$S1/\sigma^2 = \left[\sum_{i=1}^{n} (Y_i - \hat{\alpha}x_i - \hat{\beta})^2 \right] / \sigma^2$$

has the χ^2 distribution with $n - 2$ degrees of freedom. Moreover, $S1/\sigma^2$ and $d^2/\text{Var}[d]$ are independent. Therefore, the ratio

$$(d^2/\text{Var}[d])/\{S1/[\sigma^2(n-2)]\}$$
$$= d^2/(S1\{[(x - \bar{x})^2/S_x] + (1/n) + 1\}/(n - 2)),$$

has the F distribution with parameters 1 and $n - 2$. This leads to a confidence interval for Y:

$$P(\hat{Y} - (\gamma Q)^{1/2} \leqslant Y < \hat{Y} + (\gamma Q)^{1/2}) = 1 - \delta, \qquad (7.26)$$

where γ and δ have the same meaning as in (7.23), and

$$Q = S1\{[(x - \bar{x})^2/S_x] + (1/n) + 1\}/(n - 2).$$

Note that the width of the confidence interval increases with the distance of x from $\bar{x}$: the further the prediction point from the centre of the explored region, the less accurate is the prediction. This situation is illustrated in figure 7.2.

In the analysis so far, there has been no assumption that the values x_i of the controlled variable are distinct. It is perfectly possible to take several (independent) observations at each distinct value of the controlled variable. Indeed, if one wishes to test for the linearity of the regression function, it is necessary

Figure 7.2. Confidence intervals for predictions.

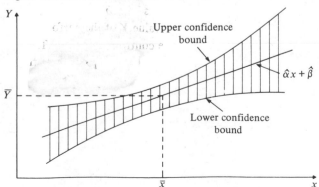

to do so. Assume that there are k distinct x-values, $x_1, x_2, \ldots, x_k$, and that there are m observations, $Y_{i1}, Y_{i2}, \ldots, Y_{im}$ taken at point x_i ($i = 1, 2, \ldots, k$). The total number of observations is $n = km$. Let $\bar{Y}_i = (Y_{i1} + Y_{i2} + \ldots + Y_{im})/m$ be the sample mean corresponding to x_i. The overall sample mean is $Y = (\bar{Y}_1 + \bar{Y}_2 + \ldots + \bar{Y}_k)/k$ and the mean x-value is $\bar{x} = (x_1 + x_2 + \ldots + x_k)/k$.

The estimates (7.19) and (7.20) for the regression line parameters become

$$\hat{\alpha} = \left[\sum_{i=1}^{k} \bar{Y}_i(x_i - \bar{x}) \right] \bigg/ \left[\sum_{i=1}^{k} (x_i - \bar{x})^2 \right]; \quad \hat{\beta} = \bar{Y} - \hat{\alpha}\bar{x}. \tag{7.27}$$

The sum, $S1$, of the squares of deviations from the estimated regression line can now be decomposed further:

$$S1 = \sum_{i=1}^{k} \sum_{j=1}^{m} (Y_{ij} - \hat{\alpha}x_i - \hat{\beta})^2$$

$$= \sum_{i=1}^{k} \sum_{j=1}^{m} (Y_{ij} - \bar{Y}_i)^2 + m \sum_{i=1}^{k} (\bar{Y}_i - \hat{\alpha}x_i - \hat{\beta})^2$$

$$= S12 + S11. \tag{7.28}$$

We have seen already that $S1/\sigma^2$ has the χ^2 distribution with $n - 2$ degrees of freedom. In the right-hand side of (7.28), the sum of squares $S12$ has $n - k$ degrees of freedom (because the sum over j of $Y_{ij} - \bar{Y}_i$ is zero for each $i = 1, 2, \ldots, k$), and $S11$ has $k - 2$ degrees of freedom (because of the relations (7.27)). Hence, by Cochran's theorem, $S12/\sigma^2$ and $S11/\sigma^2$ are independent random variables having the χ^2 distribution with $n - k$ and $k - 2$ degrees of freedom respectively.

Thus, under the null hypothesis of a linear regression function, the ratio

$$F_{k-2, n-k} = [S11/(k - 2)]/[S12/(n - k)] \tag{7.29}$$

has the F distribution with parameters $k - 2$ and $n - k$. That statistic can therefore be used to test for linearity: for a given level of confidence, $1 - \beta$, the null hypothesis is rejected if the evaluated right-hand side of (7.29) exceeds the $(1 - \beta)$-percentile of the F distribution.

The linear regression model can be generalised by including more than one controlled variable. The resulting analysis is usually referred to as 'multiple regression'. Several procedures have been devised for deciding which, out of a number of controlled variables, have a significant effect on the performance measure.

Exercises

1. Prove the identity (7.3) in section 7.1.

2. In the analysis of a variance model with two factors described by equation (7.7), devise a test for the null hypothesis

$H_0: a_i = b_j = ab_{ij} = 0$ (all i, j).

(Hint: consider the sum $SS2 + SS1_1 + SS1_2$.)

3. Show that the least-square estimates $\hat{\alpha}$ and $\hat{\beta}$ of the linear regression parameters are unbiased, i.e.

$E[\hat{\alpha}] = a; \quad E[\hat{\beta}] = b.$

Are these estimates consistent?

4. Prove the partitioning (7.21).

5. Suppose that, when collecting observations for a linear regression analysis, one can choose the n values of the controlled variable arbitrarily in the range $x_{min} \leqslant x \leqslant x_{max}$. How should those values be chosen so as to maximise the predictive accuracy of the estimated regression line? (Hint: the width of the confidence interval (7.26) decreases when the sum of squares S_x increases.)

APPENDIX 1.   A SIMULA PRIMER

For our purposes, the structure of SIMULA (or SIMULA 67), can be loosely described by the following pyramid:

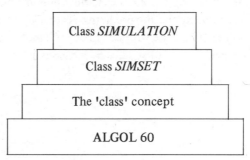

At the base of the pyramid is the (very slightly modified) general purpose programming language **ALGOL 60**. A major addition to that is the notion of 'class', which allows one to define composite objects containing both data and actions. Two system-defined classes follow: *SIMSET* and *SIMULATION*. The first provides facilities for manipulating linked lists and the second a clock routine, an event list and parallel processes. In the interests of keeping this appendix reasonably short, we shall assume that the reader is familiar with a language of the **ALGOL** family (e.g. ALGOL 60, ALGOL W, ALGOL 68, PASCAL). Standard programming constructs will be taken largely for granted and attention will be directed mainly towards the higher levels of the pyramid. A formal definition of SIMULA may be found in Dahl, Myhrhaug & Nygaard [8]; the book by Birtwistle, Dahl, Myhrhaug & Nygaard [3] is an excellent self-contained text with many examples.

1.   **General features. Input/Output**
        A SIMULA program is a block of the type

    begin 'declarations';
            'statements';
    end;

That block may optionally be prefixed by either *SIMSET* or *SIMULATION*. The

128

declarations define the objects (reals, integers, booleans, characters, texts, arrays, procedures, classes) that the statements operate upon. A statement may itself be a block, with declarations and other statements. Both declarations and statements are separated by semicolons (blanks may be inserted for ease of reading; they are ignored by the compiler).

To name an object one uses an identifier: an arbitrary sequence of letters and/or digits beginning with a letter (no blanks or other special symbols). The following are some valid declarations:

> **integer** $I, K11$;
> **real** $ALPHA, B2, LENGTH$;
> **boolean** $OCCUPIED, FULL, LEFT$;
> **real array** $A(0:N), BOARD(1:8, 1:K+1)$;

One difference between ALGOL 60 and SIMULA is that in the latter all variables are initialised at declaration time: thus, in the above examples, I and $K11$ will be set to zero (integer), $ALPHA$, $B2$ and $LENGTH$ to zero (real), $OCCUPIED$, $FULL$ and $LEFT$ to **false** and the arrays A and $BOARD$ will be filled with real zeros.

Arithmetic expressions are formed using the operations $+, -, *$ (multiplication), $/$ (division), $//$ (integer division), $**$ (exponentiation), as well as user- or system-defined procedures (such as $SQRT$, SIN, ABS, etc.). For boolean expressions, the standard comparators and conjunctives are available: $<, >, =, <=$ (less than or equal), $>=$ (greater than or equal), $\neg =$ (not equal), **and, or, imp** (implies), $\neg$ (not); the comparison of references will be discussed later.

The value of an expression can be assigned to a variable by means of the assignment statement:

> 'variable':='expression';

Certain rules of compatibility have to be borne in mind. Thus, if X is declared to be an integer, Y a real and Z a boolean variable, the assignments $X:=Z$, $Y:=Z$, $Z:=X$ and $Z:=Y$ are illegal. It is possible to write $Y:=X$ and $X:=Y$, but in the latter case the value of Y is rounded off (so that it becomes integer) before assigning it to X.

Conditional operations and iterations are done by means of **if, while** and **for** statements. The general format of these statements is

> **if** b **then** s;
> **if** b **then** $s1$ **else** s;
> **while** b **do** s;
> **for** $v:=e1$ **step** $e2$ **until** $e3$ **do** s;

where b is a boolean expression (having value **true** or **false**), s is any statement, $s1$ is any statement except **if, while, for** or **inspect** (to be described later), v is a simple variable (usually integer) and $e1$, $e2$ and $e3$ are arithmetic expressions.

Arithmetic and boolean expressions may also involve conditional clauses, as in the following assignments:

$E1$:=**if** $X<0$ **then** -1 **else** 1;
$E2$:=**if** $X=Y$ **then** **true** **else** **false**;

Procedures are declared as follows:

'type' **procedure** 'identifier' ('formal parameters'); 'specifications';
'procedure body';

If 'type' is omitted, then the procedure behaves like a normal statement: when the name is called (supplying actual parameters in place of the formal ones), the body is executed. If 'type' is specified (e.g. **real**, **integer**, **boolean** or a reference to a class), then at the time of call not only is the body executed but the procedure identifier is given a value which may be used directly in expressions. That value is the last assigned to the procedure identifier in the procedure body, or if no assignment is made, it is the default value associated with the procedure type (e.g. zero for **real**, etc.). The procedure is then said to be a function.

The formal parameters are listed in parentheses, separated by commas. Parameters may be passed by value (the actual parameter is evaluated and a copy of it is made available to the procedure body), by reference (a pointer to the actual parameter is passed to the procedure body) or by name (the actual parameter is textually substituted for the formal one throughout the procedure body). The default modes are: by value for value-type parameters (e.g. **real**, **integer**, **boolean**) and by reference for text and class objects, arrays and procedures. Value-type parameters cannot be passed by reference and class references, reference arrays and procedures cannot be passed by value; any parameter can be passed by name. Parameter passings other than by the default mode are stated immediately after the formal parameter list (thus, **value** followed by a list of parameters and/or **name** followed by a list of parameters). Thereafter, the types of all formal parameters must be stated, although not necessarily in the order in which they appear in this list.

This part of the procedure declaration, i.e. the part preceding the body, is called a 'header'. The following are some examples of procedure headers:

procedure $P1$;
real procedure $P2(X)$; **real** X;
integer procedure $P3(X,Y)$; **name** X; **integer** X,Y;
procedure $P4(A,N)$; **integer** N; **real array** A;
procedure $P5(Q,S)$; **real procedure** Q; **ref**$(SERVER)S$;

Two of the above procedures, $P2$ and $P3$, are functions; their bodies would normally contain assignments of the form $P2$:='real value', $P3$:='integer value' respectively. The parameter S of procedure $P5$ is a reference to an object of a certain class called $SERVER$ (classes will be introduced in the next section).

The procedure body is a statement, normally a block. It may contain a call on the procedure being defined, in which case the definition is said to be recursive.

Some of the commonly used system-defined procedures are listed at the end of this appendix. Here we shall mention a set of procedures providing simple input and output facilities. These are part of a more general file and text manipulation package.

The procedures *ININT* and *INREAL* read from the input stream the next integer and the next real number respectively. Both are functions: their value is the number read. Thus, if *N* and *X* have been declared as **integer** and **real** respectively, they can be assigned values from the input:

> *N:=ININT*;
> *X:=INREAL*;

The input file, be it on a deck of cards, on a keyboard terminal or on a secondary storage device, should contain integers and reals in the order in which they are read, separated by arbitrary numbers of blanks. Reals are typed in a decimal point format, with or without a sign, e.g. $0.5, -31.73, 25.0$.

The boolean procedure *LASTITEM* searches for the next item in the input stream and returns the value **false** if it finds one otherwise it returns the value **true**. If the number of items to be read is not known, that procedure can be used to detect the end of the input stream. For instance, to read an unspecified number of integers and accumulate their total in the variable *SUM*, one could use the statement

> **while** ¬ *LASTITEM* **do** *SUM:=SUM+ININT*;

The output procedures *OUTINT*, *OUTFIX* and *OUTTEXT* put integers, reals and pieces of text, respectively, on the output stream. *OUTINT* has two parameters: the integer to be output and the width of the field (in number of characters) that it is to occupy. If an expression is supplied as the first parameter, that expression is evaluated and the result is output.

Thus,

> *OUTINT(2*J,7)*;

outputs the value of $2*J$ in a field of width 7. The output is always right-justified in the field and any unused spaces to the left are filled with blanks. If, however, the number is too big to fit in the designated space, the latter is filled with asterisks and an error message is printed.

The procedure *OUTFIX* has three parameters: the real value (variable or expression) to be output, the number of digits after the decimal point to be included and the width of the field that the value is to occupy (right-justified). The format of the output is $[-]dd\cdots d.dd\cdots d$. The width of the field should be sufficient to accommodate all the digits, the decimal point and the sign (if present); otherwise the field is filled with asterisks and an error message is printed. For example,

$$OUTFIX(SIN(X),3,5);$$

attempts to output the value of $SIN(X)$ in a field of width 5, with 3 digits after the decimal point; if that value is, say, -0.318, then the width will be insufficient.

It is also possible to output real values in the 'mantissa and characteristic' format, thus $[-]d.dd\cdots d\pm Edd$, by using the procedure $OUTREAL$. This also has three parameters which have the same meaning as for $OUTFIX$. The width of the field should now accommodate the digits of the mantissa and characteristic and the letter E.

A piece of text can be output by enclosing it in double quotation marks and passing it as a parameter to the procedure $OUTTEXT$, e.g.

$$OUTTEXT(\text{"CUSTOMER ENTERS QUEUE"});$$

All characters, digits and special symbols are allowed in the text, and are placed in the output stream exactly as given.

It should be emphasised that a call on one of the above output procedures does not necessarily guarantee that the corresponding item will appear on the line printer paper or on the video screen. Those procedures put their items, in order of call, into an output buffer corresponding to a line in the output file. A new line is added to the file either when the buffer is full or when such an action is explicitly requested. Thus, if the program should fail for some reason with the current output buffer only partially filled, the items in it will not appear in the output file.

To force the current buffer to be added to the output file (and a new empty buffer to be made available), one calls procedure $OUTIMAGE$. In particular, successive calls on $OUTIMAGE$ immediately following one another produce blank lines in the output file.

Consider the following examples:

(a) $OUTINT(I,10); OUTINT(J,10); OUTINT(K,10);$
       $OUTIMAGE;$
(b) $OUTINT(I,10); OUTIMAGE; OUTINT(J,10);$
       $OUTIMAGE; OUTINT(K,10); OUTIMAGE;$

In the case (a), the values of the integers I, J and K are output on one line and a new line is started. In case (b), the same integers are output under each other on separate lines, before starting a new line.

The above input and output procedures are contained in the system-defined classes $INFILE$ and $OUTFILE$. For further text handling and file manipulation facilities in SIMULA the interested reader is directed to Birtwistle, Dahl, Myhrhaug & Nygaard [3].

132

2. The class concept

One of the meanings of the word 'class' is a set of similar things. In SIMULA, a class is a collection of zero or more objects, all constructed according to the same pattern. That pattern is determined by the class declaration, which has the following form (some additions will be mentioned later):

> **class** 'identifier' ('formal parameters'); 'specifications';
> **begin** 'declarations';
>   'statements';
> **end**;

As in the case of procedures, the declaration is composed of a header (containing the class identifier, formal parameters and their specifications) and a body (which may be a single statement or a block). The parameter passing and specification is similar to that of procedures, except that procedures may not be passed as parameters to classes, nor may any parameter be passed by name.

The declaration provides a template from which objects – class instances – can be created. This is done by invoking the object generator, **new**, followed by the class identifier and, if necessary, by a list of actual parameters in parentheses. Thus, if the header of a class declaration is

> **class** $MAN(AGE,HEIGHT,WEIGHT)$; **integer** AGE; **real** $HEIGHT$, $WEIGHT$;

then an instance of that class is created by writing, for example,

> **new** $MAN(42,1.75,65.5)$;

If the class body contains any 'actions', i.e. statements beyond the declarations part, these are executed upon creation of a new class instance. However, that instance may continue to exist long after the moment of its creation; there may be several instances of the same class in existence concurrently.

In order to work with an object, one should be able to refer to it. A variable can be declared as a reference, or a pointer, to instances of a given class. The form of the declaration is

> **ref**('class identifier') 'list of identifiers';

Thus, to declare TOM, $DICK$ and $HARRY$ as pointers to instances of class MAN, we write

> **ref**$(MAN)TOM,DICK,HARRY$;

It is also possible to declare arrays of pointers, e.g.

> **ref**(MAN) **array** $EMPLOYEES(1:N)$;

As with all declarations, reference variables are initialised at the time of declaration: their initial value is **none**, i.e. a null pointer. All elements of a reference array are initialised to **none**.

Objects can be assigned to reference variables by using an assignment statement with a different assignment symbol:

'reference variable':—'reference expression';

where 'reference expression' should produce an instance of the appropriate class. The following are three assignments of *MAN* instances:

TOM:—**new** *MAN*(0,0.4,3.1);
DICK:—**new** *MAN*(*ININT,INREAL,INREAL*);
HARRY:—*TOM*;

The actual parameters of the object assigned to *DICK* are read from the input stream; *HARRY* points to the same object as *TOM*.

Anything declared as part of a class declaration, be it in the parameter part or in the body (but not in blocks which are nested inside the body), is an 'attribute' of that class. For instance, the class *MAN* mentioned above has attributes *AGE, HEIGHT, WEIGHT* (it may also have other attributes declared in the body). The attributes may be value types (e.g. reals, integers, booleans), arrays, procedures, references to other class instances or arrays or such references.

Normally, variables declared within a block cannot be accessed from outside that block. One can, however, access the attributes of an object from the outside. This is done by 'dot' expressions, which have the form

'reference'.'attribute'

In the above examples, *TOM.AGE, TOM.HEIGHT* and *TOM.WEIGHT* are 0, 0.4 and 3.1 respectively, whereas *DICK.AGE, DICK.HEIGHT* and *DICK.WEIGHT* have the values read in from the input stream. The attributes of attributes, etc., can be accessed in a similar way. Thus, if class *MAN* has an attribute *SON*, which is a reference to a *MAN* object (by including a declaration **ref**(*MAN*)*SON* in the body of class *MAN*), then the age of the son of *TOM* can be accessed by the expression *TOM.SON.AGE*.

If an object has a procedure as an attribute, then accessing that procedure via a dot expression is equivalent to invoking it from within the object. Appropriate actual parameters should be supplied.

It is instructive to illustrate these concepts with a simple, yet non-trivial example. Suppose that we wish to manipulate rational fractions of the type p/q, where p and q are integers. A class *FRACTION* is to be defined, taking a pair of integers as parameters. The body of the class will contain procedures, say *ADD*, *MULT* and *DISPLAY*. The first two are functions which, when invoked from within a *FRACTION* object and passed another *FRACTION* object as a parameter, produce a result that is again a *FRACTION* object. The third procedure just displays the fraction from within which it is invoked in the form p/q.

The declaration of class *FRACTION* is as follows:

```
class  FRACTION(P,Q); integer P,Q;
begin ref(FRACTION)procedure ADD(F); ref(FRACTION)F;
      begin ADD:—new FRACTION(P*F.Q+Q*F.P,Q*F.Q)
      end of procedure ADD;
      ref(FRACTION)procedure MULT(F); ref(FRACTION)F;
      begin MULT:—new FRACTION(P*F.P, Q*F.Q);
      end of procedure MULT;
      procedure DISPLAY;
      begin OUTINT(P,10); OUTTEXT("/"); OUTINT(Q,10);
            OUTIMAGE;
      end of procedure DISPLAY;
   end of class FRACTION;
```

Note that, while the procedures *ADD*, *MULT* and *DISPLAY* can access the *P* and *Q* attributes of their own *FRACTION* object directly, the same attributes of another *FRACTION* object – the one referred to by the parameter *F* – have to be accessed by a dot expression.

Let us now use class *FRACTION*. Three pairs of integers representing three rational fractions *F1*, *F2* and *F3*, are to be read from the input stream and the fraction $(F1+F2)*F3$ is to be printed out:

```
ref(FRACTION)F1,F2,F3;
F1:—new FRACTION(ININT,ININT);
F2:—new FRACTION(ININT,ININT);
F3:—new FRACTION(ININT,ININT);
F1.ADD(F2).MULT(F3).DISPLAY;
```

The last statement invokes procedure *ADD* from within *F1* and passes it *F2* as a parameter; this produces a new *FRACTION* object from within which procedure *MULT* is invoked, passing it *F3* as a parameter; finally, procedure *DISPLAY* is invoked from the resulting *FRACTION* object. The same effect could have been achieved by writing

```
F3.MULT(F1.ADD(F2)).DISPLAY;
```

Here *MULT* is invoked from *F3* and is passed the result of *F1.ADD(F2)* as a parameter.

Another way of 'entering' the environment of an object and accessing its local attributes is provided by the **inspect** statement. The simplest form of the **inspect** statement is as follows:

inspect *R* **do** *S* **otherwise** *T*;

where *R* is a reference to an object and *S* and *T* are statements. If *R* is not **none** then *S* is executed as if it were local to *R* and can access all the attributes of *R*. The statement *T* is optional; it is executed if *R* is **none**. For example, to print out the fraction *F1* above, one could write

> **inspect** *F1* **do** *DISPLAY* **otherwise** *OUTTEXT*("∗∗∗");

This normally has the same effect as *F1.DISPLAY*. However, the latter will cause a run-time error if *F1* is **none**, whereas the former will print three asterisks as a warning message.

It is often desirable to refer to an object from within that object (while executing its actions or while executing a local procedure). Such a possibility is provided by the system-defined reference **this** 'class identifier'. Suppose, for example, that we wished to include as an attribute of class *FRACTION* a functional procedure *SQUARE* which, when invoked from within a *FRACTION* object, would return a new fraction equal to the old one squared. We could then add to the body of class *FRACTION* the declaration

> **ref** (*FRACTION*)**procedure** *SQUARE*;
> **begin** *SQUARE:−MULT*(**this** *FRACTION*);
> **end**;

which achieves the desired objective by multiplying the fraction with itself.

In contrast to the explicit creation of objects (using **new** ...), their destruction is done implicitly. If the actions of any objects have been executed and if there are no references pointing to it, that object is considered as having ceased to exist (in fact, the space it occupies is eventually freed by the run-time system garbage collection routines). For instance, to destroy the *FRACTION* object pointed to by *F1* (assuming that there are no other pointers to it) one could assign another object to *F1*, or write *F1:−***none**.

Two reference comparators are available, == and =/=, corresponding to 'equal' and 'not equal', respectively. Let *R1* and *R2* be two references. The boolean expression *R1==R2* has the value **true** if they both point to the same object, otherwise it has the value **false**. Conversely, the expression *R1=/=R2* has the value **true** if *R1* and *R2* point to different objects, **false** if they point to the same object. For example, the above **inspect** statement is in all respects equivalent to the following conditional one:

> **if** *F1* =/= **none** **then** *F1.DISPLAY* **else** *OUTTEXT*("∗∗∗");

3.   Prefixing. Hierarchical structures

SIMULA classes can be combined with one another by means of a prefixing mechanism. If the declaration of a certain class, say *CL1*, is prefixed by the identifier of another class, say *CL0*,

> *CL0* **class** *CL1* ...;

then a *CL1*-object contains, as well as its own attributes, all the attributes of *CL0*. In this combination, *CL0* is said to be the 'outer class' and *CL1* the 'inner class'. The class *CL1*, in turn, can be used as a prefix to yet another class, say *CL2*:

    CL1 **class** *CL2* ...;

A *CL2*-object would then have, as well as its own attributes, those of *CL1* and those of *CL0*. Class *CL1* is inner with respect to *CL0* but outer with respect to *CL2*.

In this manner one can construct tree-like hierarchical structures. The outer-most class can be thought of as being at the root of the tree; a class at a given node has as descendants all classes which are inner with respect to it.

When a new object of a prefixed class is created, the actions (if any) of the outer class are executed first, followed by the actions (if any) of the prefixed class. If the outer class requires actual parameters, these are given, in the appropriate order, before the parameters of the prefixed class. For example, a new object of class *CL1* is created by

    new *CL1*('parameters of *CL0*','parameters of *CL1*');

the actions of the newly created object are the *CL0*-actions followed by the *CL1*-actions.

A reference assignment statement in which the left-hand side has the same scope as the right-hand side, or is outer with respect to it, is always legal. Thus, given the declarations

    ref(*CL0*)*P0*;
    ref(*CL1*)*P1*;

the following assignments are legal:

    P0:—**new** *CL0*; *P0*:—**new** *CL1*; *P1*:—**new** *CL1*;

(assuming that no parameters are required). The assignment

    P1:—*P0*;

may, or may not be legal, depending on whether *P0* points to a *CL1*-object or a *CL0*-object (this has to be checked at run time). The assignment *P1*:—**new** *CL0* is illegal, as is any assignment between incompatible references. Any assignment whose right-hand side is **none** is legal (**none** is treated as inner to all classes).

Suppose that classes *CL0* and *CL1* have attributes *A0* and *A1* respectively. Then, if the reference *P1* declared above points to a *CL1*-object, one can access both *A1* and *A0* by dot expressions

    P1.A1; *P1.A0*;

since the attributes of *CL0* are made available to *CL1*. On the other hand, regardless of whether *P0* points to a *CL0*-object or a *CL1*-object, only *A0* can be accessed via *P0.A0*; the expression *P0.A1* is invalid.

The above situation appears unsatisfactory. A reference variable may point to a composite object (e.g. *P0*:—**new** *CL1*), although it was declared as a pointer to objects of the outer class (**ref**(*CL0*)*P0*). If this is the case, why should one not use that reference to access attributes of the inner class? Indeed, the possibility exists. However, one has to state explicitly that the access is via the inner class, e.g. by means of the qualifier **qua**:

> *P0* **qua** *CL1.A1*;

Such a qualification satisfies the compiler; the run-time system will object if *P0* does not, in fact, point to a *CL1*-object. Alternatively, a version of the **inspect** statement can be used to gain access to the attributes of an inner class:

> **inspect** *P0* **when** *CL1* **do** ... *A1* ...;

The prefixing mechanism is very well suited to the application of structured programming techniques. Certain general facilities can be provided in an outer class, without having to specify who is going to need them. Those facilities are then made available by using that class as a prefix. As well as other classes, one can also prefix blocks, e.g.

> *CL0* **begin**
>
> ⋮
>
> **end**;

Then all the attributes of the prefixing class are directly accessible in the prefixed block (as if they were declared in an outer block).

The following two sections will supply examples of such provision of general facilities and of the use of prefixing. Before proceeding, however, we shall mention two programming constructs which add flexibility to the class hierarchies. These are the **inner** and the **virtual** constructs.

The rule that, when creating a composite object, the actions of an outer class must be executed before those of an inner one is sometimes too restrictive. That rule can be circumvented by the use of **inner**. One can specify an arbitrary point in the actions of an outer class, where the actions of an inner class are to be inserted, e.g.

> **class** *CL0*:
> **begin**
>
> ⋮
>
> **inner**;
>
> ⋮
>
> **end**;

Then, if this class is subsequently used as a prefix and a composite object is created, e.g.

> *CL0* **class** *CL1*;
> **begin**
>
> ⋮
>
> **end**;

$- - -$

new *CL1*;

the actions of the new object are executed in the following order:

CL0-actions prior to **inner**; *CL1*-actions; *CL0*-actions after **inner**.

There are occasions when it is desirable to use in the body of an outer class a procedure that is declared in an inner class (for instance, dealing at a general level with an object 'server', one may wish to invoke a procedure 'service', without having to define what it does; that definition will be left to a specialised 'server' whose characteristics are contained in an inner class). This can be done by specifying the procedure in question as **virtual**, in the header of the outer class declaration, e.g.

> **class** *CL0*; **virtual**: **procedure** *P*;
> **begin**
> $\qquad \vdots$
> $\qquad$ *P*;
> $\qquad \vdots$
> **end**;
> *CL0* **class** *CL1*;
> **begin procedure** *P* . . . ;
> $\qquad \vdots$
> **end**;

The **virtual** specification must come after all formal parameter specifications (if any). More than one procedure can be included in it, separated by semicolons.

4.   **Class *SIMSET***

The system-defined class *SIMSET* implements doubly linked lists (see chapter 2). The elements of such a list are called *LINK*-objects, while the list itself is a *HEAD*-object. The forward and backward pointers are provided by two functional procedures, *SUC* and *PRED* (for 'successor' and 'predecessor' respectively), which return references to *LINK*-objects, or **none**:

> **ref**(*LINK*)**procedure** *SUC*; . . .;
> **ref**(*LINK*)**procedure** *PRED*; . . .;

These two procedures are the attributes of a class called *LINKAGE*, which prefixes both class *LINK* and class *HEAD*. They can therefore be invoked from within *LINK*- and *HEAD*-objects. Suppose that *L* and *H* are references to a *LINK*- and a *HEAD*-object respectively. If *L* belongs to a linked list and is not the last element in it, then *L.SUC* returns a reference to the successor of *L*; similarly, if *L* is not the first element in the list, *L.PRED* returns a reference to the predecessor of *L*; otherwise *L.SUC* and *L.PRED* return **none**. If *H* refers to a linked list which is not empty, *H.SUC* and *H.PRED* return references to the first and last *LINK*-objects in the list respectively; if *H* is empty then *H.SUC* and

H.PRED return **none**. The relations among objects in a list structure are illustrated in figure A1.1. Note the distinction between a non-existent list and an empty list. When a *HEAD* reference variable is declared (say **ref**(*HEAD*)*H*;), it is initialised to **none**, i.e. there is no list associated with it. After the assignment statement *H:*—**new**(*HEAD*), there is a linked list referred to by *H* but it is an empty list. It will cease to be empty when some *LINK*-objects are placed in it.

In addition to *SUC* and *PRED*, the classes *LINK* and *HEAD* have the following attributes of their own:

Attributes of class *LINK*

procedure *OUT*;

If *L* refers to a *LINK*-object which belongs to a linked list (it cannot belong to more than one list), *L.OUT* removes it from that list; otherwise *L.OUT* has no effect.

procedure *INTO(HD)*; **ref**(*HEAD*)*HD*;

If *H* refers to an existing linked list, *L.INTO(H)* results in *L* becoming the last *LINK*-object in *H*; otherwise *L* is just removed from any previous list it might have belonged to.

procedure *PRECEDE(X)*; **ref**(*LINKAGE*)*X*;

The actual parameter of this procedure may be either a *LINK*-object or a *HEAD*-object (since both are prefixed by *LINKAGE*). If *L1* is a *LINK*-object, *L.PRECEDE(L1)* inserts *L* into the same linked list that *L1* belongs to, in the position immediately preceding *L1* (if *L1* does not belong to a linked list, the result is the same as for *L.OUT*). If *H* is a *HEAD*-object, *L.PRECEDE(H)* is

Figure A1.1

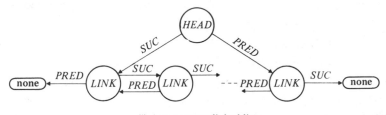

(i) A non-empty linked list

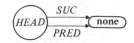

(ii) An empty linked list

equivalent to *L.INTO(H)*.

procedure *FOLLOW(X)*; **ref**(*LINKAGE*)*X*;

This has a similar action to *PRECEDE*, except that *L.FOLLOW(L1)* inserts *L* immediately after *L1* and *L.FOLLOW(H)* places *L* as the first *LINK*-object in *H*.

Attributes of class *HEAD*

ref(*LINK*)**procedure** *FIRST*;
ref(*LINK*)**procedure** *LAST*;

These two functional procedures return references to the first and last *LINK*-object in the list respectively. If the list is empty, they return **none**. In other words, *H.FIRST* and *H.LAST* (where *H* is a *HEAD*-object) are equivalent to *H.SUC* and *H.PRED* respectively.

integer procedure *CARDINAL*;

H.CARDINAL returns the number of *LINK*-objects in the list *H* (zero if *H* is empty).

boolean procedure *EMPTY*;

H.EMPTY returns **true** if *H* is empty, **false** otherwise.

procedure *CLEAR*;

This procedure removes all *LINK*-objects (if any) from the list. If *H.EMPTY* is invoked after *H.CLEAR* (but before any new *LINK*-objects have been put into *H*), it will return the value **true**.

To recapitulate, class *SIMSET* has the following structure:

```
class SIMSET;
begin class LINKAGE;
        begin ... procedures SUC,PRED...
        end of LINKAGE;
        LINKAGE class LINK;
        begin ... procedures OUT,INTO,PRECEDE,FOLLOW...
        end of LINK;
        LINKAGE class HEAD;
        begin ... procedures FIRST,LAST,CARDINAL,EMPTY,CLEAR ...
        end of HEAD;
end of class SIMSET;
```

These facilities are made available to a program by prefixing the program block with *SIMSET* (or with another class which is prefixed by *SIMSET*):

```
SIMSET begin
            :
        end;
```

The most common applications of class *SIMSET* have to do with queues: a queue of items is represented by a *HEAD*-object, while the items themselves are (or are prefixed by) *LINK*-objects. The scheduling strategy (First-In-First-Out, Last-In-First-Out, etc.) is determined by the pattern of insertions of items into, and their removals from, the queue. Here we shall give a slightly different example.

Suppose that we wish to perform set-theoretic operations (union, intersection, etc.) on sets of integers. Since the size of the sets is not fixed, it is reasonable to implement them by means of linked lists. A class *SET* can be declared and prefixed by *HEAD*, thereby providing it with all the attributes of the latter. The desired operations will be carried out by procedures local to class *SET*. We shall give only one, a functional procedure *INTERSECT*, which when invoked from within one *SET*-object and passed another *SET*-object as a parameter, will return a new *SET*-object containing the intersection of the two. To represent the integer elements of a set, a class *ELEMENT* is declared, prefixed by *LINK* and taking an integer as a parameter. It is also convenient to declare in class *ELEMENT* a boolean procedure, say *BELONGS*, which when invoked from an *ELEMENT*-object and passed a *SET*-object as a parameter, will return **true** or **false** depending on whether the element's integer already belongs to the set or not.

The declarations of classes *SET* and *ELEMENT* are given below:

```
HEAD class SET;
begin ref(SET) procedure INTERSECT(S); ref(SET)S;
    begin ref(SET)TEMP;
        TEMP:—new SET;
        if ¬(EMPTY or S.EMPTY) then
        begin ref(ELEMENT)E;
            E:—FIRST;
            while E =/= none do
            begin if E.BELONGS(S) then
                    new ELEMENT(E.K).INTO(TEMP);
                    E:—E.SUC;
            end;
        end;
        INTERSECT:—TEMP;
    end of INTERSECT;
end of class SET;

LINK class ELEMENT(K); integer K;
begin boolean procedure BELONGS(S); ref(SET)S;
    begin boolean FOUND;
        if ¬S.EMPTY then
```

```
        begin ref(ELEMENT)E;
            E:−S.FIRST;
            while E=/=none and ¬FOUND do
            begin FOUND:=K=E.K;
                E:−E.SUC;
            end;
        end;
        BELONGS:=FOUND;
    end of BELONGS;
end of class ELEMENT;
```

The reason for writing, in procedure *INTERSECT*,

new *ELEMENT(E.K).INTO(TEMP)*

(instead of just *E.INTO(TEMP)*) is that we wish the two intersecting sets to be left intact after the intersection operation. Since each *LINK*-object can belong to at most one linked list, one must create a duplicate *ELEMENT*, carrying the same integer, and place it in the intersection set. Note also that *E* is declared as a reference to *ELEMENT*, while *FIRST* and *SUC* return references to *LINK*-objects. The validity of the assignment *E:−FIRST*, for instance, has to be checked at run time. An alternative approach would be to declare **ref**(*LINK*)*E* and later use **qua**, e.g. *E* **qua** *ELEMENT.BELONGS(S)*; this would avoid getting compiler warning messages.

The program block containing the declarations of *SET* and *ELEMENT* would be prefixed by *SIMSET*. For such a package to be useful, class *SET* should contain input/output procedures – say *INITIALISE* and *DISPLAY* – as well as other set operation procedures. Procedure *INITIALISE* might read in a number *N*, telling it how many elements are to be put in the set initially, and then use a **for** loop to fill the set:

```
for I:=1 step 1 until N do
    new ELEMENT(ININT).INTO(this SET);
```

If, for example, we wish to read in two sets and print out their intersection, we can write

```
ref(SET)S1,S2;
S1:−new SET; S2:−new SET;
S1.INITIALISE; S2.INITIALISE;
S1.INTERSECT(S2).DISPLAY;
```

5.   Class *SIMULATION*

The simulation facilities of SIMULA, namely clock, event list and process management routines, are contained in the system-defined class *SIMULATION*. Moreover, that class is prefixed by *SIMSET*, so that the attributes of classes *LINKAGE*, *LINK* and *HEAD* are available too.

In a process-oriented simulation (see chapter 2), the behaviour of a system is modelled by a number of interacting sequential processes. Accordingly, class *SIMULATION* contains a class *PROCESS*, prefixed by *LINK* (so that processes can be inserted into and removed from linked lists). A user-defined class can thus be turned into a process by prefixing it with *PROCESS*.

At any point in time, a process can be in one, and only one, of the following states:

Active. The process is at the head of the event list and its actions are being executed. Only one process can be active at any one time.

Suspended. The process is on the event list, scheduled to become active at a specified time in the future. The event list is ordered according to these 'event times'. The event time of a suspended process may be equal to that of the active process, in which case its actions will be executed before the clock is advanced.

Passive. The process is not on the event list. Unless another process brings it back on to the list by means of an activation statement, its further actions will not be executed.

Terminated. The process is not on the event list and has no further actions to execute.

A process that is either active or suspended is said to be 'scheduled'.

Local to class *PROCESS* are four functional procedures:

boolean procedure *IDLE*;

P.IDLE returns **true** if the process *P* is passive or terminated, **false** if it is scheduled.

boolean procedure *TERMINATED*;

P.TERMINATED returns **true** if *P* is terminated, **false** if it is scheduled or passive.

real procedure *EVTIME*;

If *P* is a scheduled process, *P.EVTIME* returns the time when *P* will become active. An attempt to invoke *EVTIME* from within a passive process results in a run-time error.

ref(*PROCESS*)**procedure** *NEXTEV*;

If *P* is scheduled and is not the last process on the event list, *P.NEXTEV* returns a reference to the next process on the list (i.e. the one that will become active after *P*). Otherwise *P.NEXTEV* returns **none**.

The general structure of class *PROCESS* is as follows:

LINK **class** *PROCESS*;
begin ... procedures *IDLE,TERMINATED,EVTIME,NEXTEV*...;
       :
       :

    inner;
       :
       :

  end;

The user actions, i.e. the actions of a user-defined class prefixed by *PROCESS*, are wedged in the place of **inner** (see section 3). Before and after **inner** there are actions ensuring the initial and final passing of control to the clock routine.

To allow the scheduling, de-scheduling and re-scheduling of processes, class *SIMULATION* provides several procedures and language constructs:

> **procedure** *HOLD(T)*; **real** *T*;

This procedure, when invoked by the active process, removes that process from the head of the event list and schedules it to become active *T* units of time later. In other words, the active process re-schedules itself after a delay *T*.

> **procedure** *PASSIVATE*;

Also acting on behalf of the active process, *PASSIVATE* removes it from the event list altogether. If that process is to be scheduled again in the future, an intervention from another process is required.

> **procedure** *WAIT(S)*; **ref** *(HEAD)S*;

The active process is inserted at the end of the linked list pointed to by *S* (remember that *PROCESS* is prefixed by *LINK*) and then it is immediately *PASSIVATE*d.

> **procedure** *CANCEL(X)*; **ref** *(PROCESS)X*;

This procedure takes a reference to a process as a parameter. If that process is scheduled, the procedure removes it from the event list (thus making it passive); otherwise it has no effect.

Other ways of scheduling processes are provided by the 'activation statements' (these are treated as language primitives, rather than procedure calls). The simplest activation statements are

> **activate** *P*;
> **reactivate** *P*;

where *P* is a reference to a process. In both cases *P* is brought to the head of the event list and becomes the active process. The first statement has an effect only if *P* was passive, whereas the second applied also to processes already scheduled.

More general activation commands are given by

> **activate** *P* **at** *T*;
> **reactivate** *P* **at** *T*;

or

> **activate** *P* **delay** *T*;
> **reactivate** *P* **delay** *T*;

where *P* is a reference to a process and *T* is a real value. The timing clauses **at** and **delay** specify the moment when *P* should become active: in the former case it will be at time *T* and in the latter at the current time + *T*. Again, **activate** applies only to passive processes while **reactivate** applies to passive and scheduled ones. If one or more other processes are already scheduled for the time that *P* is to be activated, it will become active after them. However, one can reverse that order by adding the word **prior**, e.g.

reactivate *P* **delay** *T* **prior**;

If, in an **at**-clause, the value of *T* is less than the current time, or, in a **delay**-clause, the value of *T* is negative, then *P* is activated at the current time (but it does not become the active process unless **prior** is present).

Another way of specifying the time of activation is by referring to a process that is already scheduled. The corresponding statements are

activate *P* **before** *Q*;
reactivate *P* **before** *Q*;

or

activate *P* **after** *Q*;
reactivate *P* **after** *Q*;

where *P* and *Q* are references to processes. Process *P* is scheduled for the same clock time as *Q* and will become active either immediately before or immediately after *Q*, depending on the preposition employed. If *Q* is **none**, or refers to a passive process, or to the same process as *P*, then the above statements have the same effect as *CANCEL(P)*.

It is not unusual for more than one process to be scheduled at the same clock time. This is because a change of state in the system being simulated can easily affect more than one process (for instance, both a server and a customer process may have to take some action at a service completion instant). The programmer should be aware that, although the actions of all such processes occur conceptually at the same instant of time, they are in fact executed one after the other, in the order implied by the event list. That order may or may not be important for the correct running of the simulation; if it is, the constructs **before**, **after** and **prior** should be used as appropriate.

The simulation program itself, i.e. the block prefixed by *SIMULATION*, is also treated as a process (although it is not one really) and is referred to by the system-defined reference *MAIN*. This allows the main program to be scheduled like any other process. The simulation starts by placing *MAIN* at the head of the event list at time zero; it ends when the main program finishes all its actions.

There are three more procedures in class *SIMULATION*; they are not absolutely necessary but make the programmer's task easier.

ref *(PROCESS)***procedure** *CURRENT*;

This procedure returns a reference to the active process. Since it is invoked either from the active process or from the main program, its invocation is equivalent to writing **this** *PROCESS* or *MAIN* respectively.

real procedure *TIME*;

returns the current value of the clock. Since that is the event time of the active process, *TIME* is obtained as *CURRENT.EVTIME*.

146

procedure *ACCUM(A,B,C,D)*; **name** *A,B,C*; **real** *A,B,C,D*;

accumulates the area under a step function and updates the function itself (see section 5.1). Parameter *A* contains the accumulated area, *B* is the time of the last jump, *C* is the current value of the step function (i.e. just before it jumps again) and *D* is the size of the jump it is about to make. Thus a customer–hour integral like the one pictured in figure 5.1 would be updated by

$$ACCUM(AREA,LASTEVENT,N,1);$$

at an arrival instant, and

$$ACCUM(AREA,LASTEVENT,N,-1);$$

at a departure instant.

The overall structure of class *SIMULATION* is as follows:

> *SIMSET* **class** *SIMULATION*;
> **begin** *LINK* **class** *PROCESS* ...;
>   ... procedures *HOLD,PASSIVATE,WAIT,CANCEL,CURRENT,*
>   *TIME,ACCUM* ...;
>   ... **activate** and **reactivate** statements ...;
>   *PROCESS* **class** 'main program' ...;
>   **ref**('main program')*MAIN*;
>   ... actions: set up event list, placing *MAIN* at its head with event
>   time zero ...;
> **end** of class *SIMULATION*;

A simulation program is a block prefixed by *SIMULATION*:

> *SIMULATION* **begin**
>   ⋮
>   **end**;

Several simulation programs are presented and discussed in chapter 3. They illustrate most of the concepts mentioned here and the reader is urged to examine them carefully.

6. System-defined procedures

The list below is not exhaustive. The character and text-handling procedures have been omitted, as well as the procedures in classes *SIMSET* and *SIMULATION*, which have been described already.

Arithmetic functions

ABS(X);	absolute value ($|X|$)
EXP(X);	exponent (e^X)
LN(X);	natural logarithm ($\ln X$)
SQRT(X);	square root ($\sqrt{X}$)
SIN(X);	sine
COS(X);	cosine $\Big\}$ X is in radians
TAN(X);	tangent

$$ARCSIN(X); \quad \text{arc-sine}$$
$$ARCCOS(X); \quad \text{arc-cosine}$$
$$ARCTAN(X); \quad \text{arc-tangent}$$

ARCSIN(X);   arc-sine ⎫
ARCCOS(X);   arc-cosine ⎬ principal value, in radians
ARCTAN(X);   arc-tangent ⎭
SINH(X);   hyperbolic sine $(\frac{1}{2}(e^X - e^{-X}))$
COSH(X);   hyperbolic cosine $(\frac{1}{2}(e^X + e^{-X}))$

The argument in the above functions can be a variable or an expression whose value is **integer**, **real** or **long real**. Accordingly, the computation is performed in either single or double precision and the result is either **real** or **long real**.

SIGN(X);   returns 1, 0 or -1, for $X > 0$, $X = 0$ and $X < 0$ respectively.

ENTIER(X);   largest integer $\leqslant X$ (e.g. $ENTIER(-3.2) = -4$).

MOD(M,N);   remainder of integer division of M by N (M mod N).

The last three procedures return an **integer** as a result.

Random drawing procedures

All the following procedures take as one of their parameters a random number seed, U, which should be an odd integer. At every procedure call, the SIMULA pseudo-random number generator is invoked (see chapter 4) and the next number in the sequence corresponding to the initial seed value is used by the procedure that was called.

boolean procedure $DRAW(A,U)$; **name** U; **real** A; **integer** U;

returns **true** with probability A if $0 \leqslant A \leqslant 1$, with probability 0 if $A < 0$ and with probability 1 if $A > 1$.

integer procedure $RANDINT(A,B,U)$; **name** U; **integer** A,B,U;

returns one of the integers $A, A + 1, \ldots, B$ (with equal probability).

integer procedure $DISCRETE(A,U)$; **name** U; **real array** A; **integer** U;

inverts a cumulative discrete distribution function specified by the array A. If the subscripts of A are $1, 2, \ldots, N$, the procedure returns 1 with probability $A(1)$, 2 with probability $A(2) - A(1), \ldots$, and N with probability $1 - A(N - 1)$ (see section 4.2; it is assumed that $A(N) = 1$).

integer procedure $HISTD(A,U)$; **name** U; **real array** A; **integer** U;

inverts a distribution given in the form of a frequency histogram, in the array A. If the subscripts of A are $1, 2, \ldots, N$, the procedure returns I with probability $A(I)/[A(1) + A(2) + \ldots + A(N)], I = 1, 2, \ldots, N$.

real procedure $LINEAR(A,B,U)$; **name** U; **real array** A,B; **integer** U;

inverts a piecewise linear approximation of a cumulative distribution function $F(x)$ whose values are given at a number of points: the two arrays A and B have the same subscripts, say $1, 2, \ldots, N$, and $A(I) = F(B(I)), I = 1, 2, \ldots, N$. The procedure returns a real number whose distribution function, $\tilde{F}(x)$, coincides with $F(x)$ at points $B(I)$ and between those points is obtained by linear interpolation. It is necessary that $A(1) = 0$ and $A(N) = 1$.

real procedure *UNIFORM(A,B,U)*; **name** *U*; **real** *A,B*; **integer** *U*;

returns a real number distributed uniformly on the interval (A,B).

real procedure *NEGEXP(A,U)*; **name** *U*; **real** *A*; **integer** *U*;

returns a real number distributed exponentially with mean $1/A$.

real procedure *ERLANG(A,B,U)*; **name** *U*; **real** *A,B*; **integer** *U*;

returns a real number having the Erlang distribution with mean $1/A$ and standard deviation $1/(AB^{1/2})$, i.e. the sum of B exponentially distributed random variables, each with mean $1/(AB)$.

real procedure *NORMAL(A,B,U)*; **name** *U*; **real** *A,B*; **integer** *U*;

returns a real number distributed normally with mean A and standard deviation B. The polar coordinates method (see section 4.2) is employed.

integer procedure *POISSON(A,U)*; **name** *U*; **real** *A*; **integer** *U*;

returns an integer having the Poisson distribution with mean (and variance) A.

APPENDIX 2.   A PROBABILITY THEORY PRIMER

This appendix does not pretend to do more than present in a concise form, and mostly without proofs, a few basic results from probability theory, some of which are referred to in the rest of the book. There is, of course, an extensive literature on the subject; the interested reader might consult for example the classic book by Feller [11]. A more recent and very readable text by Whittle [42], is also recommended.

1.   **Sample points, events and probabilities**
We think of an 'experiment' as some activity which has an outcome. The collection of all possible outcomes is called the 'sample space' of the experiment; a particular outcome is a 'sample point'. For example, in a simulation experiment, the sample points are the operation paths produced by the program and the sample space is the set of all possible operation paths. The sample space is usually denoted by Ω.

Certain sets of sample points, i.e. subsets of Ω, are called 'events' (this notion of the term event is different from the one introduced in chapter 1; here, an event is thought to have 'occurred' if the outcome of the experiment was one of the sample points in the set defining the event). The whole sample space Ω is an event (certain to occur), as is also the empty set, $\emptyset$ (it never occurs). If A is an event, its complement, $\neg A = \Omega - A$, is also an event ($\neg A$ occurs when A does not, and vice versa). If $\{A_1, A_2, \ldots\}$ is a denumerable set of events, then the union

$$A_U = \sum_{i=1}^{\infty} A_i$$

is an event (it occurs when at least one of the $A_1, A_2, \ldots$ occurs). Similarly, the intersection

$$A_I = \prod_{i=1}^{\infty} A_i = \neg \sum_{i=1}^{\infty} (\neg A_i)$$

is an event (A_I occurs when all of the $A_1, A_2, \ldots$ occur).

150

Two events, A and B, are said to be 'disjoint' or 'exclusive' if their intersection is empty: $AB = \emptyset$. The events in a denumerable set, $\{A_1, A_2, \ldots\}$, are
said to be 'mutually exclusive' if for every $i \neq j$, A_i and A_j are exclusive. The set
$\{A_1, A_2, \ldots\}$ constitutes a 'partition' of the sample space Ω if the events in it
are mutually exclusive and if at least one of them is certain to occur:

$$\sum_{i=1}^{\infty} A_i = \Omega.$$

The sample space, together with the set of events that are allowed in it,
becomes a 'probability space' by the addition of a function, P, which maps
events into real numbers. That function, called 'probability', must satisfy the
following three axioms:

(i) For every event A, $0 \leqslant P(A) \leqslant 1$;
(ii) $P(\Omega) = 1$;
(iii) If $A_1, A_2, \ldots$ are mutually exclusive events, then

$$P\left(\sum_{i=1}^{\infty} A_i\right) = \sum_{i=1}^{\infty} P(A_i).$$

In particular, if $A_1, A_2, \ldots$ form a partition of the event space, then

$$\sum_{i=1}^{\infty} P(A_i) = 1.$$

Thus, for every event A, $P(\neg A) = 1 - P(A)$. The probability of the null event is
zero: $P(\emptyset) = 1 - P(\Omega) = 0$. For two arbitrary events, A and B,

$$P(A + B) = P(A) + P(B) - P(AB)$$

(this is obtained by writing $A + B = A + (B - AB)$, where A and $B - AB$ are
exclusive, and noting that $P(B - AB) = P(B) - P(AB)$).

Two events, A and B, are said to be 'independent' if the probability that they
both occur is equal to the product of their respective probabilities:

$$P(AB) = P(A)P(B),$$

otherwise they are 'dependent'. More generally, n events, $A_1, A_2, \ldots, A_n$, are
independent if for every subset of k events,

$$P(A_{i_1} A_{i_2} \ldots A_{i_k}) = P(A_{i_1}) P(A_{i_2}) \ldots P(A_{i_k}), \quad k = 2, 3, \ldots, n$$

(it is not enough to require pairwise independence); otherwise they are
dependent.

This concept of dependence corresponds to the intuitive idea that the occurrence of certain events may influence the likelihood of occurrence of others. For
example, the probability that the throw of a die will yield an even number is $\frac{1}{2}$;
the probability that it will yield a number less than or equal to 3 is also $\frac{1}{2}$; however, the probability that the throw will yield an even number less than or equal

151

to 3 is $\frac{1}{6}$ and not $\frac{1}{4}$. The two events 'even' and 'less than or equal to 3' are not independent.

Closely related to dependence is the notion of 'conditional probability'. Consider the intersection of two events, A and B, and suppose that $P(B) > 0$. We can write

$$P(AB) = [P(AB)/P(B)]\, P(B).$$

The term in the square brackets is defined as the 'conditional probability of A, given that B has occurred', and is denoted by

$$P(A|B) = P(AB)/P(B)$$

(note that $A|B$ is not an event; the above equation is just a definition). Thus the probability of intersection is given by

$$P(AB) = P(A|B)\, P(B).$$

If A and B are independent, then $P(A|B) = P(A)$; the occurrence or non-occurrence of B does not influence that of A.

The product formula generalises easily to more than two events:

$$P(A_1 A_2 \ldots A_n) = P(A_1|A_2 A_3 \ldots A_n)P(A_2|A_3 \ldots A_n)\ldots P(A_{n-1}|A_n)P(A_n).$$

. If the events $A_1, A_2, \ldots$ constitute a partition of Ω (i.e. they are mutually exclusive and their union is Ω) then an arbitrary event B can be expressed as

$$B = BA_1 + BA_2 + \ldots$$

where the events BA_i are also mutually exclusive. Hence,

$$P(B) = \sum_i P(BA_i) = \sum_i P(B|A_i)\, P(A_i).$$

On the other hand, the conditional probability of A_i, given B, is equal to

$$P(A_i|B) = P(BA_i)/P(B)$$
$$= [P(B|A_i)\, P(A_i)] \bigg/ \left[\sum_i P(B|A_i)\, P(A_i)\right].$$

The last two expressions are known as the 'complete probability formula' and the 'Bayes formula' respectively.

A probability space is thus a triple consisting of a sample space, Ω, a set of events in Ω and a probability function, P, defined on that set of events. From now on, it will be assumed that such a probability space is given.

2.   **Random variables**

A real-valued function, X, defined on Ω (i.e. mapping sample points, or outcomes, into real numbers), is called a 'random variable', provided that the following condition is satisfied: the set of sample points for which $X \leqslant x$ is an event for every real x. This last condition is indeed satisfied in all cases of practical interest, so we shall not refer to it explicitly in the future.

152

Since X maps sample points into real numbers, it maps events into sets of real numbers, and vice versa. One can talk, therefore, about the probability of X belonging to a given set of real numbers. In particular, the probability that X does not exceed x is a function of x:

$$P(X \leqslant x) = F(x).$$

That function is called the 'distribution function' of the random variable X. It has the following properties:

(i) $F(-\infty) = 0$; $\quad F(\infty) = 1$. This is another way of saying that the value of X is certain to be finite.

(ii) If $x \leqslant y$ then $F(x) \leqslant F(y)$. This is because the event $X \leqslant x$ implies (is included in) the event $X \leqslant y$.

(iii) $F(x)$ is continuous from the right. If $y_1, y_2, \ldots$ is a decreasing sequence converging to x, then the event $X \leqslant x$ is the intersection of the events $X \leqslant y_i$, $\quad i = 1, 2, \ldots$.

The probability that X takes a value in the interval $(a, b]$, where $a < b$, is given by

$$P(a < X \leqslant b) = F(b) - F(a).$$

Letting $a \to b$ in this equation we get, in the limit,

$$P(X = b) = F(b) - F(b^-),$$

where $F(b^-)$ is the limit from the left of $F(x)$ at $x = b$. If $F(x)$ is continuous at $x = b$ then of course $P(X = b) = 0$.

A random variable, X, is said to be 'discrete' if its distribution function has jumps at points $x_1, x_2, \ldots$, of magnitudes $p_1, p_2, \ldots$ respectively, and in between those points remains constant. In other words, X can only take the values $x_1, x_2, \ldots$, with probabilities $p_1, p_2, \ldots$ respectively. These probabilities satisfy

$$p_1 + p_2 + \ldots = 1.$$

A random variable, X, is said to be 'continuous' if its distribution function is continuous everywhere. Another important characteristic of the random variable is then the 'probability density function', $f(x)$, which is defined as the derivative of the distribution function, $F'(x)$, at the points where the latter exists. The probability that X takes a value in the interval $(a, b]$ (it does not matter now whether the interval is open, half-open or closed) can be expressed in terms of the density function:

$$P(a < X \leqslant b) = F(b) - F(a) = \int_a^b f(x)\, \mathrm{d}x.$$

From property (i) of the distribution function it follows that

$$\int_{-\infty}^{\infty} f(x)\, \mathrm{d}x = 1.$$

153

The term 'density' reflects the fact that $f(x)$ is approximately the ratio between the probability of X taking a value in a small interval around x, and the length of that interval:

$$f(x) \approx [F(x + \Delta x) - F(x)]/\Delta x = P(x < X \leqslant x + \Delta x)/\Delta x.$$

In the limit $\Delta x \to 0$, the approximate equality becomes equality (assuming that the distribution function is differentiable at x). This is often expressed by introducing the infinitesimal quantity dx and writing

$$f(x) = P(X = x)/dx, \quad \text{or} \quad P(X = x) = f(x)\, dx.$$

If X and Y are two random variables, their 'joint' distribution function is defined for all real x and y as

$$F(x, y) = P(X \leqslant x, Y \leqslant y)$$

(where the comma in the right-hand side should be interpreted as an *and*, i.e. an intersection). The joint distribution function takes into account the dependency that might exist between X and Y:

$$F(x, y) = P(X \leqslant x \mid Y \leqslant y)\, P(Y \leqslant y)$$
$$= P(Y \leqslant y \mid X \leqslant x)\, P(X \leqslant x).$$

The distribution of X on its own – the 'marginal' distribution of X – is given by

$$F_X(x) = P(X \leqslant x) = F(x, \infty).$$

Similarly, the marginal distribution of Y is

$$F_Y(y) = P(Y \leqslant y) = F(\infty, y).$$

The random variables X and Y are said to be independent if their joint distribution function factorises into a product of their marginal distribution functions, i.e. if for all x and y,

$$F(x, y) = F(x, \infty)\, F(\infty, y).$$

When X and Y are continuous, their joint probability density function is given by

$$f(x, y) = \frac{\partial^2 F(x, y)}{\partial x\, \partial y}.$$

As in the case of a single random variable, the concept of joint density can be expressed by writing

$$P(X = x, Y = y) = f(x, y)\, dx\, dy$$

(it should be remembered, however, that this is only a shorthand notation for the limiting ratio of probability in a small rectangle to the area of that rectangle).

The probability that a random point (X, Y) falls in a region S of the two-dimensional plane is evaluated as

$$P[(X, Y) \in S] = \int_S f(x, y)\, dx\, dy.$$

3.   Mean, variance and covariance. Inequalities

Intuitively, one thinks of the mean (or the average, or the expectation) of a random variable, as a weighted sum of all its values, where the weight of a value is the probability with which it is taken. Thus, if X is discrete, taking values $x_1, x_2, \ldots$ with probabilities $p_1, p_2, \ldots$ respectively, its mean is equal to

$$E[X] = \sum_{i=1}^{\infty} x_i p_i,$$

(the sum in the right-hand side may be finite or infinite). If X is continuous, then the contribution of each value is infinitesimal and the sum becomes an integral:

$$E[X] = \int_0^{\infty} x f(x) \, dx.$$

In the general case when the distribution function of X has continuous (non-constant) portions as well as jumps, the expectation involves integration over the continuous portions plus terms of the type $x_i p_i$, where x_i is a discontinuity point for $F(x)$ and p_i is the magnitude of the jump there.

An important property of the expectation is its linearity. If X and Y are two random variables, then

$$E[X + Y] = E[X] + E[Y],$$

regardless of whether X and Y are dependent or independent. If X is a random variable and α is a constant, then

$$E[\alpha X] = \alpha E[X].$$

If a random variable X is, in fact, a constant (i.e. if it takes a single value, x, with probability 1) then its expectation is equal to that constant:

$$E[x] = x.$$

If a random variable takes only non-negative values, then its expectation is also non-negative. This, plus the linearity property, implies that the expectation preserves inequalities among random variables:

$$\text{if } X \leqslant Y \text{ then } E[X] \leqslant E[Y].$$

There is a very close relation between expectation and probability. Consider an event A and define the random variable, I_A, which takes the value 1 for the sample points in A and 0 elsewhere (i.e. 1 when A occurs and 0 when it does not occur). That random variable is called the 'indicator', or the 'indicator function' of the event A. It is readily seen that the expectation of the indicator of an event is equal to the probability of that event:

$$E[I_A] = 1 \cdot P(I_A = 1) + 0 \cdot P(I_A = 0)$$
$$= P(I_A = 1) = P(A).$$

Two very useful inequalities can be derived as simple consequences from the

155

above properties of expectation. Let X be a non-negative random variable and α be a positive constant. The indicator of the event $X > \alpha$ obviously satisfies (for all values of X)

$$I_{(X>\alpha)} \leqslant X/\alpha.$$

Taking expectations we obtain

$$P(X > \alpha) \leqslant E[X]/\alpha.$$

This is known as 'Markov's inequality'. It provides an upper bound for the probability that a non-negative random variable exceeds a given constant.

Suppose now that X is an arbitrary random variable (not necessarily non-negative). Let α be a positive constant and β be any constant. Then the indicator of the event $|X - \beta| > \alpha$ satisfies

$$I_{(|X-\beta|>\alpha)} \leqslant (X-\beta)^2/\alpha^2.$$

This yields an inequality for the expectations:

$$P(|X - \beta| > \alpha) \leqslant E[(X-\beta)^2]/\alpha^2$$
$$= \{E[X^2] - 2\beta E[X] + \beta^2\}/\alpha.$$

The right-hand side of the above inequality is minimised for $\beta = E[X]$; the expression in the curly brackets then becomes $E[X^2] - (E[X])^2$. The quantity

$$\mathrm{Var}[X] = E[(X-E[X])^2] = E[X^2] - (E[X])^2$$

is called the 'variance' of the random variable X. The variance can be regarded as a measure of the spread of X around its mean. The square root of the variance is also such a measure; it is called the 'standard deviation' of X.

Our inequality thus becomes

$$P(|X - E[X]| > \alpha) \leqslant \mathrm{Var}[X]/\alpha^2.$$

This is known as 'Chebichev's inequality'. It gives a bound for the probability that X deviates from its mean by more than a given amount, in terms of the variance of X. In particular, if $\mathrm{Var}[X] = 0$ then X is equal to its mean, with probability 1.

The definition of the variance involved the expectation of the square of the random variable, $E[X^2]$, which is referred to as its 'second moment'. In general, the expectation of the nth power of X,

$$M_n = E[X^n],$$

is called the 'nth moment' of X. If all the moments of a random variable are finite and known, they determine the distribution of that random variable completely.

If the random variables X and Y are independent, then from the definition of expectation it follows that

$$E[XY] = E[X]\,E[Y].$$

The reverse implication, however, is not true. Random variables that satisfy the above equation are said to be 'uncorrelated'. It is possible for two variables to be uncorrelated, yet dependent.

The quantity

$$Cov[X,Y] = E[(X - E[X])(Y - E[Y])]$$
$$= E[XY] - E[X]E[Y]$$

is called the 'covariance' of X and Y. If the latter are uncorrelated, then their covariance is zero.

The accepted measure of correlation between X and Y is their 'correlation coefficient', $r_{x,y}$, defined as

$$r_{x,y} = Cov[X, Y]/(Var[X] Var[Y])^{1/2}.$$

The correlation coefficient is always in the range

$$-1 \leqslant r_{x,y} \leqslant 1.$$

This follows from the fact that, for any two random variables U and V,

$$(E[UV])^2 \leqslant E[U^2] E[V^2]$$

(substitution of $U = X - E[X]$, $V = Y - E[Y]$ yields the desired result). The last inequality is known as the inequality of Cauchy–Bounyakovski–Schwarz. To derive it, note that

$$E[(U - \alpha V)^2] = E[U^2] - 2\alpha E[UV] + \alpha^2 E[V^2]$$

is non-negative for every α. Therefore the discriminant of the quadratic form in the right-hand side is less than or equal to zero, which establishes the inequality. Moreover, if the discriminant is zero, i.e. if $(E[UV])^2 = E[U^2] E[V]^2$, then there is an α such that $E[(U - \alpha V)^2] = 0$. This, in turn, implies that $U = \alpha V$ with probability 1.

Thus, if the correlation coefficient of two random variables is equal to 1 or to -1, then those random variables are linearly related, with probability 1.

The following properties of the variance and covariance are straightforward consequences of the definitions (X and Y are random variables and α and β are constants):

(i) $Var[\alpha X] = \alpha^2 Var[X]$;
(ii) $Cov[X, X] = Var[X]$;
(iii) $Cov[\alpha X, \beta Y] = \alpha\beta Cov[X, Y]$;
(iv) $Var[X + Y] = Var[X] + 2Cov[X, Y] + Var[Y]$;
(v) $Var[\alpha X + \beta Y] = \alpha^2 Var[X] + 2\alpha\beta Cov[X, Y] + \beta^2 Var[Y]$.

The last equality generalises to any finite linear combination: If $X_1, X_2, \ldots, X_n$ are random variables and $\alpha_1, \alpha_2, \ldots, \alpha_n$ are constants, then

$$Var\left[\sum_{i=1}^{n} \alpha_i X_i\right] = \sum_{i=1}^{n} \sum_{j=1}^{n} \alpha_i \alpha_j Cov[X_i, X_j].$$

The $n \times n$ matrix whose elements are $Cov[X_i X_j]$, $i, j = 1, 2, \ldots, n$, is the 'co-

157

variance matrix' of $X_1, X_2, \ldots, X_n$. If the covariance matrix is diagonal, i.e. if the random variables are pairwise uncorrelated, then

$$\text{Var}\left[\sum_{i=1}^{n} \alpha_i X_i\right] = \sum_{i=1}^{n} \alpha_i^2 \, \text{Var}[X_i].$$

In particular, if the random variables are pairwise independent, then the above equality certainly holds.

4.   **Bernoulli trials. The geometric and binomial distributions**

Suppose that a certain experiment has two possible outcomes, say 'success' and 'failure', and that these occur with probabilities q and $1 - q$ respectively. Consider a sequence of repeated performances of that experiment, all taking place under identical conditions and independently of each other (i.e. the ith outcome is independent of outcomes $1, 2, \ldots, i - 1$). This is said to be a sequence of 'Bernoulli trials'. Tosses of a coin or a die, or taking samples from a population with replacement are examples of Bernoulli trials.

A random variable of interest in connection with a sequence of Bernoulli trials is the number, K, of trials that are made until the occurrence of the first success. That random variable takes the value k with probability

$$p_k = P(K = k) = P(k - 1 \text{ failures followed by a success})$$
$$= (1 - q)^{k-1} q, \quad k = 1, 2, \ldots.$$

This is the 'geometric distribution'. The expectation of K is obtained as

$$E[K] = \sum_{k=1}^{\infty} k p_k = q \sum_{k=1}^{\infty} k(1-q)^{k-1} = 1/q.$$

As one would expect, the lower the probability of success, the longer one has to wait, on the average, until the first success. The variance of K is given by

$$\text{Var}[K] = (1 - q)/q^2.$$

From the nature of Bernoulli trials it is obvious that the following 'memoryless' property holds: if a success has not occurred after k trials, the probability that at least another j trials will be required, does not depend on k. This can also be seen from the distribution of K:

$$P(K \geqslant k + j \mid K > k) = P(K \geqslant k + j, K > k)/P(K > k)$$
$$= P(K \geqslant k + j)/P(K > k)$$
$$= q^{k+j-1}/q^k = q^{j-1} = P(K \geqslant j).$$

The geometric distribution is the only discrete distribution that has this property.

Another random variable of interest is the number, S, of successes that occur among the first n trials. The probability that a given set of s trials result in

158

successes and the other $n - s$ are failures is equal to $q^s(1-q)^{n-s}$. Summing this over all possible ways of selecting s out of n trials we obtain

$$P(S = s) = \binom{n}{s} q^s(1-q)^{n-s}, \quad s = 0, 1, \ldots, n.$$

This is known as the 'binomial distribution'. Note that the random variable S can be expressed as

$$S = \sum_{i=1}^{n} S_i$$

where S_i is the number of successes that occurred at the ith trial; that number is either 0 or 1. Moreover, the S_is are identically distributed and independent. Since $E[S_i] = P(S_i = 1) = q$, and $\text{Var}[S_i] = q - q^2 = q(1-q)$, we immediately obtain

$$E[S] = nq; \quad \text{Var}[S] = nq(1-q).$$

Of course, these quantities can also be derived directly from the binomial distribution.

There are three famous limiting results concerning the behaviour of the random variable S as n tends to infinity. The first of these is the 'strong law of large numbers'. It asserts that the ratio of the number of successes to the number of trials tends to the probability of success, with probability one:

$$P\left[\lim_{n \to \infty} \left(\frac{S}{n}\right) = q \right] = 1.$$

This law provides justification for the intuitive idea that the probability of an event is the fraction of outcomes in which the event occurs.

The second limiting result refers to the random variable $X_n = (S - nq)/[nq(1-q)]^{1/2}$. As $n \to \infty$, the distribution of X_n tends to the standard normal distribution. This is a special case of the central limit theorem (section 6). The third results applies in the case when $n \to \infty$ and $q \to 0$ in such a way that $nq \to \lambda$, for some positive λ. Then the distribution of S tends to the Poisson distribution with parameter λ (see section 5).

Closely related to the random variable S is the number, N, of trials required to achieve s successes. This can obviously be expressed as a sum of s identically distributed independent random variables

$$N = \sum_{i=1}^{s} K_i$$

where K_i is the number of trials between the $(i-1)$th and the ith success; that number has the geometric distribution with parameter q. Hence,

$$E[N] = s/q; \quad \text{Var}[N] = s(1-q)/q^2.$$

The distribution of N has the form

$$P(N = n) = \binom{n-1}{s-1} q^s(1-q)^{n-s}, \quad n = s, s+1, \ldots.$$

This is known as the 'negative binomial distribution'.

159

5.   The exponential distribution and the Poisson process

A random variable X is said to be distributed exponentially if its distribution function is of the form

$$F(x) = P(X \leqslant x) = \begin{cases} 1 - e^{-\lambda x}, & x \geqslant 0 \\ 0, & x < 0. \end{cases}$$

The corresponding probability density function is given by

$$f(x) = \lambda e^{-\lambda x}, \quad x \geqslant 0.$$

The mean and variance of the exponential distribution are

$$E[X] = 1/\lambda; \quad \text{Var}[X] = 1/\lambda^2.$$

Exponentially distributed random variables are widely used in modelling. Some of the reasons for this were discussed in chapter 4. Another important reason is the 'memoryless property' of the exponential distribution: if an exponentially distributed activity is known to have been in progress for time x, then the probability that it will continue for at least time y more, is independent of x. This is analogous to the memoryless property of the geometric distribution and is established in a similar way:

$$\begin{aligned} P(X > x + y \mid X > x) &= P(X > x + y)/P(X > x) \\ &= [1 - F(x + y)]/[1 - F(x)] \\ &= e^{-\lambda(x+y)}/e^{-\lambda x} = e^{-\lambda y} = P(X > y). \end{aligned}$$

The exponential distribution is the only continuous distribution that has this property.

If X and Y are two independent random variables distributed exponentially with parameters λ and μ respectively, then the random variable $V = \min(X, Y)$ is distributed exponentially with parameter $\lambda + \mu$. This follows immediately from

$$P(V > v) = P(X > v, Y > v) = e^{-\lambda v} e^{-\mu v} = e^{-(\lambda + \mu) v},$$

and generalises easily to more than two random variables. Thus, the time until the earliest completion among a number of independent, exponentially distributed activities proceeding in parallel, is distributed exponentially. Moreover, it does not matter when each of those activities started.

Consider an increasing sequence of random points on the positive real line, $a_1, a_2, \ldots, a_n, \ldots$, such that the intervals between consecutive points, $(a_{i+1} - a_i)$, are independent of each other and are all distributed exponentially with mean $1/\lambda$. Such a sequence is called a 'Poisson process', or 'Poisson stream'. To fix ideas, we shall think of the positive real line as the time axis; something takes place at each of the instants $a_1, a_2, \ldots$; say a new customer arrives into a system. Let N be the number of arrivals that take place during the interval $(0, 1)$. That random variable has the 'Poisson distribution':

$$P(N = n) = P(a_n \leqslant 1 < a_{n+1}) = (\lambda^n/n!) e^{-\lambda}, \quad n = 0, 1, \ldots.$$

160

From the memoryless property of the exponential distribution it follows that this is also the distribution of the number of arrivals during any interval of length 1. The mean and variance of N are easily seen to be

$$E[N] = \lambda; \quad \text{Var}[N] = \lambda.$$

As there are, on the average, λ arrivals per unit time, λ is called the 'rate' of the Poisson stream.

More generally, the number of arrivals during an arbitrary (but fixed) period of length t - denote that number by $N(t)$ - has the Poisson distribution with parameter λt:

$$P(N(t) = n) = [(\lambda t)^n/n!]\, e^{-\lambda t}, \quad n = 0, 1, \ldots.$$

Conversely, if this is true then the intervals between consecutive arrivals are distributed exponentially with parameter λ.

Suppose now that we have a time interval whose length, X, is a random variable with distribution function $F(x)$. Let N_X be the number of arrivals that occur during that random interval. The distribution of N_X is obtained by conditioning on the value of X:

$$P(N_X = n) = \int_0^\infty P(N_X = n \,|\, X = x)\, \mathrm{d}F(x)$$

$$= \int_0^\infty [(\lambda x)^n/n!]\, e^{-\lambda x}\, \mathrm{d}F(x), \quad n = 0, 1, \ldots.$$

From this distribution one can determine, without too much difficulty, the mean and variance of N_X in terms of the mean and variance of X:

$$E[N_X] = \lambda E[X]; \quad \text{Var}[N_X] = \lambda E[X] + \lambda^2 \,\text{Var}[X].$$

If N_1 and N_2 are two independent Poisson random variables with parameters λ_1 and λ_2 respectively, then their sum, $N = N_1 + N_2$, has the Poisson distribution with parameter $\lambda_1 + \lambda_2$:

$$P(N = n) = \sum_{i=0}^n P(N_1 = i)\, P(N_2 = n - i)$$

$$= \sum_{i=0}^n (\lambda_1^i/i!)\, e^{-\lambda_1}(\lambda_2^{n-i}/(n-i)!)\, e^{-\lambda_2}$$

$$= [(\lambda_1 + \lambda_2)^n/n!]\, e^{-(\lambda_1 + \lambda_2)}.$$

In particular, the total number of arrivals from a Poisson stream (rate λ) during two disjoint intervals of length t_1 and t_2 respectively, has the Poisson distribution with parameter $\lambda(t_1 + t_2)$. Also, the total number of arrivals from two independent Poisson streams with rates λ_1 and λ_2 respectively, during an interval of length t, has the Poisson distribution with parameter $(\lambda_1 + \lambda_2)\,t$. In other words, the result of merging two (or more) independent Poisson streams is a Poisson stream.

An operation which is in a sense inverse to merging is the splitting, or 'decomposition' of Poisson streams. At each arrival instant of a Poisson stream (rate λ), a Bernoulli trial is performed, with a probability of success q; if the trial is successful, the arrival is labelled 'type 1', otherwise it is labelled 'type 2'. Then the type 1 arrivals and the type 2 arrivals form two independent Poisson streams with rates λq and $\lambda(1-q)$ respectively. Indeed, let N, N_1 and N_2 be the number of original, type 1 and type 2 arrivals that take place during the interval $(0, 1)$, and let S_n be the number of successes among n Bernoulli trials. Then

$$P(N_1 = n_1, N_2 = n_2) = P(N = n_1 + n_2) \, P(S_{n_1+n_2} = n_1)$$
$$= [\lambda^{n_1 + n_2}/(n_1 + n_2)!] \, e^{-\lambda} \binom{n_1 + n_2}{n_1} q^{n_1}(1-q)^{n_2}$$
$$= [(\lambda q)^{n_1}/n_1!] \, e^{-\lambda q} \, [(\lambda(1-q))^{n_2}/n_2!] \, e^{-\lambda(1-q)},$$

which is the product of the respective probabilities in two Poisson streams. This result also generalises to splitting into more than two sub-streams. The merging and splitting of Poisson streams is illustrated in figure A2.1.

Poisson processes have another, rather remarkable property, which is very useful in modelling. If customers arrive in a Poisson stream into a system, then the system state distribution which they observe as they come in is the same as would be observed by someone who is entirely unconnected with the system. This is sometimes referred to as the 'random observer' property. Its importance lies in allowing one to obtain estimates for customer-oriented performance measures by collecting system-oriented statistics (and vice versa).

The time Y_n until the nth arrival in a Poisson stream, which is equal to the sum of n independent exponentially distributed random variables (the first n interarrival intervals) has the 'n-stage Erlang distribution'. The probability density function of Y_n is

$$f(x) = [\lambda(\lambda x)^{n-1}/(n-1)!] \, e^{-\lambda x}$$

and the mean and variance are

$$E[Y_n] = n/\lambda; \quad \text{Var}[Y_n] = n/\lambda^2.$$

Figure A2.1. Merging and splitting of Poisson streams.

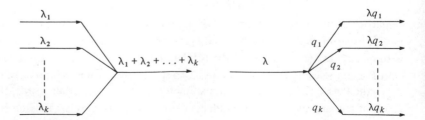

6. The normal distribution and related topics

A random variable X is said to have the 'standard normal distribution' if its probability density function is given by

$$f(x) = \frac{1}{(2\pi)^{1/2}} e^{-x^2/2}.$$

That random variable has mean 0 and variance 1. A linear transformation of X, with coefficients μ and σ,

$$Y = \mu + \sigma X$$

produces a random variable with mean μ and variance σ^2. The variable Y has the general normal distribution, denoted by $N(\mu, \sigma^2)$. Its probability density function is

$$g(x) = \frac{1}{\sigma(2\pi)^{1/2}} \exp\left[-\frac{1}{2}\left(\frac{x-\mu}{\sigma}\right)^2\right].$$

If the random variable Y has the normal distribution $N(\mu, \sigma^2)$ and α is a constant, then αY has the normal distribution $N(\alpha\mu, \alpha^2\sigma^2)$. If Y_1 and Y_2 are independent random variables with distributions $N(\mu_1, \sigma_1^2)$ and $N(\mu_2, \sigma_2^2)$ respectively, then $Y_1 + Y_2$ has the distribution $N(\mu_1 + \mu_2, \sigma_1^2 + \sigma_2^2)$. Hence arbitrary linear combinations of independent normally distributed random variables are normally distributed. Moreover, the only continuous distribution with this property is the normal one.

The great importance of the normal distribution stems from the fact that, under quite general assumptions, the sum of a large number of independent random variables is approximately normally distributed. The result that is the basis for this assertion is known as the 'central limit theorem'. We shall state it in less than its full generality.

Central limit theorem

Let $X_1, X_2, \ldots$ be independent and identically distributed random variables with finite mean and variance, $E[X]$ and $\mathrm{Var}[X]$, and let S_n be the partial sum $S_n = X_1 + X_2 + \ldots + X_n$. Then the distribution of the random variable

$$(S_n - nE[X])/(n\,\mathrm{Var}[X])^{1/2}$$

approaches the standard normal distribution, $N(0,1)$, as $n \to \infty$.

Thus, for large n, the distribution of S_n is approximately $N(nE[X], n\,\mathrm{Var}[X])$, regardless of the distribution of X_i. The condition that the random variables $X_1, X_2, \ldots$ should be independent and identically distributed can be relaxed considerably.

Certain distributions, derived from the normal, play a major role in the statistical analysis of data. Consider a sample of independent random variables, $Y_1, Y_2, \ldots, Y_n$, all having the normal distribution $N(\mu, \sigma^2)$. Clearly, the sample

163

mean, $\bar{Y} = (Y_1 + Y_2 + \ldots + Y_n)/n$, is distributed according to $N(\mu, \sigma^2/n)$. Let us examine the sample variance, s^2, given by

$$s^2 = \left[\sum_{i=1}^{n} (Y_i - \bar{Y})^2 \right] \bigg/ (n-1)$$

$$= \frac{\sigma^2}{n-1} \left[\sum_{i=1}^{n} \left(\frac{Y_i - \mu}{\sigma} \right)^2 - \left(\frac{\mu - \bar{Y}}{\sigma/n^{1/2}} \right)^2 \right]$$

The terms in the square brackets are all squares of standard normal random variables. These are not independent, since they satisfy the linear relationship

$$\sum_{i=1}^{n} \frac{Y_i - \mu}{\sigma} = n(\bar{Y} - \mu)/\sigma.$$

It can be shown, however, that the quantity in the square brackets has the same distribution as the random variable

$$\chi^2_{n-1} = \sum_{i=1}^{n-1} X_i^2,$$

where $X_1, X_2, \ldots, X_{n-1}$ are independent random variables, all having the standard normal distribution, $N(0, 1)$. The sample variance can therefore be expressed as

$$s^2 = [\sigma^2/(n-1)] \chi^2_{n-1}$$

The distribution of χ^2_n, called the 'chi-square distribution', depends on a single parameter, n, referred to as the 'degrees of freedom'. The probability density function of χ^2_n is

$$f_n(x) = [x^{(n/2)-1} e^{-x/2}]/[2^{n/2} \Gamma(n/2)],$$

where $\Gamma(n/2)$ is defined by $\Gamma(\frac{1}{2}) = \pi^{1/2}$, $\Gamma(1) = 1$ and, for all y, $\Gamma(y) = (y-1)\Gamma(y-1)$ (in the special case $n = 2$, the chi-square distribution is an exponential distribution with parameter $\frac{1}{2}$; when n is even, it is an $(n/2)$-stage Erlang distribution with parameters $\frac{1}{2}, n/2$). The mean and variance of χ^2_n are

$$E[\chi^2_n] = n; \quad \mathrm{Var}[\chi^2_n] = 2n.$$

From the central limit theorem it follows that the distribution of $(\chi^2_n - n)/(2n)^{1/2}$ approaches the standard normal one as $n \to \infty$.

If X and χ^2_n are two independent random variables having the standard normal and the chi-square (with n degrees of freedom) distributions respectively, then the random variable

$$t_n = X/(\chi^2_n/n)^{1/2}$$

is said to have 'Student's t distribution' with n degrees of freedom. Returning to the sample of independent random variables $Y_1, Y_2, \ldots, Y_n$ with distribution $N(\mu, \sigma^2)$, it can be shown that

$$(\bar{Y} - \mu)/(s/n^{1/2}) = [(\bar{Y} - \mu)/(\sigma/n^{1/2})](\sigma/s)$$
$$= [(\bar{Y} - \mu)/(\sigma/n^{1/2})]/[\chi_{n-1}^2/(n-1)]^{1/2}$$
$$= t_{n-1}$$

(the last equation presumes that $\bar{Y}$ and s^2 are independent, which, although not obvious, is in fact the case). One can thus use Student's t distribution to derive confidence intervals for the parameter μ (see chapter 5), or to test for equality of the means of two normal populations.

The probability density function of t_n is given by

$$g_n(x) = [1 + (x^2/n)]^{-(n+1)/2}\Gamma((n+1)/2)/[\Gamma(n/2)(n\pi)^{1/2}].$$

The mean and variance of t_n, for $n > 2$, are

$$E[t_n] = 0; \quad \mathrm{Var}[t_n] = n/(n-2)$$

(when $n = 1$, Student's distribution has no moments; when $n = 2$ it has a mean but no variance). When $n \to \infty$, the distribution of t_n approaches the standard normal distribution.

If χ_n^2 and χ_m^2 are two independent random variables with chi-square distributions (degrees of freedom n and m respectively), then the random variable

$$F_{n,m} = [\chi_n^2/n]/[\chi_m^2/m]$$

is said to have 'Fisher's distribution' (or simply the 'F distribution') with degrees of freedom n, m.

Fisher's distribution is used in statistical tests based on ratios of variances. If one is given two independent samples of n and m random variables from the distributions $N(\mu_1, \sigma_1^2)$ and $N(\mu_2, \sigma_2^2)$ respectively, and if the two sample variances are s_1^2 and s_2^2 respectively, then

$$[s_1^2/s_2^2]/[\sigma_1^2/\sigma_2^2] = F_{n-1, m-1}.$$

One can, therefore, test for the equality of σ_1^2 and σ_2^2.

The probability density function of $F_{n,m}$ has the form

$$f_{n,m}(x) = \Gamma\left(\frac{n+m}{2}\right)\left(\frac{n}{m}\right)^{n/2} x^{(n/2)-1}\left(1 + \frac{nx}{m}\right)^{-(n+m)/2} \Big/ \left[\Gamma\left(\frac{n}{2}\right)\Gamma\left(\frac{m}{2}\right)\right].$$

The mean and variance of $F_{n,m}$ are given by

$$E[F_{n,m}] = m/(m-2) \text{ for } m > 2,$$
$$\mathrm{Var}[F_{n,m}] = 2m^2(n+m-2)/[n(m-2)^2(m-4)] \text{ for } m > 4$$

(there is no mean for $m \leqslant 2$ and no variance for $m \leqslant 4$).

When $n \to \infty$ and $m \to \infty$, $F_{n,m}$ tends (in distribution) to the constant 1.

7. Simple queueing systems

The derivations of the results presented here can be found, for example, in Gelenbe & Mitrani [17].

Consider a system where customers arrive according to a Poisson stream with rate λ and are served, in order of arrival, by a single server. The distribution of service times is exponential, with mean $1/\mu$ (thus the rate of service, when the server is busy, is μ customers per unit time). There is no limit to the number of customers that may be queueing. The interarrival and service times are mutually independent.

We are interested in the long-run, or steady-state, behaviour of this system. Let N be the number of customers present (if $N > 0$ then one of them is in service and the rest are waiting). When a steady-state exists, the distribution of N is geometric:

$$P(N = n) = \rho^n(1 - \rho), \quad n = 0, 1, \ldots,$$

where $\rho = \lambda/\mu$ (this last quantity, referred to as the 'traffic intensity', represents the average amount of work brought into the system per unit time). The condition of the existence of a steady-state is $\rho < 1$. The mean and variance of N are obtained as

$$E[N] = \rho/(1 - \rho); \quad \mathrm{Var}[N] = \rho/(1 - \rho)^2.$$

Another random variable of interest in this system is the time, W, that customers spend in it (waiting and being served). That time is distributed exponentially, with parameter $\mu - \lambda$. Hence,

$$E[W] = 1/(\mu - \lambda); \quad \mathrm{Var}[W] = 1/(\mu - \lambda)^2.$$

The utilisation of the server is equal to

$$U = P(N > 0) = \rho.$$

This last result holds for general interarrival and service times (as long as their means are $1/\lambda$ and $1/\mu$ respectively).

Let us generalise the model by allowing the service times to have an arbitrary distribution with finite mean, $1/\mu$, and variance, V. Denote by C^2 the coefficient of variation of the service time distribution: $C^2 = \mu^2 V$. The arrival stream is still Poisson with rate λ.

The average number of customers in the system is now given by

$$E[N] = \rho + \frac{\rho^2(1 + C^2)}{2(1 - \rho)}.$$

This is known as 'Pollaczek–Khintchine's formula'. The average time that customers spend in the system is, as before,

$$E[W] = E[N]/\lambda.$$

The condition for the existence of a steady-state is again $\rho < 1$.

Suppose that there are different types of customers, numbered $1, 2, \ldots, R$, and that type i customers have non-preemptive priority over type j customers if $i < j$ (such a model is simulated in chapter 3). Type i customers arrive in a Poisson stream with rate λ_i and have generally distributed service times with finite mean, $1/\mu_i$, and second moment, m_{2i}. Denote by $\rho_i = \lambda_i/\mu_i$ the traffic intensity for type i, by N_i the number of type i customers in the system and by W_i the time that type i customers spend in the system. We have the following expressions:

$$E[N_i] = \rho_i + \lambda_i w_0 \Big/ \left[\left(1 - \sum_{j=1}^{i-1} \rho_j\right) \left(1 - \sum_{j=1}^{i} \rho_j\right) \right], \quad i = 1, 2, \ldots, R,$$

where

$$w_0 = \frac{1}{2} \sum_{j=1}^{R} \lambda_j m_{2j}.$$

The expected times spent in the system are

$$E[W_i] = E[N_i]/\lambda_i, \quad i = 1, 2, \ldots, R.$$

A steady-state exists if $\rho_1 + \rho_2 + \ldots + \rho_R < 1$. Note, however, that this system may be saturated with respect to some customer types (i.e. infinite queues and waiting times for those types) and in equilibrium with respect to others. Of course, if it is saturated with respect to type j, i.e. if $\rho_1 + \rho_2 + \ldots + \rho_j \geq 1$, then it will be saturated with respect to all types $j + 1, j + 2, \ldots, R$.

Finally, consider a queueing network with M modes (see the example in chapter 3). Customers come into node j from outside in a Poisson stream with rate γ_j; there is a single server at node j, whose service times are distributed exponentially with mean $1/\mu_j$ ($j = 1, 2, \ldots, M$). On completing service at node j, customers go to node k with probability q_{jk} ($j, k = 1, 2, \ldots, M$); they leave the network with probability $1 - (q_{j1} + q_{j2} + \ldots + q_{jM})$.

Let λ_j be the total average number of customers arriving into node j per unit time (from outside and from other nodes). If the network is in a steady-state, λ_j is also the total average number of customers leaving node j per unit time. These rates of traffic satisfy the following system of 'flow balance equations':

$$\lambda_j = \gamma_j + \sum_{k=1}^{M} \lambda_k q_{kj}, \quad j = 1, 2, \ldots.$$

One can, in general, determine the λ_js from the flow balance equations, provided that $\gamma_j \neq 0$ for at least one j. The traffic intensity at node j is $\rho_j = \lambda_j/\mu_j$ ($j = 1, 2, \ldots, M$). The joint distribution of the numbers of customers at the various nodes, $N_1, N_2, \ldots, N_M$, is then given by

$$P(N_1 = n_1, N_2 = n_2, \ldots, N_M = n_M) = \prod_{j=1}^{M} [\rho_j^{n_j}(1 - \rho_j)].$$

This result is known as 'Jackson's theorem'. It implies that each node behaves as if it was an independent single-server queueing system with Poisson arrival stream and exponentially distributed service times. It is a rather surprising result because the total stream of arrivals into a node is not, in general, Poisson.

The total average number of customers in the network is equal to

$$E[N_1 + N_2 + \ldots + N_M] = \sum_{j=1}^{M} \rho_j/(1-\rho_j).$$

The total average time, $E[W]$, that customers spend in the network is obtained from

$$E[W] = (E[N_1 + N_2 + \ldots + N_M])/(\gamma_1 + \gamma_2 + \ldots + \gamma_M).$$

Note that in any queueing system in a steady-state, we have the relation

$$E[\text{number in system}] = (\text{arrival rate}) E[\text{time in system}].$$

This is 'Little's result', which is discussed in chapter 5.

TABLES

The Kolmogorov-Smirnov table is adapted from D. Knuth, *The Art of Computer Programming*, Vol. 2, 2nd edn., Addison-Wesley (Reading, Mass.), 1981. All other tables are adapted from the *Biometrika Tables for Statisticians* (eds. E. S. Pearson & H. O. Hartley), Cambridge University Press, 1954.

Percentiles of the standard normal distribution

For a given probability, β, the table gives a value x such that
$P[N(0, 1) \leqslant x] = \beta$.

β	x
0.50	0
0.55	0.126
0.60	0.253
0.65	0.385
0.70	0.524
0.75	0.674
0.80	0.842
0.85	1.036
0.90	1.282
0.95	1.645
0.96	1.751
0.97	1.881
0.98	2.054
0.99	2.326
0.995	2.576
0.999	3.090

For a given probability, β, and degree of freedom, n, the table gives a value x such that

$$P(t_n \leqslant x) = \beta.$$

β / n	0.9	0.95	0.975	0.99	0.995	0.9975	0.999
1	3.078	6.314	12.706	31.821	63.657	127.32	318.31
2	1.886	2.920	4.303	6.965	9.925	14.089	22.326
3	1.638	2.353	3.182	4.541	5.941	7.453	10.213
4	1.533	2.132	2.776	3.747	4.604	5.598	7.173
5	1.476	2.015	2.571	3.365	4.032	4.773	5.893
6	1.440	1.943	2.447	3.143	3.707	4.317	5.208
7	1.415	1.895	2.365	2.998	3.499	4.029	4.785
8	1.397	1.860	2.306	2.896	3.355	3.833	4.501
9	1.383	1.833	2.262	2.821	3.250	3.690	4.297
10	1.372	1.812	2.228	2.764	3.169	3.581	4.144
11	1.363	1.796	2.201	2.718	3.106	3.497	4.025
12	1.356	1.782	2.179	2.681	3.055	3.428	3.930
13	1.350	1.771	2.160	2.650	3.012	3.372	3.852
14	1.345	1.761	2.145	2.624	2.977	3.326	3.787
15	1.341	1.753	2.131	2.602	2.947	3.286	3.733
16	1.337	1.746	2.120	2.583	2.921	3.252	3.686
17	1.333	1.740	2.110	2.567	2.898	3.222	3.646
18	1.330	1.734	2.101	2.552	2.878	3.197	3.610
19	1.328	1.729	2.093	2.539	2.861	3.174	3.579
20	1.325	1.725	2.086	2.528	2.845	3.153	3.552
21	1.323	1.721	2.080	2.518	2.831	3.135	3.527
22	1.321	1.717	2.074	2.508	2.819	3.119	3.505
23	1.319	1.714	2.069	2.500	2.807	3.104	3.485
24	1.318	1.711	2.064	2.492	2.797	3.091	3.467
25	1.316	1.708	2.060	2.485	2.787	3.078	3.450
26	1.315	1.706	2.056	2.479	2.779	3.067	3.435
27	1.314	1.703	2.052	2.473	2.771	3.057	3.421
28	1.313	1.701	2.048	2.467	2.763	3.047	3.408
29	1.311	1.699	2.045	2.462	2.756	3.038	3.396
30	1.310	1.697	2.042	2.457	2.750	3.030	3.385
40	1.303	1.684	2.021	2.423	2.704	2.971	3.307
60	1.296	1.671	2.000	2.390	2.660	2.915	3.232
120	1.289	1.658	1.980	2.358	2.617	2.860	3.160
∞	1.282	1.645	1.960	2.326	2.576	2.807	3.090

Percentiles of the χ^2 distribution

For a given probability, β, and degree of freedom, n, the table gives a value x such that

$$P(\chi_n^2 \leqslant x) = \beta.$$

n \ β	0.01	0.025	0.05	0.1	0.9	0.95	0.975	0.99
1	0.00	0.00	0.00	0.02	2.71	3.84	5.02	6.63
2	0.02	0.05	0.10	0.21	4.61	5.99	7.38	9.21
3	0.11	0.22	0.35	0.58	6.25	7.81	9.35	11.34
4	0.30	0.48	0.71	1.06	7.78	9.49	11.14	13.28
5	0.55	0.83	1.15	1.61	9.24	11.07	12.83	15.09
6	0.87	1.24	1.64	2.20	10.64	12.59	14.45	16.81
7	1.24	1.69	2.17	2.83	12.02	14.07	16.01	18.48
8	1.65	2.18	2.73	3.49	13.36	15.51	17.53	20.09
9	2.09	2.70	3.33	4.17	14.68	16.92	19.02	21.67
10	2.56	3.25	3.94	4.87	15.99	18.31	20.48	23.21
15	5.23	6.26	7.26	8.55	22.31	25.00	27.49	30.58
20	8.26	9.59	10.85	12.44	28.41	31.41	34.17	37.57
25	11.52	13.12	14.61	16.47	34.38	37.65	40.65	44.31
30	14.95	16.79	18.49	20.60	40.26	43.77	46.98	50.89
40	22.16	24.43	26.51	29.05	51.81	55.76	59.34	63.69
50	29.71	32.36	34.76	37.69	63.17	67.50	71.42	76.15
60	37.48	40.48	43.19	46.46	74.40	79.08	83.30	88.38
70	45.44	48.76	51.74	55.33	84.53	90.53	95.02	100.43
80	53.54	57.15	60.39	64.28	96.58	101.88	106.63	112.33
90	61.75	65.65	69.13	73.29	107.57	113.15	118.14	124.12
100	70.06	74.22	77.93	82.35	118.50	124.34	129.56	135.81
X	-2.33	-1.96	-1.64	-1.28	1.28	1.64	1.96	2.32

For $n > 100$, take

$$x = \tfrac{1}{2}[X + (2n - 1)^{1/2}]^2,$$

where X is given in the bottom line of the table.

90% percentiles of the F distribution

For a given n_1 and n_2, the table gives a value x such that
$$P(F_{n_1,n_2} \leqslant x) = 0.9.$$

Degree of freedom of the numerator

n_1 / n_2	1	2	3	4	5	6
1	39.86	49.50	53.59	55.83	57.24	58.2(
2	8.53	9.00	9.16	9.24	9.29	9.3:
3	5.54	5.46	5.39	5.34	5.31	5.2{
4	4.54	4.32	4.19	4.11	4.05	4.0:
5	4.06	3.78	3.62	3.52	3.45	3.4(
6	3.78	3.46	3.29	3.18	3.11	3.0:
7	3.59	3.26	3.07	2.96	2.88	2.8:
8	3.46	3.11	2.92	2.81	2.73	2.6:
9	3.36	3.01	2.81	2.69	2.61	2.5:
10	3.29	2.92	2.73	2.61	2.52	2.4(
11	3.23	2.86	2.66	2.54	2.45	2.3:
12	3.18	2.81	2.61	2.48	2.39	2.3:
13	3.14	2.76	2.56	2.43	2.35	2.2{
14	3.10	2.73	2.52	2.39	2.31	2.2‹
15	3.07	2.70	2.49	2.36	2.27	2.2:
16	3.05	2.67	2.46	2.33	2.24	2.1{
17	3.03	2.64	2.44	2.31	2.22	2.1:
18	3.01	2.62	2.42	2.29	2.20	2.1:
19	2.99	2.61	2.40	2.27	2.18	2.1]
20	2.97	2.59	2.38	2.25	2.16	2.0:
21	2.96	2.57	2.36	2.23	2.14	2.0{
22	2.95	2.56	2.35	2.22	2.13	2.0(
23	2.94	2.55	2.34	2.21	2.11	2.0:
24	2.93	2.54	2.33	2.19	2.10	2.0‹
25	2.92	2.53	2.32	2.18	2.09	2.0:
26	2.91	2.52	2.31	2.17	2.08	2.0]
27	2.90	2.51	2.30	2.17	2.07	2.0(
28	2.89	2.50	2.29	2.16	2.06	2.0(
29	2.89	2.50	2.28	2.15	2.06	1.9:
30	2.88	2.49	2.28	2.14	2.05	1.9{
40	2.84	2.44	2.23	2.09	2.00	1.9:
60	2.79	2.39	2.18	2.04	1.95	1.8:
120	2.75	2.35	2.13	1.99	1.90	1.8:
∞	2.71	2.30	2.08	1.94	1.85	1.7:

Degree of freedom of the denominator

7	8	9	10	15	20	30
58.91	59.44	59.86	60.19	61.22	61.74	62.26
9.35	9.37	9.38	9.39	9.42	9.44	9.46
5.27	5.25	5.24	5.23	5.20	5.18	5.17
3.98	3.95	3.94	3.92	3.87	3.84	3.82
3.37	3.34	3.32	3.30	3.24	3.21	3.17
3.01	2.98	2.96	2.94	2.87	2.84	2.80
2.78	2.75	2.72	2.70	2.63	2.59	2.56
2.62	2.59	2.56	2.54	2.46	2.42	2.38
2.51	2.47	2.44	2.42	2.34	2.30	2.25
2.41	2.38	2.35	2.32	2.24	2.20	2.16
2.34	2.30	2.27	2.25	2.17	2.12	2.08
2.28	2.24	2.21	2.19	2.10	2.06	2.01
2.23	2.20	2.16	2.14	2.05	2.01	1.96
2.19	2.15	2.12	2.10	2.01	1.96	1.91
2.16	2.12	2.09	2.06	1.97	1.92	1.87
2.13	2.09	2.06	2.03	1.94	1.89	1.84
2.10	2.06	2.03	2.00	1.91	1.86	1.81
2.08	2.04	2.00	1.98	1.89	1.84	1.78
2.06	2.02	1.98	1.96	1.86	1.81	1.76
2.04	2.00	1.96	1.94	1.84	1.79	1.74
2.02	1.98	1.95	1.92	1.83	1.78	1.72
2.01	1.97	1.93	1.90	1.81	1.76	1.70
1.99	1.95	1.92	1.89	1.80	1.74	1.69
1.98	1.94	1.91	1.88	1.78	1.73	1.67
1.97	1.93	1.89	1.87	1.77	1.72	1.66
1.96	1.92	1.88	1.86	1.76	1.71	1.65
1.95	1.91	1.87	1.85	1.75	1.70	1.64
1.94	1.90	1.87	1.84	1.74	1.69	1.63
1.93	1.89	1.86	1.83	1.73	1.68	1.62
1.93	1.88	1.85	1.82	1.72	1.67	1.61
1.87	1.83	1.79	1.76	1.66	1.61	1.54
1.82	1.77	1.74	1.71	1.60	1.54	1.48
1.77	1.72	1.68	1.65	1.55	1.48	1.41
1.72	1.67	1.63	1.60	1.49	1.42	1.34

For a given n_1 and n_2, the table gives a value x such that
$$P(F_{n_1, n_2} \leqslant x) = 0.95.$$

Degree of freedom of the numerator

n_1 n_2	1	2	3	4	5	6
1	161.4	199.5	215.7	224.6	230.2	234.0
2	18.51	19.00	19.16	19.25	19.30	19.33
3	10.13	9.55	9.28	9.12	9.01	8.94
4	7.71	6.94	6.59	6.39	6.26	6.16
5	6.61	5.79	5.41	5.19	5.05	4.95
6	5.99	5.14	4.76	4.53	4.39	4.28
7	5.59	4.74	4.35	4.12	3.97	3.87
8	5.32	4.46	4.07	3.84	3.69	3.58
9	5.12	4.26	3.86	3.63	3.48	3.37
10	4.96	4.10	3.71	3.48	3.33	3.22
11	4.84	3.98	3.59	3.36	3.20	3.09
12	4.75	3.89	3.49	3.26	3.11	3.00
13	4.67	3.81	3.41	3.18	3.03	2.92
14	4.60	3.74	3.34	3.11	2.96	2.85
15	4.54	3.68	3.29	3.06	2.90	2.79
16	4.49	3.63	3.24	3.01	2.85	2.75
17	4.45	3.59	3.20	2.96	2.81	2.70
18	4.41	3.55	3.16	2.93	2.77	2.66
19	4.38	3.52	3.13	2.90	2.74	2.63
20	4.35	3.49	3.10	2.87	2.71	2.60
21	4.32	3.47	3.07	2.84	2.68	2.57
22	4.30	3.44	3.05	2.82	2.66	2.55
23	4.28	3.42	3.03	2.80	2.64	2.53
24	4.26	3.40	3.01	2.78	2.62	2.51
25	4.24	3.39	2.99	2.76	2.60	2.49
26	4.23	3.37	2.98	2.74	2.59	2.47
27	4.21	3.35	2.96	2.73	2.57	2.46
28	4.20	3.34	2.95	2.71	2.56	2.45
29	4.18	3.33	2.93	2.70	2.55	2.43
30	4.17	3.32	2.92	2.69	2.53	2.42
40	4.08	3.23	2.84	2.61	2.45	2.34
60	4.00	3.15	2.76	2.53	2.37	2.25
120	3.92	3.07	2.68	2.45	2.29	2.17
∞	3.84	3.00	2.60	2.37	2.21	2.10

Degree of freedom of the denominator

7	8	9	10	15	20	30
236.8	238.9	240.5	241.9	245.9	248.0	250.1
19.35	19.37	19.38	19.40	19.43	19.45	19.46
8.89	8.85	8.81	8.79	8.70	8.66	8.62
6.09	6.04	6.00	5.96	5.86	5.80	5.75
4.88	4.82	4.77	4.74	4.62	4.56	4.50
4.21	4.15	4.10	4.06	3.94	3.87	3.81
3.79	3.73	3.68	3.64	3.51	3.44	3.38
3.50	3.44	3.39	3.35	3.22	3.15	3.08
3.29	3.23	3.23	3.14	3.01	2.94	2.86
3.14	3.07	3.02	2.98	2.85	2.77	2.70
3.01	2.95	2.90	2.85	2.72	2.65	2.57
2.91	2.85	2.80	2.75	2.62	2.54	2.47
2.83	2.77	2.71	2.67	2.53	2.46	2.38
2.76	2.70	2.65	2.60	2.46	2.39	2.31
2.71	2.64	2.59	2.54	2.40	2.33	2.25
2.66	2.59	2.54	2.49	2.35	2.28	2.19
2.61	2.55	2.49	2.45	2.31	2.23	2.15
2.58	2.51	2.46	2.41	2.27	2.19	2.11
2.54	2.48	2.42	2.38	2.23	2.16	2.07
2.51	2.45	2.39	2.35	2.20	2.12	2.04
2.49	2.42	2.37	2.32	2.18	2.10	2.01
2.46	2.40	2.34	2.30	2.15	2.07	1.98
2.44	2.37	2.32	2.27	2.13	2.05	1.96
2.42	2.36	2.30	2.25	2.11	2.03	1.94
2.40	2.34	2.28	2.24	2.09	2.01	1.92
2.39	2.32	2.27	2.22	2.07	1.99	1.90
2.37	2.31	2.25	2.20	2.06	1.97	1.88
2.36	2.29	2.24	2.19	2.04	1.96	1.87
2.35	2.28	2.22	2.18	2.03	1.94	1.85
2.33	2.27	2.21	2.16	2.01	1.93	1.84
2.25	2.18	2.12	2.08	1.92	1.84	1.74
2.17	2.10	2.04	1.99	1.84	1.75	1.65
2.09	2.02	1.96	1.91	1.75	1.66	1.55
2.01	1.94	1.88	1.83	1.67	1.57	1.46

97.5% percentiles of the F distribution

For a given n_1 and n_2, the table gives a value x such that
$$P(F_{n_1,n_2} \leqslant x) = 0.975.$$

Degree of freedom of the numerator

n_2 \ n_1	1	2	3	4	5	6
1	647.8	799.5	864.2	899.6	921.8	937.1
2	38.51	39.00	39.17	39.25	39.30	39.33
3	17.44	16.04	15.44	15.10	14.88	14.73
4	12.22	10.65	9.98	9.60	9.36	9.20
5	10.01	8.43	7.76	7.39	7.15	6.98
6	8.81	7.26	6.60	6.23	5.99	5.82
7	8.07	6.54	5.89	5.52	5.29	5.12
8	7.57	6.06	5.42	5.05	4.82	4.65
9	7.21	5.71	5.08	4.72	4.48	4.32
10	6.94	5.46	4.83	4.47	4.24	4.07
11	6.72	5.26	4.63	4.28	4.04	3.88
12	6.55	5.10	4.47	4.12	3.89	3.73
13	6.41	4.97	4.35	4.00	3.77	3.60
14	6.30	4.86	4.24	3.89	3.66	3.50
15	6.20	4.77	4.15	3.80	3.58	3.41
16	6.12	4.69	4.08	3.73	3.50	3.34
17	6.04	4.62	4.01	3.66	3.44	3.28
18	5.98	4.56	3.95	3.61	3.38	3.22
19	5.92	4.51	3.90	3.56	3.33	3.17
20	5.87	4.46	3.86	3.51	3.29	3.13
21	5.83	4.42	3.82	3.48	3.25	3.09
22	5.79	4.38	3.78	3.44	3.22	3.05
23	5.75	4.35	3.75	3.41	3.18	3.02
24	5.72	4.32	3.72	3.38	3.15	2.99
25	5.69	4.29	3.69	3.35	3.13	2.97
26	5.66	4.27	3.67	3.33	3.10	2.94
27	5.63	4.24	3.65	3.31	3.08	2.92
28	5.61	4.22	3.63	3.29	3.06	2.90
29	5.59	4.20	3.61	3.27	3.04	2.88
30	5.57	4.18	3.59	3.25	3.03	2.87
40	5.42	4.05	3.46	3.13	2.90	2.74
60	5.29	3.93	3.34	3.01	2.79	2.63
120	5.15	3.80	3.23	2.89	2.67	2.52
∞	5.02	3.69	3.12	2.79	2.57	2.41

Degree of freedom of the denominator

7	8	9	10	15	20	30
948.2	956.7	963.3	968.6	984.9	993.1	1001
39.36	39.37	39.39	39.40	39.43	39.45	39.46
14.62	14.54	14.47	14.42	14.25	14.17	14.08
9.07	8.98	8.90	8.84	8.66	8.56	8.46
6.85	6.76	6.68	6.62	6.43	6.33	6.23
5.70	5.60	5.52	5.46	5.27	5.17	5.07
4.99	4.90	4.82	4.76	4.57	4.47	4.36
4.53	4.43	4.36	4.30	4.10	4.00	3.89
4.20	4.10	4.03	3.96	3.77	3.67	3.56
3.95	3.85	3.78	3.72	3.52	3.42	3.31
3.76	3.66	3.59	3.53	3.33	3.23	3.12
3.61	3.51	3.44	3.37	3.18	3.07	2.96
3.48	3.39	3.31	3.25	3.05	2.95	2.84
3.38	3.29	3.21	3.15	2.95	2.84	2.73
3.29	3.20	3.12	3.06	2.86	2.76	2.64
3.22	3.12	3.05	2.99	2.79	2.68	2.57
3.16	3.06	2.98	2.92	2.72	2.62	2.50
3.10	3.01	2.93	2.87	2.67	2.56	2.44
3.05	2.96	2.88	2.82	2.62	2.51	2.39
3.01	2.91	2.84	2.77	2.57	2.46	2.35
2.97	2.87	2.80	2.73	2.53	2.42	2.31
2.93	2.84	2.76	2.70	2.50	2.39	2.27
2.90	2.81	2.73	2.67	2.47	2.36	2.24
2.87	2.78	2.70	2.64	2.44	2.33	2.21
2.85	2.75	2.68	2.61	2.41	2.30	2.18
2.82	2.73	2.65	2.59	2.39	2.28	2.16
2.80	2.71	2.63	2.57	2.36	2.25	2.13
2.78	2.69	2.61	2.55	2.34	2.23	2.11
2.76	2.67	2.59	2.53	2.32	2.21	2.09
2.75	2.65	2.57	2.51	2.31	2.20	2.07
2.62	2.53	2.45	2.39	2.18	2.07	1.94
2.51	2.41	2.33	2.27	2.06	1.94	1.82
2.39	2.30	2.22	2.16	1.94	1.82	1.69
2.29	2.19	2.11	2.05	1.83	1.71	1.57

For a given n_1 and n_2, the table gives a value x such that
$$P(F_{n_1, n_2} \leqslant x) = 0.99.$$

Degree of freedom of the numerator

n_2 \ n_1	1	2	3	4	5	6
1	4052	4999.5	5403	5625	5764	5859
2	98.50	99.00	99.17	99.25	99.30	99.33
3	34.12	30.82	29.46	28.71	28.24	27.91
4	21.20	18.00	16.69	15.98	15.52	15.21
5	16.26	13.27	12.06	11.39	10.97	10.67
6	13.75	10.92	9.78	9.15	8.75	8.47
7	12.25	9.55	8.45	7.85	7.46	7.19
8	11.26	8.65	7.59	7.01	6.63	6.37
9	10.56	8.02	6.99	6.42	6.06	5.80
10	10.04	7.56	6.55	5.99	5.64	5.39
11	9.65	7.21	6.22	5.67	5.32	5.07
12	9.33	6.93	5.95	5.41	5.06	4.82
13	9.07	6.70	5.74	5.21	4.86	4.62
14	8.86	6.51	5.56	5.04	4.69	4.46
15	8.68	6.36	5.42	4.89	4.56	4.32
16	8.53	6.23	5.29	4.77	4.44	4.20
17	8.40	6.11	5.18	4.67	4.34	4.10
18	8.29	6.01	5.09	4.58	4.25	4.01
19	8.18	5.93	5.01	4.50	4.17	3.94
20	8.10	5.85	4.94	4.43	4.10	3.87
21	8.02	5.78	4.87	4.37	4.04	3.81
22	7.95	5.72	4.82	4.31	3.99	3.76
23	7.88	5.66	4.76	4.26	3.94	3.71
24	7.82	5.61	4.72	4.22	3.90	3.67
25	7.77	5.57	4.68	4.18	3.85	3.63
26	7.73	5.53	4.64	4.14	3.82	3.59
27	7.68	5.49	4.60	4.11	3.78	3.56
28	7.64	5.45	4.57	4.07	3.75	3.53
29	7.60	5.42	4.54	4.04	3.73	3.50
30	7.56	5.39	4.51	4.02	3.70	3.47
40	7.31	5.18	4.31	3.83	3.51	3.29
60	7.08	4.98	4.13	3.65	3.34	3.12
120	6.85	4.79	3.95	3.48	3.17	2.96
∞	6.63	4.61	3.78	3.32	3.02	2.80

Degree of freedom of the denominator

7	8	9	10	15	20	30
5928	5982	6022	6056	6157	6209	6261
99.36	99.37	99.39	99.40	99.43	99.45	99.47
27.67	27.49	27.35	27.23	26.87	26.69	26.50
14.98	14.80	14.66	14.55	14.20	14.02	13.84
10.46	10.29	10.16	10.05	9.72	9.55	9.38
8.26	8.10	7.98	7.87	7.56	7.40	7.23
6.99	6.84	6.72	6.62	6.31	6.16	5.99
6.18	6.03	5.91	5.81	5.52	5.36	5.20
5.61	5.47	5.35	5.26	4.96	4.81	4.65
5.20	5.06	4.94	4.85	4.56	4.41	4.25
4.89	4.74	4.63	4.54	4.25	4.10	3.94
4.64	4.50	4.39	4.30	4.01	3.86	3.70
4.44	4.30	4.19	4.10	3.82	3.66	3.51
4.28	4.14	4.03	3.94	3.66	3.51	3.35
4.14	4.00	3.89	3.80	3.52	3.37	3,21
4.03	3.89	3.78	3.69	3.41	3.26	3.10
3.93	3.79	3.68	3.59	3.31	3.16	3.00
3.84	3.71	3.60	3.51	3.23	3.08	2.92
3.77	3.63	3.52	3.43	3.15	3.00	2.84
3.70	3.56	3.46	3.37	3.09	2.94	2.78
3.64	3.51	3.40	3.31	3.03	2.88	2.72
3.59	3.45	3.35	3.26	2.98	2.83	2.67
3.54	3.41	3.30	3.21	2.93	2.78	2.62
3.50	3.36	3.26	3.17	2.89	2.74	2.58
3.46	3.32	3.22	3.13	2.85	2.70	2.54
3.42	3.29	3.18	3.09	2.81	2.66	2.50
3.39	3.26	3.15	3.06	2.78	2.63	2.47
3.36	3.23	3.12	3.03	2.75	2.60	2.44
3.33	3.20	3.09	3.00	2.73	2.57	2.41
3.30	3.17	3.07	2.98	2.70	2.55	2.39
3.12	2.99	2.89	2.80	2.52	2.37	2.20
2.95	2.82	2.72	2.63	2.35	2.20	2.03
2.79	2.66	2.56	2.47	2.19	2.03	1.86
2.64	2.51	2.41	2.32	2.04	1.88	1.70

For a given probability, β, and sample size, n, the table gives a value x such that

$$P(K_n^+ \leqslant x) = \beta.$$

K_n^- has the same distribution as K_n^+, so the same table applies. The statistics K_n^+ and K_n^- are computed according to (4.24).

n \ β	0.01	0.05	0.95	0.99
1	0.01	0.05	0.95	0.99
2	0.01	0.07	1.10	1.27
3	0.02	0.08	1.13	1.36
4	0.02	0.09	1.14	1.38
5	0.02	0.10	1.15	1.40
6	0.02	0.10	1.15	1.41
7	0.03	0.10	1.16	1.42
8	0.03	0.11	1.16	1.43
9	0.03	0.11	1.16	1.44
10	0.03	0.11	1.17	1.44
15	0.03	0.12	1.18	1.46
20	0.04	0.13	1.18	1.47
30	0.04	0.14	1.19	1.48
X	0.07	0.16	1.22	1.52

For $n > 30$, take $x = X - [1/(6\sqrt{n})]$, where X is given in the bottom row of the table. For arbitrary β and $n > 30$, take

$$x = [-\tfrac{1}{2}\ln(1-\beta)]^{1/2} - [1/(6n^{1/2})].$$

REFERENCES

[1] Aho, A. V., Hopcroft, J. E. & Ullman, J. D. *The Design and Analysis of Computer Algorithms*, Addison-Wesley, Reading, Mass., 1974.

[2] Birtwistle, G. M. *DEMOS: A System for Discrete Event Modelling on SIMULA*, Macmillan, 1979.

[3] Birtwistle, G. M., Dahl, O. J., Myhrhaug, B. & Nygaard, K. *SIMULA BEGIN*, Auerbach, Philadelphia, Pa., 1973.

[4] Buxton, J. N. 'Writing Simulations in CSL', *Computer Journal*, **9**, 2, pp. 137–43, 1966.

[5] Cochran, W. & Cox, G. *Experimental Designs*, 2nd edn., Wiley, New York, 1957.

[6] Cox, D. R. 'A Use of Complex Probabilities in the Theory of Stochastic Processes', *Proc., Cambridge Phil. Soc.*, **51**, pp. 313–19, 1955.

[7] Crane, M. A. & Iglehart, D. L. 'Simulating Stable Stochastic Systems, III: Regenerative Processes and Discrete Event Simulations', *Opns. Res.*, **23**, 1, pp. 33–45, 1975.

[8] Dahl, O. J., Myhrhaug, B. & Nygaard, K. 'SIMULA 67 Common Base Language', *NCC pub.* S-22, Oslo, 1971.

[9] Dahl, O. J. & Nygaard, K. 'SIMULA – An ALGOL-Based Simulation Language', *CACM*, **9**, 9, pp. 671–8, 1966.

[10] Engelbrecht-Wiggans, R. & Maxwell, W. 'Analysis of the Time Indexed List Procedure for Synchronisation of Discrete Event Simulations', *Manag. Sci.*, **24**, 13, pp. 1417–27, 1978.

[11] Feller, W. *Introduction to Probability Theory and Its Applications*, Vol. 1, 3rd edn., Wiley, New York, 1968.

[12] Fishman, G. S. *Concepts and Methods in Discrete Event Digital Simulation*, Wiley, New York, 1973.

[13] Franta, W. R. *The Process View of Simulation*, Elsevier North Holland, New York, 1977.

[14] Franta, W. R. & Maly, K. 'An Efficient Data Structure for the Simulation Event Set', *CACM*, **20**, 8, pp. 596–602, 1977.

[15] Freeman, H. *Introduction to Statistical Inference*, Addison-Wesley, Reading, Mass., 1963.

[16] Gaver, D. P. & Shedler, G. S. 'Control Variable Methods in the Simulation of a Model of a Multiprogrammed Computer System', *Naval Res. Log. Quart.*, **18**, pp. 435–50, 1971.

[17] Gelenbe, E. & Mitrani, I. *Analysis and Synthesis of Computer Systems*, Academic Press, London, 1980.

[18] Gonnet, G. H. 'Heaps Applied to Event Driven Mechanisms', *CACM*, **19**, 7, pp. 417–18, 1976.

[19] Gordon, G. *The Application of GPSS V to Discrete System Simulation*, Prentice-Hall, Englewood Cliffs, N.J., 1975.

[20] Gordon, G. *System Simulation*, Prentice-Hall, Englewood Cliffs, N.J., 1978.

[21] Hammersley, J. M. & Handscomb, D. C. *Monte Carlo Methods*, Methuen, London, 1964.

[22] Heidelberger, P. & Welch, P. D., 'A Spectral Method for Confidence Interval Generation and Run Control in Simulations', *CACM*, **24**, 4, pp. 233–45, 1981.

[23] Hills, P. R. 'SIMON – A Computer Simulation Language in ALGOL', *Digital Simulation in Operations Research* (Hollingdale, S. H., ed.), Elsevier North Holland, New York, 1967.

[24] Hull, T. E. & Dobell, A. R. 'Random Number Generation', *SIAM Review*, **4**, 3, pp. 230–54, 1962.

[25] Iglehart, D. L. 'The Regenerative Method for Simulation Analysis', *Current Trends in Programming Methodology* (Chandy, K. M. & Yeh, R. T., eds.), Prentice-Hall, Engelwood Cliffs, N.J., 1978.

[26] Karr, H. W., Kleine, H. & Markowitz, H. *SIMSCRIPT I.5*, Consolidated Analysis Centers, Inc., Santa Monica, Ca., 1965.

[27] Kiviat, P. J., Villanueva, R. & Markowitz, H. *The SIMSCRIPT II Programming Language*, Prentice-Hall, Englewood Cliffs, N. J., 1969.

[28] Kiviat, P. J., Villanueva, R. & Markowitz, H. *The SIMSCRIPT II.5 Programming Language*, Consolidated Analysis Centers, Los Angeles, Ca., 1973.

[29] Kleijnen, J. P. C. *Statistical Techniques in Simulation, Part 1*, Marcel Dekker, New York, 1974.

[30] Knuth, D. *The Art of Computer Programming, Vol. 2*, Addison-Wesley, Menlo Park, Ca., 1969.

[31] Knuth, D. *The Art of Computer Programming, Vol. 3*, Addison-Wesley, Menlo Park, Ca., 1973.

[32] Kobayashi, H. *Modelling and Analysis: An Introduction to System Performance Evaluation Methodology*, Addison-Wesley, Reading, Mass., 1978.

[33] Lehmer, D. H. *Proceedings, 2nd Sympsoium on Large-Scale Digital Computing Machinery*, pp. 141–6, Harvard University Press, Cambridge, Mass., 1951.

[34] Lindgren, B. W. *Statistical Theory,* Macmillan, New York, 1968.

[35] Page, E. S. 'On Monte Carlo Methods in Congestion Problems, II: Simulation of Queueing Systems', *Opns. Res.*, **13**, pp. 300–5, 1965.

[36] Page, E. S. & Wilson, L. B. *Information Representation and Manipulation in a Computer*, 2nd edn., Cambridge University Press, 1978.

[37] Samuelson, P. A. *Economics*, 10th edn., McGraw-Hill, New York, 1976.

[38] Shreider, Y. A. *Monte Carlo Methods*, Pergamon Press, London, 1966.

[39] Tognetti, K. P. & Brett, C. 'SIMSCRIPT II and SIMULA 67 – A Comparison', *The Australian Computer Journal*, **4**, 2, 1972.

[40] Vaucher, J. G. & Duval, P. 'A Comparison of Simulation Event List Algorithms, *CACM*, **18**, 4, pp. 223–30, 1975.

[41] Virjo, A. *A Comparative Study of Some Discrete Event Simulation Languages*, Finnish State Computing Centre, Helsinki, Finland, 1972.

[42] Whittle, P. *Probability*, Penguin Books, Middlesex, 1970.

[43] Wyman, F. P., 'Improved Event Scanning Mechanisms for Discrete Event Simulation', *CACM*, **18**, 6, pp. 350–3, 1975.

INDEX

activate, 45–62
activities, 15, 23
   scheduling, 23
activity-oriented simulation, 23
additive congruential generator, 69
ALGOLW, 23
ALGOL60, 39, 128
ALGOL68, 23
analysis of variance, *see* variance
antithetic variates, 111, 112
arithmetic functions, 147, 148
assignment, 129
   reference, 134
attribute, 8, 13, 19, 23–5, 134–43

batched means method, 97, 103
Bernoulli trials, 5, 158, 159
binomial distribution, 158, 159
Brownian motion, 41
Buffon's needle, 3, 4

Cauchy–Bounyakovski–Schwarz
   inequality, 157
Cauchy distribution, 85
central limit theorem, 75, 92, 102, 159,
   163, 164
Chebichev's inequality, 5, 95, 156
chi-square, 77
   distribution, 78, 117–20, 124–6, 164,
      165
   test, 77, 78, 80
class, 24, 31, 39, 45–62, 133–43
clock, 16, 18, 31, 35, 37
cobweb models, 11, 15
coefficient of variation, 166
composition method, 73, 74, 84
conditional probability, 152
confidence interval, 5, 6, 14, 92–5, 101,
   102, 106–15
correlation, 67, 107, 111–13
   coefficient, 81, 115, 157
control variable, 113–15
   concomitant, 114
covariance, 98, 111, 155–8
   function, 98

Coxian distribution, 84

decomposition theorem, 118, 120
degrees of freedom, 77, 117, 118, 120, 164,
   165
demand law, 11, 12
DEMOS, 39
density function, 7, 73–5, 153
   joint, 75, 154
distribution function, 70–2, 82, 153
   joint, 154

entity, 8, 13, 19
equilibrium, 11
Erlang distribution, 76, 84, 105, 149, 162
estimate, 14
   consistent, 87, 88
   interval, 87, 101, 103
   jackknife, 101, 103
   point, 14, 87, 101
   unbiased, 87, 88, 107, 113
event, 8, 13, 150–2
   continuous, 8, 9, 17
   discrete, 9, 10, 17
event list, 17–21, 31–5
event-oriented simulation, 15, 18, 41

F distribution, 118–21, 124–6, 165
Fibonacci sequence, 69
FIFO, 36, 42, 57
Fisher's distribution, 165
fixed time increments, 16, 17, 41
flow balance equations, 167
for, 49, 54, 61, 62, 129
frequency histogram, 104, 105

gap test, 81
geometric distribution, 70–2, 158, 159
Greco-Latin squares, 121
GPSS, 20, 34, 37–40
graph, 27
   cyclic, 27
   directed, 27

HEAD, 139–42
heap, 27–30, 34, 41
hyperexponential distribution, 73, 84, 104

if, 45–62, 129, 130
importance sampling, 8
independent replications method, 96
inspect, 129, 135, 136, 138
interval estimate, *see* estimate
inverse transformation method, 71, 72

jackknife estimate, *see* estimate
Jackson's theorem, 167
Jacobian determinant, 75

Kolmogorov–Smirnov test, 79, 80

Latin squares, 121
law (strong) of large numbers, 4, 159
least squares estimates, 123
LIFO, 36, 42
linear congruential algorithm, 66, 67
linear regression, 121–7
LINK, 139–43
linked list, 24–6, 31–3
    indexed, 32
    two-level, 33
Little's result, 90, 91, 168
long-run performance, 95, 96, *see also*
    steady-state

machine interference model, 46, 100
marginal distribution, 154
Markov's inequality, 156
maximum of k test, 81
mean, 35, 37, 82, 92, 97, 101, 107, 117,
    155–8
memoryless property, 100, 109, 160
middle-square algorithm, 66
Monte Carlo method, 2–4, 6, 15, 66
multiplicative congruential algorithm, 68

negative binomial distribution, 159
network, 27, 84
    closed, 63
    mixed, 63
    queuing, 57, 167
new, 24, 46–62, 133–43
none, 25, 133, 135, 139, 140
normal distribution, 74, 75, 83, 93, 149,
    163–5
    standard, 93, 117, 163

operation path, 8, 9, 13

PASCAL, 23
performance measure, 16, 43, 47, 51, 58,
    89, 100
    customer-oriented, 88, 90, 92
    system-oriented, 88, 89, 92, 100

Poisson distribution, 76, 149, 159, 160
Poisson stream, 83, 109, 160–2, 166, 167
poker test, 81
Pollaczeck–Khintchine's formula, 166
polar method, 75
potency, 67, 68
prefixing, 136–9
priorities, 50
    non-preemptive, 51
    preemptive, 51, 54, 55
probability function, 151, 152
procedure, 130
process, 15, 20, 43–62
    scheduling, 20
PROCESS, 45–61, 144–7
process-oriented simulation, 15, 20, 21
pseudo-random number sequence, 65

queueing systems, 165–8

random drawing procedures, 148, 149
random number sequences, 15, 35, 65, 107
random observer property, 162
random variable, 152–8
record, 23, 25, 27
reference, 133–43
    expression, 134
    variable, 133, 134
regenerative method, 99–103
regression function, 122
rejection method, 73

sample mean, 15
sample path, 8
short-run performance, 95, 96
SIMON, 23
SIMSCRIPT, 17, 34–7, 40, 68
SIMSET, 39, 128, 139–43
SIMULA, 20, 21, 24, 34, 39, 40, 42, 45,
    128
SIMULATION, 39, 45, 48, 53, 60, 128,
    143–7
simulator, 16
spectrum, 99
steady-state, 166–8
Student's t distribution, 94, 95, 98, 107,
    164, 165
supply law, 11, 12
system state, 8, 89

t-distribution, *see* Student's t
    distribution
traffic intensity, 166
tree, 27–9
    binary, 28, 29

uniform distribution, 59, 66, 69, 73, 75, 78,
    149

variable time increments, 16, 17, 41

variance, 5, 35, 82, 87, 92, 94, 107, 117, 155–8
   analysis of, 116–21, 123
variance reduction, 8, 15, 95, 106–15

virtual, 139

Weibull distribution, 85
while, 25, 45–9, 53–6, 60–2, 129, 131

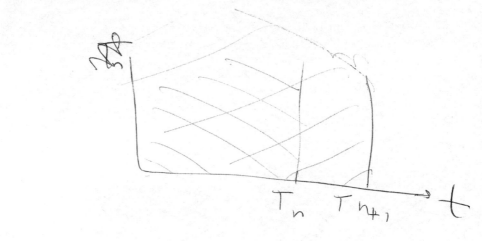

$$S = - \boxed{b} + \frac{f}{2} - 2\frac{f}{3} + 2\frac{f}{3} \cdot 3f_{n+1}$$

$$S = -f$$

G.A. Cope

The Modelling of Circuit-switched
Multi-stage interconnecting networks.

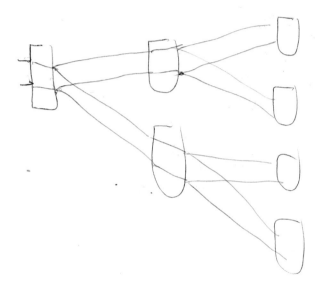